10-MINUTE TECH
VOLUME 3

MORE THAN 600 PRACTICAL AND MONEY-SAVING IDEAS FROM FELLOW RVERS

TRAILER LIFE BOOKS

Editorial Director: Bob Livingston
Editor: Eileen Hubbard
Marketing Director: Kim Souza
Production Director: Christine Bucher
Production Manager: Carol Sankman
Interior Illustrations: Bill Tipton/CompArt Design
Cover Design: Brian Burchfield
Interior Design: MSA Digital Graphics Group

This book was set in AkzidenzGroteskBE, New Caledonia and Vectora LH
and printed by Ripon Printers.

9 8 7 6 5 4 3 2 1

ISBN: 0-934798-80-X

contents

Cleaning & Protecting

Devices & Gadgets

Doors, Handles & Hatches

In Camp

Livability

Maintenance

Mobile Computing

Safety & Security

Sanitation

Storage

Systems

Towing

TRAILER LIFE BOOKS

10 minute tech

accessories

And Now for Something Completely Different ...

PIERRE NANTELL, MAGALIA, CALIFORNIA

▶ After years of setting up my dish antenna using a collapsible tripod, I decided to try something different.

Using the mount that originally came with the satellite system, I installed it on my fifth-wheel's pin box, as far forward as possible. I used self-tapping screws, but nuts and bolts could also be used.

Now, at most parks I go to, I seldom have to remove the dish. I simply dial in the proper settings by ZIP code, and in no time I have reception. When we leave, I don't even have to reposition it for travel.

If I am in a park where something is blocking the signal, I simply remove the dish from the arm and do it the old-fashioned way, using the tripod.

Dish Anchor

PIERRE NANTELL,
MAGALIA, CALIFORNIA

▶ So many times, I see RVers using gallon bottles to hold their satellite-dish tripods down to anchor them in strong winds.

I bought a 10-pound mushroom boat anchor, which I hang from the bottom of the tripod, where the pole is cradled into the pole holder. It has held up in winds as high as 45 miles per hour.

Not only is it effective, but it is more aesthetically pleasing to the eye and gives your setup a more professional appearance. It is also easy to store.

Tote-Tank Carrier

ALAN LINDHORST, KATY, TEXAS

▶ Here's an idea for carrying your tote tank using a modified bumper-mounted bike rack. The only tank holder I could find in RV-supply catalogs was a costly setup which required drilling into the trailer skin and into wall studs.

I purchased a bike rack, drilled new ½-inch diameter holes lower on the vertical square tubes and moved the support bars down to this location by rotating them 180 degrees. Coincidentally, the curvature of the bars fit the contour of my 25-gallon tote.

I installed two new ½-inch-diameter bolts, nuts and lock washers to secure the brace to the tubes at the top corners. The tank is supported by the relocated bars, and held in place by bungee cords.

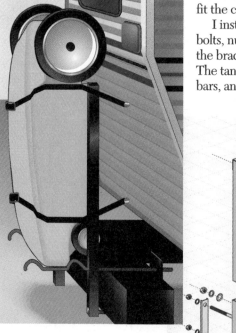

DirecTV Access Card Repair

ERNIE KLEVEN, LIVINGSTON, TEXAS

▶ I recently had problems with the access card on my RV's satellite television DirecTV system. When I replaced an expired card with a new card from DirecTV, it went bad in just a few days. The screen displayed the message "Please insert a valid access card." DirecTV shipped me another new card, but it did not alleviate the problem, and the screen continued to display the same message. After trying everything DirecTV representatives suggested, another new card was sent out. By that time, I suspected poor contacts between the receiver and the access card to be the culprit.

To clean the contacts in the receiver, I folded an index card twice to get the necessary thickness. I then saturated one end of the card with alcohol, inserted it into the vacant access card slot, and gently moved it in and out several times to clean the contacts. Eureka! The problem was solved.

Dishes On the Table

HARVEY HETRICK, TORRANCE, CALIFORNIA

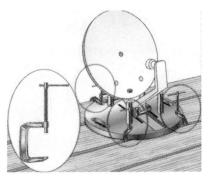

▶ The roof-mounted dish antenna on our RV works well most of the time, but there is always the occasion when trees or other obstacles block the reception.

We purchased a temporary dish set-up and found that on most occasions, inexpensive 3-inch C-clamps hold the dish firmly to most picnic tables even in severe winds. And, so long as the table is nearly level, I can locate the satellite on the first try.

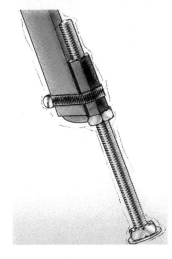

Satellite-Dish Levelers

DENNIS HARDING, VANCOUVER, WASHINGTON

▶ Here's an ideal way to make leveling a satellite dish on uneven ground easy. From the hardware store, buy three each: ⅜-inch threaded couplers, ⅜ × 8-inch-long carriage bolts and small hose clamps. Make sure the bolts are threaded all the way. Clamp the coupler to the bottom of the tripod leg, and thread in the bolt to make an adjustable point for each leg. When setting up the dish, just turn the bolt in or out to get it level.

Tangled TV Cable?

BILL WRIGHT, SANTA ROSA, CALIFORNIA

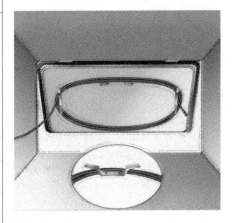

▶ After years of fighting tangled TV cables, wrapped-around hoses, etc., I decided to make life a little easier. From a hardware store, I purchased three tie-down clevis hooks that are usually used on boats and wherever cords need to be tied down. I fastened them to the inside of the door of the compartment that contains the motorhome's cable connection. I attached one end of the cable to the cable connection, and then just wound the rest of the cable around the three tie-downs, where it stays ready for action.

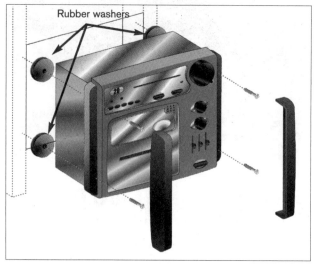

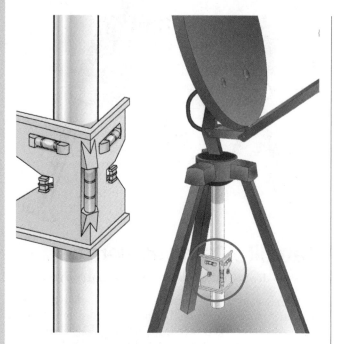

Level With Me

ERNIE KLEVEN, STEVENSVILLE, MONTANA

▶ Having difficulty leveling and setting up my satellite dish, I found this inexpensive fence-post level at a home-improvement center.

It attaches to the dish pole with a rubber band, which allows the level to rotate easily around the post as you level the dish.

Simply Silly

DAVE SIMMONDS, AVENEL, NEW JERSEY

▶ My trailer has a combination radio and CD player. This unit is mounted in an upper cabinet. When playing a CD, I noticed that if you didn't close the cabinet door very carefully, it would cause the CD to skip.

What I did to fix the problem was almost silly in its simplicity. I took the trim off the unit and removed the screws holding the unit into the cabinet and put a rubber washer between the unit and cabinet at each screw. I tightened them down, replaced the trim, and the CD hasn't skipped since.

Boy, It's Hot (Or Cold)!

LEONARD GUZZO, OXNARD, CALIFORNIA

▶ We bought an indoor/outdoor thermometer system. Finding a good place to mount the outside sender on a trailer was a challenge.

The sender must be protected from the elements, it must be able to get a true outdoor-temperature reading (without being affected by radiant heat from inside the RV or directly from the sun) and it must be able to communicate by radio frequency with the indoor display.

I found a spot under my LP-gas cylinder cover that allowed the mounting of the sender to the vertical front wall between the two cylinders. To preclude the influence of the sun heating this front wall and to isolate the system from vibration, I mounted it on a piece of ¾-inch thick foam. I looped a plastic cable tie around the bracket and the sender to add extra security to keep the sender mounted to the bracket.

A word of caution: Test out the communication between the outside sender and the inside module for your vehicle before you permanently mount anything. Since the system uses a radio frequency, metal sides, wiring, walls and appliances may affect the communication.

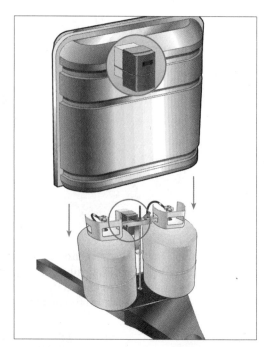

Grounded For Life

CHARLES HELLER, BARD, CALIFORNIA

▶ When my wife and I bought a new fifth-wheel, my wife said, "Nothing is to be put on the roof," so I built a lazy Susan, to be used on the ground, and mounted my solar panels on it. I made them adjustable to get the angle of the sun and they can also be turned to follow the sun all day long.

Take a 4 × 8-foot sheet of ¾-inch outdoor plywood and cut it to make two 4 × 4-inch pieces. Around the edge of the top sheet fasten lengths of 1 × 2s to make a support for the solar panels' hinge and back supports.

Find the center of each panel and bolt together, so you can turn them to follow the sun. Bolt the solar panels together, using lengths of aluminum angles. Make back supports adjustable to the angle of the sun. You could put feet on the bottom sheet, which would make it easier to keep this assembly reasonably level.

Save a Batwing

Z.M. PIKE, SALIDA, COLORADO

▶ I was forced to make a change to my Winegard batwing-style TV antenna. I had to replace three of them because they ended up with the leading edge bent back 90 degrees due to wind pressure and/or air turbulence from big trucks. To reinforce the antenna wing, I took two pieces of metal strip and bolted them on the wing and housing, being careful to avoid shorting out any wires in the housing. The metal strips strengthen the metal antenna wing and reduce its ability to flex in the wind, so it's now extra durable and still works great.

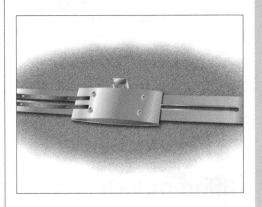

Wind Diverter

ROBERT FAULKS, APPLE VALLEY, CALIFORNIA

▶ To a great degree, motorhomes have their TV antennas mounted near the front of the vehicle. In the down position, this can cause the leading wing of the antenna to lift under certain wind conditions.

On a recent trip, we discovered the leading wing of our TV antenna bent straight up. This happened twice. What was needed was a wind diverter or dam, which would keep the air from getting under the front wing.

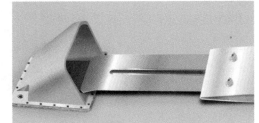

At the local hardware store, we found the solution. It is a small vent hood for a clothes dryer that costs about $3. The white-plastic hood with an attached aluminum tube normally goes through the laundry-room wall and is attached to the dryer's flexible vent hose. Some vents are aluminum and could be painted to match the RV roof.

First, disconnect the aluminum tubing and the cold-air vent flapper from the plastic housing. Grind off the small ridge that held the aluminum tubing so the bottom will be flat. Position the housing in front of the antenna wing, and have someone crank the antenna up and down, so that the wing does not touch the hood but is still very close to its sloping front. (You want the wing to be protected as much as possible.)

Apply a bead of silicone adhesive to the bottom of the vent. Position the vent in front of the antenna, and then push it down onto the RV roof for a good seal. If the antenna wing is touching the roof and making some noise, add a bit of foam rubber just under the wing inside the vent, and presto — no more bent antenna wing or noise.

(Bike) Rack 'Em Up

DENNY HUFFMAN, GRAND JUNCTION, COLORADO

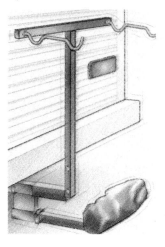

▶ My wife and I are avid mountain bikers, but I've been reluctant to hang the weight of two bicycles off my roof ladder for long hauls. Since my dinghy tow package required a drop-receiver, I had a short piece of 2-inch-square tubing welded to the top of the receiver. The same receiver-based bike rack I use behind my pickup and car is now solidly attached to the rear of the motorhome — where our bikes are out of the direct effects of the weather.

The bikes and rack are completely out of the way of the tow bar, and the bikes are easy to get down when we want them. Plus, we can easily remove the rack from behind the motorhome and insert it in the dinghy's receiver for day trips.

Simple Solution

JACK FOX, CARTHAGE, TEXAS

Hook-and-loop fasteners

▶ When we purchased our new fifth-wheel, we didn't want to hold the television and satellite receiver in place with bungee cords or unsightly straps.

The solution was simple — industrial-strength hook-and-loop fastener. After 6,000 miles, all units are firmly in place after traveling over some roads that could have qualified for an earthquake-magnitude rating.

I recommend using hook-and-loop fastener to hold anything in place in any RV. Another good thing is that appliances can be moved if necessary and the hook-and-loop fastener is easily removed.

Different Jack Pads

GRAHAM MITCHELL,
HAY RIVER, NORTHWEST TERRITORIES

▶ This is a good idea for leveling jack pads. Instead of carrying around blocks of wood with rope handles, I use plastic cutting boards. These cutting boards can be found in any housewares department. They're flat, strong, easy to store, have built-in handles and, when muddy, can be hosed off!

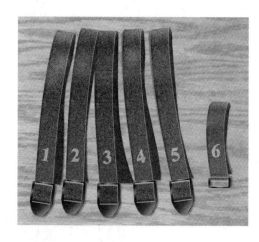

End the Confusion

RONALD CURTIS, READING, MICHIGAN

▶ Bicycle racks that strap on to RV roof ladders can be confusing to strap properly. Careful attention must be paid while trying to determine which strap goes where.

This is made easier by painting numbers on each strap, in the installation order called for by the directions. I used white correction fluid to number the straps. It's waterproof and will last a long time.

10 minute tech

appliances

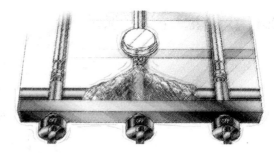

A Really Cool Message Center

MARK KUYKENDALL, LIVINGSTON, TEXAS

▶ When our motorhome's refrigerator needed to be replaced, we didn't order the typical wood-grain inserts for the front panels of the replacement fridge. Instead, we bought white bath board at Home Depot and cut it to fit. The bath board comes with a smooth finish and is about ⅛-inch thick, so it fits in the grooves on the edge of the refrigerator.

It looks clean, brightens the kitchen area — and provides a place to write messages using dry-erase markers. Taped notes don't harm it, either.

A LURKING PROBLEM

Those who spend considerable time on the road have a potential problem lurking in their home refrigerator and/or freezer – if the electricity goes down for a long period of time. Food can thaw and then re-freeze after the power comes back on, leaving no indication that the contents may have gone bad.

To find out, freeze some water in a cone-shaped paper drinking cup. After the water has frozen, cut the cup away, leaving a tapered column of ice. Place the ice in a sealable storage bag to keep the ice from evaporating, and set it where it can easily be seen.

If a thaw has happened inside the freezer, the ice cone will have some degree of melting, making it flatter. After the power comes back on, it will freeze again, only in a different shape. The shape-change is a warning that you should check with a neighbor or the power company to learn the details of the outage, and check your food for spoilage.

DON BURKLO, SOQUEL, CALIFORNIA

LURKING PROBLEM REVISITED

My freezer isn't very large. The space required for the "frozen cone" might be more space than I have available at any given time.

Why not just plug in an inexpensive electric clock? Make sure it's set to the correct time when you leave. If the power was interrupted while you were out, the time will be different and the difference between the clock time and the current time will be the amount of time the power was off.

ART BURKE, LEESBURG, FLORIDA

When HIGH Is Too Hot

HARVEY HETRICK,
TORRANCE, CALIFORNIA

▶ When using the front burner on our motorhome's stove, the pot or pan reflects a large amount of heat downward to the inside of the stove cover. When trying to adjust or turn off this burner, the shutoff mechanism is so hot and the internal adjustment rod is so tight (due to its expanding from the excess heat), it will hardly move or not at all. This stuck rod, if forced, results in a stripped knob.

A simple solution I have found is to place two layers of aluminum foil (shiny side up) between the mechanism and the stove cover. It reflects the heat away from the rod and tubing. We have been using this for more than a year and have never again had a stuck rod.

Editor's note: *The instructions for that stove explain that it has a limit of a 10-inch-diameter pan to avoid excess heat reflection into the stove mechanism. And if the valve is that tight, it should be inspected and replaced by an authorized dealer.*

Make Room

JOE ZENZ, LIVINGSTON, TEXAS

▶ My Fridge-Mate fan was taking up too much space on the refrigerator shelf, and was also falling off the shelf when I'd open the door.

I used a plastic cable fastener to attach the fan to the bottom side of our lower refrigerator shelf. It is now out of the way and can do its job while hanging beneath the shelf.

Stop That Flapper

FRED OLSON, LONGVIEW, WASHINGTON

▶ An easy way to keep your range vent flapper from rattling in the wind is to install a small bead chain and decorative handle as shown in the drawing.

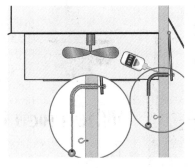

Gently (so it won't kink) bend a short piece of ¼-inch copper tubing into a 90-degree angle. Drill a hole the size of the outside diameter of the tubing through the bottom of the range hood vent compartment so that when you put the tubing in place, one end will face down (toward the stove) and the other end will project through the vent opening (toward the back of the vent flap). Fasten the tubing in place with construction adhesive or silicone sealer. All dimensions will vary according to your vehicle's setup.

Drill a tiny hole in the lower edge of the vent flap (opposite where the end of the tubing will be). Push the very end of the beaded chain (from the vent side) through the hole and glue in place.

When the adhesive has dried, pass the chain through the tubing and finish with a small knob.

Screw a small hook into the wall at the back of the stove; when you want to keep the flap closed, pull down and hook the chain. When the vent fan is on, release the chain. Be sure that this section of chain is long enough to allow the vent flap to open wide.

Slip-Sliding Away

FRANK WOYTHAL,
ANDOVER, NEW YORK

▶ The lower shelf in my motorhome's refrigerator door was deep enough to accommodate half-gallon containers, but any container that was narrower kept sliding off. I fixed this by fastening a piece of aluminum (with a 90-degree lip bent upward along the front edge) with a very short screw. This makes the shelf bottom as deep as the retaining bar that holds the items on the shelf.

Try a cardboard pattern first to determine the optimum depth.

Is Your Bottom Burned?

MORRIS DAHL, NILES, MICHIGAN

▶ If you have ever burned the bottom of muffins, cakes and/or pies in your LP-gas oven, I have a great tip for you. Go to your local home center or tile store and purchase four 6 × 6-inch unglazed ceramic tiles. Place them in your oven just above the fire source on that solid-steel shelf. Your troubles are over. It's that easy!

Chips Ahoy!

MAX BEDUHN, YAKIMA, WASHINGTON

▶ To keep the glass plate in the microwave safe and in place, insert an empty Pringles potato-chip can, open end up, and take a 3-inch square of ¾-inch Styrofoam or sponge rubber and wedge it between the plate and the tube.

You can trim the open end of the tube to the length needed to fit the microwave.

appliances

Pack-a-Snack

LOMA "ANN" GOODIN,
VICTORIA, TEXAS

▶ I always had trouble packing the freezer compartment of our Dometic double-door refrigerator. I found a way to utilize the available freezer space so we can carry many more frozen items.

First, we removed the racks/containers on the inside of the freezer door. Next, we purchased a freezer basket that fits the small chest-type household

freezers. We moved the freezer shelf to the lowest level and, after filling the basket, we placed it on the shelf and slid it to the back of the freezer compartment. This prevents food from falling out, and also increases your usable freezer capacity.

We still have plenty of space for ice trays as well as other items under the shelf.

Little Squirt

JOYCE BEAUDET,
FEEDING HILLS,
MASSACHUSETTS

▶ My strategy for adding water to the softener or bleach container of my motorhome's washer-dryer saves making a mess.

I use a 12-ounce plastic dish-soap bottle. After washing it out, I filled it with water and keep it near my washer; when needed, I just squirt water into the softener and/or bleach dispensers, as needed. There are no spills, and the containers are easy to reach.

Seeing Red

ROY BASSETT, SAN ANDREAS, CALIFORNIA

▶ Concerned with maintaining healthy storage temperatures for perishable food, we bought a refrigerator thermometer for our motorhome. The small gauge display made reading it difficult, however, until I hit on the idea of highlighting the food safe-temperature zone by painting a portion of the instrument face with red nail polish. Now we can see at a glance that if the thermometer needle is in the red zone, the refrigerator temperature is right where it needs to be.

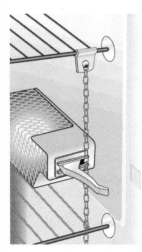

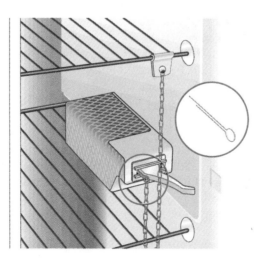

Cotter Fodder

MARY JANE MCPHILLIPS,
SAN ANTONIO, TEXAS

▶ There's no need to disconnect the battery when storing your RV with the refrigerator door open.

The light switch can be kept off by lodging a small cotter pin in it. I attached the pin to a short piece of chain and hung it on a shelf. It's out of the way when not in use, and there's no more looking for a toothpick to lodge in the switch.

10 minute tech

automotive

AMAZING COINCIDENCE!

We were returning home from a trip when the engine started to miss. I looked down and noticed low voltage. The alternator was not charging, and the engine battery was almost dead.

Since I carry a battery charger, I connected the charger to the battery, plugged the charger into a 120-volt AC outlet (on the motorhome) and started the AC generator. The missing stopped right away, and home we went.

A person could very easily make it to the next town or even finish a trip, instead of being stranded by the side of the road and/or being stuck with a large towing-and-repair bill.

DEAN FELTHAUSER, LAS VEGAS, NEVADA
& LEE PIERCE,
CHULA VISTA, CALIFORNIA

BATTERY-BOLT EXTENDER

All electronic brake-controller systems (and certain other accessories) should be wired directly to the positive and negative terminals of an automotive battery. This presents a problem when connecting the controller wires to a battery that has side posts. The result is, at best, a makeshift connection, since the side posts are not designed to accept additional connections.

I found a battery-bolt extender, sold at the local auto-parts store, that results in a solid connection for the electric system and the controller. Installation was easy, and only required that I remove the old battery bolt and replace it with the battery-bolt extender, following the instructions.

Another big advantage is that I now have a convenient place for connecting jumper cables.

DAVID SCHICK,
LAKE ALFRED, FLORIDA

DASHBOARD NOISES

Trailer Life magazine once ran a fix for dashboard noises using clear silicone. I fixed mine by spraying the joints with AMSOIL MP Metal Protector, using the little tube applicator that comes with the spray can. You do not have to spread the MP in the joint; capillary action takes care of that. Any overspray can be wiped off with a rag.

The product is clear; it dries, does not attract dust, and is harmless to wiring, plastic paint or fabrics.

MARVIN SCHNAIDT,
BEULAH, NORTH DAKOTA

Dashboard Noises II

STANLEY FREDERICK, TUCSON, ARIZONA

There was a noise in my truck's dashboard that was driving me crazy. I traced the noise to a joint in the plastic dash. I spread the joint with a screwdriver and inserted two shims made of folded card stock, so that the two pieces of plastic were held apart. The noise stopped.

For a more permanent fix, I squirted some clear silicone window sealer into the joint and smoothed it off with my finger. After I was sure the silicone had completely cured, I pulled the shims out and caulked where they were.

Heart-Pounding Experience

JAMES GORMAN,

COOS BAY, OREGON

Before traveling, I check the air pressure in all tires, including the spare. The spare is located in one of my basement-storage compartments.

The carpeted floor, combined with the 55-pound weight of the 19.5-inch tire, made it a heart-pounding experience to move.

To help eliminate the friction between the carpet and the tire, I purchased a piece of heavy-gauge plastic sheeting large enough to cover the bottom and sides of the tire and come together on the top of the tire. I used a piece of duct tape to hold the corners of the plastic sheet down. I added a rope tied to a lug hole to make it easier to pull the tire out for inspection. Besides reducing the friction, the plastic sheeting protects the carpet from the tire.

Two Ways to Aid Wheel-Cover Removal

RAY BARTHEL, TINLEY PARK, ILLINOIS

▶ Our new motorhome came equipped with stainless-steel wheel liners. To eliminate the guesswork of which two lugs actually hold the liner on, I put a dimple on the two with a center punch and put paint on the ends of the matching studs.

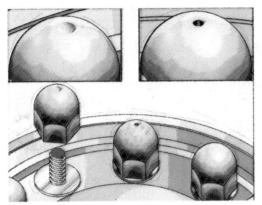

FRANK WOYTHAL, ANDOVER, NEW YORK

▶ Whenever I removed my front wheel covers to do any type of service or inspection work, I was faced with determining which two stainless-steel nut covers to remove. All 10 looked alike, but only two actually contain a real steel nut that threads onto the stud.

After locating the two key ones (I used a magnet), I removed them and drilled a ¹⁄₁₆-inch hole into the end of each nut cover. The hole is barely noticeable, acts as the identifier and, in the event of internal rust, allows me to squirt in a bit of WD-40 to free things up.

Neck-in-Neck

JAMES OZENBERGER, ST. JOSEPH, MISSOURI

▶ I was dismayed to discover that the spouts on new quart-sized motor oil containers had been increased substantially in diameter — to the point where they no longer fit into the oil-filler tube on my motorhome.

Since the fill-tube opening is at a shallow angle, various funnels and other methods were tried, resulting in many drips and spills but little success. After comparing their sizes, however, I determined that the new bottle would slip inside of the old one. I cut the bottom out of an old bottle and slipped the new one inside. This forms an instant, tight, no-drip funnel!

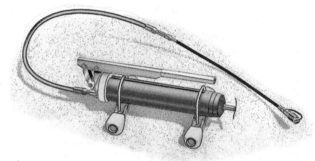

Grease-Gun Pull Toy

**PETER CHIAROLANZIO,
FLORHAM PARK, NEW JERSEY**

▶ To make greasing my motorhome easier, I put together a freestanding grease gun. Two short pieces of 1 × 1-inch hollow-stock square metal were used for the base. Two U-bolts were used to hold down the grease gun to the square metal pieces. Rubber caps (tips for chairs, crutches, canes, etc.) were used to cover the metal ends and act as wheels. My hands are now free to hold the hose and pump the grease.

LIGHTS OUT

When you drive with your motorhome's headlights on during the day, put a small plastic hang tag on the steering wheel or ignition key to remind you to turn them off when you stop. That way, you won't accidentally leave them on and drain your battery.

ARLENE JEKNAVORIAN, DAVENPORT, FLORIDA

automotive

Secure a Load

DALE SCHMIDTENDORF, TRAVERSE CITY, MICHIGAN

▶ The fifth-wheel rails on my tow vehicle make an excellent adjustable anchor point to strap down a load. By using large S hooks or one of the cam straps available at hardware stores (watch the loop size — some are too large) and a couple of ½-inch

bolts, the S hook can be placed in the rail slots and secured with a bolt (the same way the fifth-wheel is held in).

With many slots in the rail, this technique allows you to adjust the securing point to fit the load. The rails mounted to the frame under the bed of the truck are generally rated for 15,000-plus pounds, so they should hold any load the strap or rope is capable of holding.

I also add a 2 × 4 crossways in front of the tailgate if I am going to haul long boards. This takes a lot of strain off the tailgate cables.

Éliminate Heat

SAM MEGGS, MARTINEZ, GEORGIA

▶ To eliminate some of the heat buildup from the engine and exhaust manifolds in my motorhome, I installed two air ducts to force air onto the front of the exhaust manifolds.

This is helping to reduce the problem of the exhaust manifolds cracking and gaskets blowing.

In addition, it has reduced the amount of heat in the doghouse that radiates into the driver's compartment.

I used two 3-inch 45-degree PVC elbows as air scoops, nonflammable aluminum clothes-dryer-vent hose, quick ties, duct tape and two shelf brackets. Flexible exhaust tubing could be used instead of the dryer-vent hose and elbows.

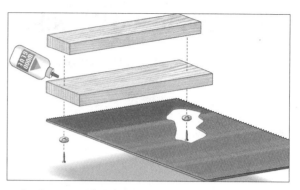

Sleigh Parking

CHARLES MULLINS, COTTONWOOD, ARIZONA

▶ To prevent bumping into the garage wall when parking vehicles, I have placed various blocks on the concrete floor for the vehicle tires to stop against.

Unfortunately, the blocks were constantly being nudged out of place when driven against, regardless of how gently they were approached.

So I decided that I needed to anchor a block to something that I could drive onto first. A carpet sample worked fine. Across one end, I attached a length of a 2 × 6-inch wood with screws and washers and then added a 2 × 4 (like a sandwich) on top of that. The weight of the tire on the carpet holds the unit in place as the tire nudges the stop.

In several years of usage, with the weight of a wheel on it, they have held together and stay where placed.

SMILE! YOU'RE ON CANDID CAMERA!

In the confined spaces of RVs, at times it is not possible to see clearly, or at all, what needs working on. I have found that by setting up my video camera (which also takes digital still pictures) on a tripod or hand-holding it, I can usually get a good view of what needs working on. It helps to illuminate the area with a flashlight or other light source, and make liberal use of the zoom lens.

I am able to easily magnify part numbers up to 300 percent by printing the picture on my computer's printer. This also gives me the ability to have a record of what I started with — and any changes I make.

ROBERT McGOWAN,
LA MESA, CALIFORNIA

automotive

10 minute tech

awnings

Awning Strap R&R

RICHARD PENCE, LATHAM, OHIO

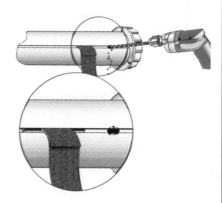

▶ Considering the amount of stress they endure, it's surprising that awning pull straps don't tear more frequently. If yours needs replacement — and the awning style allows access to the strap mount — I found an easy way to do it without disassembling the awning mechanism:

First, drill a ¼-inch hole — at a 45-degree angle — in the lip of the awning's roller track. This will allow you to remove the rubber bead that the strap is affixed to (you will have to coax the bead through the hole — the point of a knife works well). Reverse the procedure with the new rubber bead/strap until the entire rubber bead is back inside the roller track!

Kneedy Things

ROY WOHLSCHEID,
CLINTON TOWNSHIP, MICHIGAN

▶ To minimize the damage to a motorhome cover caused by the sharp awning ends, I use kneecap protectors. They are quite inexpensive, and are available at any hardware store.

I use the hook-and-loop straps they come with to hold them in place on the awning ends, although I think industrial-strength straps might do a better job. They are easier to use than trying to tie pieces of old towels or other padding to the awning ends.

AWNING CLEANER

To clean my extra-dirty awning, I use Dawn heavy-duty dish detergent in a bucket of water and scrub with an RV brush. How much Dawn soap to how much water? How dirty is your awning? Try different solutions to see what works best for you.

It cleans well with little effort.

HOWARD STEPHENS,
GRAND RAPIDS, MICHIGAN

DEFLAPPER HELP

Because the width of our trailer's awning is a little short, on very windy days our T-shape deflappers will pull away from the awning.

To eliminate this, we glued two pieces of rubberized shelf liner, cut to fit the surfaces of the deflapper. (Use glue that is compatible with the rubber liner and the deflapper material.) Now the rubber liner grips the awning material tightly and helps prevent slippage.

VERONICA WESSEL, COLUMBUS, MICHIGAN

Hold That Flap

RICHARD PENCE, LATHAM, OHIO

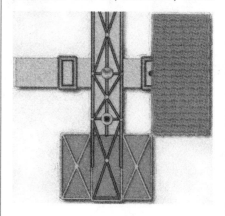

▶ If you have plastic-faced awning supports, as I do, you know that they will not hold your awning if the awning starts to flap. However, if you use two pieces of non-skid shelf liner and glue them to both faces of your awning support, using contact cement, you will find that the support will hold the awning even in 40-MPH gusts, such as we encountered this year.

Put the contact cement on the plastic face of the awning supports. Then put the liner on the plastic face.

Pull the liner backing off the plastic face, and let both surfaces dry. Once they are dry, reapply the liner to the plastic face. Do this to both pieces of each awning support. It really works.

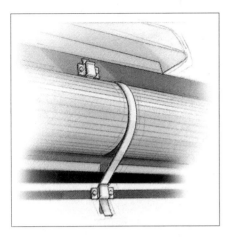

The Wind Took It

JOE COCHRAN, FOREST CITY, IOWA

▶ I have a 19-foot awning with a polar shield on my motorhome. One day in Montana the wind took it off the side while we were going down the road.

After it was replaced, I noticed that it seemed to balloon out in the slightest wind. To stop this action, I tried bungee cords, to no avail. Then I hit upon this idea.

At Camping World, I purchased Thumblock Supergrips, MRV 200 and the extra-length strap, MRV 48-inch. I installed a set about 3½ feet from each end.

We have now traveled about 10,000 miles without a problem; there is no ballooning. The only drawback is that a ladder is needed to install the straps after the awning has been rolled back up, but most of us RVers carry a ladder anyway.

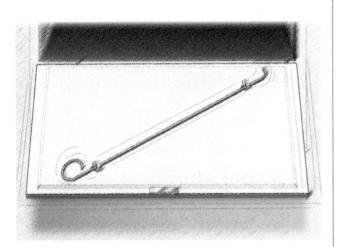

Spare the Rod

JOE PECK, MARYVILLE, TENNESSEE

▶ I always had to hunt through the compartment under the awning to try and find the awning rod. So, I mounted some spring clips on the inside of the compartment door to hold the awning rod.

Now, I just open the compartment door and presto — there is the rod!

Shake, Rattle and ... Volley?

FRED MOKRAY, HILLSBORO, OHIO

▶ The average motorhome develops a number of squeaks and rattles as they age and wear. Some you can easily eliminate, others you can't. If your awning bars have developed an irritating rattle as you go down the road, position one tennis ball under each support arm of the awning as you close it — the balls will compress and take up any slack that's occurred with age.

All Rolled Up and No Place To Go

BILL WISSINGER, MENTOR, OHIO

▶ For an inexpensive awning cover, I went to a home-improvement center and purchased two lengths of plastic rain gutter for about $5 each. I notched the ends to fit over the awning end brackets on the motorhome. It really keeps the awning clean and dry when the RV is in storage!

Snow Daze

KEVIN LUCKEY, ANCHORAGE, ALASKA

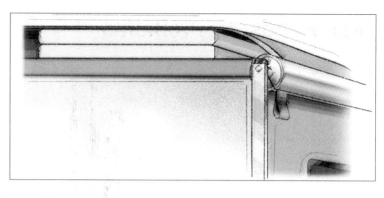

▶ We don't often drive our motorhome in the winter — but we still like to use it as a guest room for visitors. However, we never extended the slideout during this time because we were concerned that the awning, which always covers it, might be ruined from the snow.

Last year, I purchased a 4 × 8-foot sheet of open-cell Styrofoam insulation, two inches thick. This type of product is used in construction of houses and is available where lumber is sold.

I cut the sheet in half lengthwise, stacked one atop the other and slid this sandwiched assembly between the slideout roof and the awning, thereby eliminating the gap between the two. Since this now only allows the awning fabric to flex a small amount, we no longer have to worry about the snow load tearing the fabric or bending the mounts.

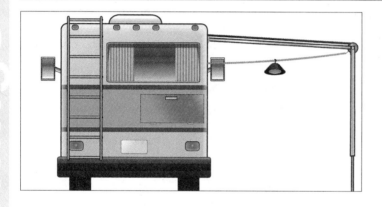

Hang-a-Light

JAMES McCLELLAN, LAPER, MICHIGAN

▶ If you want to hang a light under your awning, use the pull-down strap. Start by placing a large cup hook in place of a window-frame screw in a window under the awning. You can hook the end of the strap on the cup hook and hang the light on the strap. A bungee cord works well as an extension if your strap isn't long enough, but be sure you don't hang too much weight on the strap.

Blowing in the Wind

TALMAGE HERBERT, HILLSBORO, OREGON

▶ Occasionally we need to hang one or two items outside to dry, and we wanted to use our awning for this purpose. Unfortunately, when we would use a single clothespin, the item needed to be twisted out of shape in order to hang it from the awning edge. Also, it had a tendency to pick up dirt from the awning material.

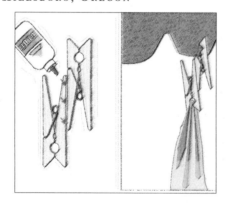

I solved the problem by gluing two clothespins together, with the heads facing opposite; now the items can be hung without twisting.

Tennis, Anyone?

ROBERT HABERERN,
SCHNECKSVILLE, PENNSYLVANIA

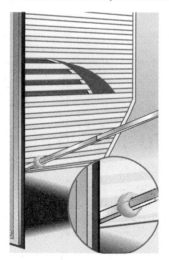

▶ When the awning is out on our trailer, the trailer door hits the awning arm, even when the door is open.

I cut a tennis ball to fit the arm, punched a hole in it on each side of the cutout, put plastic-coated wire twists through the holes and tied the ball to the arm.

Little Hands/Big Problems

RONALD FOSTER, PLATTSBURG, NEW YORK

▶ We camp at many different campgrounds and, due to various circumstances, we often put the awning support arms down in a vertical position instead at an angle to the side of the RV.

Having grandchildren, we have noticed that the awning handles are quite accessible to little hands.

I devised a quick-and-safe way to make sure that a passing child doesn't pull the handle by mistake — which could cause the awning to fall and, much worse, injure the child.

I used a ⅜-inch thick × 1½-inch wide × 3-inch long flat piece of aluminum stock with various holes drilled in it. I generally attach it to the awning arm with a stainless-steel wing nut and bolt.

Aligning the closest hole on the awning arm with one in this piece of aluminum places the aluminum block close to the upper, outer part of the awning arm, making the whole assembly safer. This is because the inner and outer arms are prevented from collapsing when the handle is accidentally pulled.

Tie One On

JOAN HENSLEY, BERTHOUD, COLORADO

▶ To eliminate the worry about our awning unrolling while going down the road, we used two hook-and-loop nylon fasteners on each awning support. This way, the awning will not come loose or unroll.

A SAPPY SOLUTION

During the summer months, I enjoy staying at campgrounds that have many tall pine trees. The trees provide very good shade, and smell wonderful. Unfortunately, these pine-tree sites have a major drawback in that the tree sap drips onto my RV's awning. The mess is further spread around when the awning is rolled up, as that smears sap on both surfaces of the awning fabric.

I finally came up with what I consider a simple and cost-effective solution. When I set up camp and before I roll down the awning, I use clothespins to attach a piece of one-mil polyethylene (plastic) at the top edge of the awning before I completely roll it down. Once the poly is attached, it unfolds (almost automatically) by itself while rolling down the awning. I then secure the remaining edges of the poly sheet to the sides of the awning. The awning wind strap can also be used to stabilize the poly sheet.

When it is time to leave, I simply discard the poly cover in the trash.

PAUL FOREST, ROCHESTER, NEW YORK

AWNING STAYS TIGHT

My awning-extension locking nuts kept sliding and allowing the awning to partially retract and slacken.

Drilling small holes at the end of the outside sliding component and through the inside sliding component of the extension arms allowed for a suitably sized hairpin clip to be inserted, thus preventing the extension arms from retracting.

Now, the awning stays tight, and the pins can easily be removed for return to the travel position.

ARCH KENNEDY,
CLINTON, PENNSYLVANIA

REMOTE CONTROL

Tired of traipsing outside to unplug/turn off the lights under our awning each evening, I purchased a remote-light switch from a building supply store.

I plugged the receiving unit into an outlet in the basement, and then plugged the outside lights into it. The sending unit looks like a regular light switch and can be fastened on the wall anywhere convenient.

DALE LYNDAHL,
GREEN BAY, WISCONSIN

awnings

A DOUBLE USE

To help protect your rig's awning while it's in storage, buy a length of 6-inch PVC sewer pipe.

Use a saw to cut it in half, lengthwise. Then lay it along the top of your rolled-up awning, and cut it to the length of your awning. If need be you can use hook-and-loop straps to secure it.

When you're on the road in the RV, take the PVC cover along to use as a support for the sewer hose.

LARRY PEROTIN, JUPITER, FLORIDA

AUTOMATIC LIGHTING

Most RVers have patio lights that we hang from our awnings for festive and/or security purposes. To enhance the latter, I purchased an outdoor timer that turns the lights on at dusk and off at my choosing (two, four or six hours later).

So even when we are away from the campsite, the lights come on automatically to provide security and after-dark lighting. The timer also turns the lights off automatically at bedtime.

To vary the brightness of my prismatic globe lights, I have installed an in-line dimmer switch between the lights and the plug. The dimmer allows us to have bright light for reading purposes and dim light for socializing.

LARRY EY, BEL AIR, MARYLAND

STAND & DELIVER

We store our awning wand in a standing section of tubing mounted unobtrusively right beside the entrance-door molding of our coach. It is out of the way, but easily retrieved from outdoors – without having to step all the way inside.

Measure the bent end of your awning wand, then buy a 15-inch length of PVC pipe with an inside diameter large enough to accommodate the bent end of the rod. Drill two ⅜-inch holes in what will become the front side of the holder (for screwdriver access), and two small holes in the back side (for the mounting screws). The screws should be countersunk so the wand won't catch on the heads as it is inserted into the pipe.

I spray-painted the pipe to blend in with the colors inside the motorhome, then mounted it a couple of inches off the floor to allow for floor cleaning.

PHILLIP CRONK, NAMPA, INDIANA

Light-Wait Shortening

DAVID NEWELL, CABOT, ARKANSAS

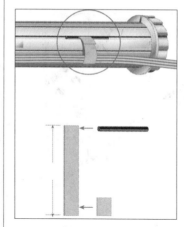

▶ While on a recent camping trip I had to store my awning away in a hurry, due to high winds and an approaching storm. As I was trying to undo the metal hooks holding up my awning lights from the holders, I thought there had to be a better way to do this.

When I got back home, I went to Wal-Mart and bought a 3-foot long, 2-inch wide piece of hook-and-loop fastener. I cut it in half (the long way) to make two strips, each 1-inch wide. I decided that a piece 6 inches long was enough to accomplish what I wanted to do.

A piece of rubber retainer is also needed. This retainer slips into the existing slot in the awning roller. You should be able to get some at an RV-supply or hardware store.

My wife then took one of the fasteners and sewed a narrow pocket in one end to hold the rubber strip, and a 1-inch piece of hook material on the other end.

Once in place these fasteners are very easily and quickly attached or removed from your lights or anything else you want to hang up. They can also be left in place without causing any damage to your rolled-up awning.

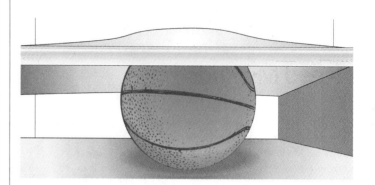

Have a Ball

EDWARD GEBEAULT, MASSENA, NEW YORK

▶ To prevent water from pooling on the awnings over the slideouts, I put a ball (about basketball size) between the awning and the slideout. That raises the awning just enough to make the water run off.

Awning-Arm Tattoo

RAY MCCALMET, DEPEW, OKLAHOMA

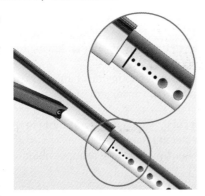

▶ When raising the RV's awning, I always leave the rear end 2⅛ inches lower than the front, for proper rain drainage. To raise it to the exact same place every time, I marked the awning extension arm.

With a permanent marker, I drew several dots and a stop line on the awning extension arm. As I raise the awning, I see the dots preceding the stop line. At the stop line, I release the locking pin, and the awning is set precisely as it was before.

It is a convenient and quick way to set the awning every time.

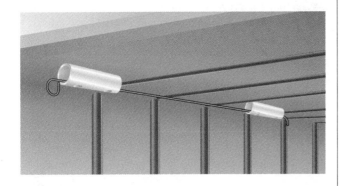

I Need My Rod

MIKE JONES, WYOMING, MICHIGAN

▶ I got tired of having to hunt for my awning rod, which had the habit of becoming buried under the other items in my largest outside storage compartment, the only compartment long enough to store it in. So I cut two short pieces (about 6 inches long) of PVC pipe, drilled two holes in each (enlarged the holes on one side for the screwdriver shaft) and attached them to the ceiling of the compartment. I measured my rod and placed the pieces of pipe so that the rod tip (bent 90 degrees) would just hang out the end. That way, there is no room for the rod to slide back and forth.

Now when I need my awning rod, I know right where it is; I don't have to hunt for it.

Awning Blowout

WES WISE, VANCOUVER, WASHINGTON

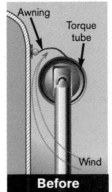

Before **After**

▶ Who ever heard of an RV awning blowing off while traveling down the road? I hadn't until I read about it happening in an earlier *10-Minute Tech*. A reader explained how he wanted to prevent that from happening again by wrapping the torque tube with bungee cord.

While traveling in my motorhome, I kept wondering how that could happen since the rolled-up awning is secure against the side of the motorhome. A short time later, I found out. My awning was hanging down the side of the motorhome and the rear support arm was broken!

The manufacturer and the dealer admitted it is not that uncommon. Unfortunately, no solution was provided. The reader's bungee-cord idea seemed to be the way to go. The problem with this approach is the additional steps needed to use the awning; I wanted a fix that would be passive.

It was explained that the wind gets between the awning and the side of the coach with enough force to blow out the awning and unroll it off the torque tube. Why not a wind spoiler, mounted in the gap between the rolled-up awning and the side of the RV?

The spoiler is made from a 10-foot section of 3-inch PVC drainpipe. It was cut lengthwise three times to form three one-third-arc (120-degree) sections. You can do this on any table saw, using a fine-tooth blade. Splice together two sections to form one piece long enough to match the length of your awning. The splice pieces are made from couplers sold to join the round PVC pipe together and, as with the 10-foot sections, are sliced into three one-third sections. Join the sections with PVC cement.

Mount this under the awning on the side of the coach with the outside of the pipe against the motorhome (see diagram). A PVC spacer, cut from the pipe, should be used under each mounting screw to hold the spoiler off the side wall to prevent moisture from collecting behind it.

The results do not detract from the motorhome's appearance, and the wind will have a hard time getting under the awning.

awnings

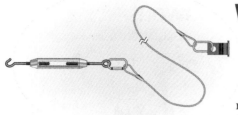

We Wish Yuma Merry Christmas

LEO MUELLER, OSHKOSH, WISCONSIN

▶ As a winter employee at an RV parts store in Yuma, Arizona, I have encountered a number of people who have had their awnings unroll while traveling down the road, in spite of having the awnings secured with rope or hook-and-loop fasteners.

Due to worn parts in the ratcheting mechanism, a weak spring or both, the awning tube can ratchet under extreme wind conditions, which allows the awning to unroll.

To prevent this from happening, I use the following method:

Attach a roller-tube hook into the unused groove in the roller tube. Attach a braided cable to the hook and a small turnbuckle at the other end. Attach the turnbuckle to the lower awning mount.

This method will exert counterclockwise pressure on the roller tube, making it impossible for the awning to unroll.

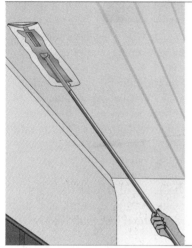

Super Swiffers

KEN PETERSON, GREEN RIVER, WYOMING

▶ Cleaning that awning just got easier with the use of a household-cleaning item called a Swiffer. You can clean both sides of the awning rather easily, and, if the pad gets dry, just add a little household cleaner.

Great idea! My wife thought of this, so I must give credit where credit is due.

Editor's note: *To make sure a household cleaner is safe to use on the awning material, test it in an inconspicuous place on the awning before using it.*

Keep It Clear

JAMES KOHLS, BELMONT, MICHIGAN

▶ The slideout awning on our coach sagged, collecting lots of debris and a puddle of water when it rained. To hold up the awning and prevent this problem, I made a support out of ¾-inch PVC pipe.

I used 2½-foot-long pieces for the top and bottom. This length was selected so that four would make the overall length about a foot less than the length of the slideout (dimension X in illustration).

Five vertical lengths were cut, so that with ¾-inch elbows attached, they would be equal to the vertical distance from the top of the slideout to the awning attachment points on the coach wall (dimension Y in illustration). Four elbows and six tees are required for the assembly.

All joints are fastened with plastic pipe cement except for one horizontal side of each of the center tees. This allows the assembly to be taken apart at the center for ease of storage.

I slide the support in from an end, so it is centered under the length and width of the awning. A note over the slide-control switch reminds me to remove the support before retracting the slide.

No cement on these joints

X

Y

$\frac{X}{4}$

awnings

10 minute tech

cleaning & protecting

Á Curved Squeegee

GARY OLSEN, HEMET, CALIFORNIA

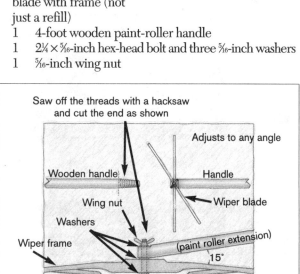

I made a squeegee for my motorhome's curved windshield that requires only three side-to-side swipes to do each half. The blade is fully adjustable for all applications.

I used a 20-inch wiper blade (available in any automotive department). Since windshields are all different sizes, buy the size that will clean your windshield in three swipes.

Materials needed:
1   20-inch wiper blade with frame (not just a refill)
1   4-foot wooden paint-roller handle
1   2¼ × ⁵⁄₁₆-inch hex-head bolt and three ⁵⁄₁₆-inch washers
1   ⁵⁄₁₆-inch wing nut

Saw off the threads with a hacksaw and cut the end as shown

Adjusts to any angle

Wooden handle
Handle
Wing nut
Wiper blade
Washers
Wiper frame
(paint roller extension)
15°
Wiper blade
2¼" × ⁵⁄₁₆" bolt

With a hacksaw, cut the threads off of the roller handle and, at this area, cut a flat spot as shown in the drawing (a hacksaw will cut a narrower, smoother cut than a larger-toothed regular saw). For the ⁵⁄₁₆-inch bolt, drill a ⁵⁄₁₆-inch hole through the handle, and assemble all parts as shown in the drawing.

Amazingly, the squeegee works great for removing the water from the sides of the motorhome after washing, and, of course, all the windows, either side to side or up and down.

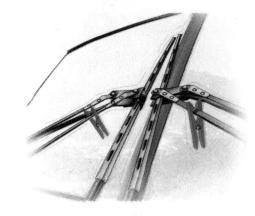

Another Clothespin Use

WILLIAM BATSON, BRIER, WASHINGTON

There are many ways to use clothespins around our motorhomes, and many ways to prolong the life of the motorhome's wiper blades. Putting these two concepts together, the illustration shows how I use two clothespins to hold the wiper blades off of the hot windshield while parked.

Everything Was a Blur

DAVID HUNT, SUNNYVALE, CALIFORNIA

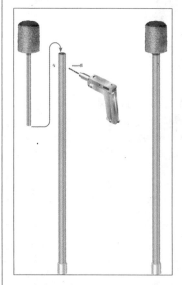

Our new motorhome has the backup camera that serves as the rearview mirror — a great thing to have! However, when we took our first trip, driving on wet and dirty highways, it was just a matter of seconds until everything became a blur. Each time we stopped, I'd climb the ladder so I could reach the camera lens and clean it. There had to be a better way!

I got a length of ¾-inch PVC pipe and put the handle of a baby bottle brush inside the PVC pipe. (The length of the PVC pipe depends on your height and the distance to the camera lens.) I drilled a hole through the pipe and handle in order to bolt the two together. Now when the camera lens gets dirty, I just moisten the brush and clean away.

Super Chlorination and You

ROBERT FAULKS, APPLE VALLEY, CALIFORNIA

⏵ *MotorHome* articles and individual motorhome owner's manuals admonish you to periodically super-chlorinate your freshwater tank using a chlorine-bleach solution (sodium hypochlorite). They usually go into great detail about the solution to use and when to do it. But they never tell you how to get that solution into the tank.

Some people use a funnel. That's OK, providing you have a clear and unobstructed access to the freshwater filler cap/neck. However, some motorhome freshwater fillers are restricted because the bay door doesn't open all the way up, especially if there is a slideout just above.

Most late-model motorhomes allow filling the freshwater tank via the water hose hooked to a water supply, so you can bypass the filler cap and go direct. Some people use this system by attaching the empty hose to the motorhome and pouring the premeasured chlorine solution into the empty hose, using a funnel, and then hooking the hose to the water source. That system works well.

We use our outside freshwater-filter canister to feed the solution into the freshwater tank. Just hook up the filter as usual, unscrew the bottom section and remove the filter element. Then fill the filter container with the chlorine solution and screw the bottom section back on.

With this system, you can use full-strength chlorine bleach without diluting it, since the water entering the filter assembly will do it.

Our filter canister holds about five cups of solution, but two cups of bleach is probably enough to super-chlorinate an 80-gallon tank. This method also chlorinates the filter container and the water lines leading to the storage tank.

Editor's note: *It's not necessary to use more than ¼ cup of chlorine for every 15 gallons of water-tank capacity. Make sure the tank is drained and rinsed with water before using. Use baking soda and water to flush out the tank again to remove the chlorine taste and smell.*

ANOTHER WAY

I have discovered another way to remove black streaks from the side of my motorhome. I usually use a commercial black-streak remover, but recently, after I had washed the motorhome, I realized that I had run out of remover. I looked in my garage and I found a small bottle of Goo Gone (by American Magic Corporation). This is a natural cleaner that removes gum, tar, stickers, etc.

I tried a little bit on a small area and the streaks came off with hardly any effort. I then wiped the freshly cleaned areas with a damp cloth.

PETER BLISSE,
SACRAMENTO, CALIFORNIA

Editor's note: *It probably is necessary to rewax after using this cleaner.*

CONVENIENT THING

Here is a convenient thing I do in our motorhome. We have towel racks on the inside of the bathroom door. To keep the moisture (from the wet towels) off the wood, we put a piece of clear vinyl, attached with small tacks, the length of the hanging towels. It sure is a lot better than spoiling the wood.

JOAN KNUTSON,
SEATTLE, WASHINGTON

GOT AN OLD SOCK?

Save an old pair of long cotton socks and place them in the compartment where you store your electric cord, so that they are available to slip over your hands when it's time to put the cord away. As you pull the cord in, just wipe away the dirt, sand and water and keep your hands, power cord and compartment clean.

BILLY WILLIAMS, PAHRUMP, NEVADA

ALL THE NEWS THAT'S FIT TO ... WIPE?

While cleaning windows in our motorhome, I remembered something my thrifty grandmother used – newspapers! I wet one with water to wash the windows, then I dry and polish the glass with a dry page. Newspapers are convenient, cheap and easily disposed of.

GLORIA CANNON,
KLAMATH FALLS, OREGON

cleaning & protecting

cleaning & protecting

SHADE-CLEANING TIPS

In February 2003, we published a request from a reader looking for ideas on how to clean day/night shades. A number of RVers responded recently with what works for them, but be sure to test any new method in an inconspicuous area first. What works on one brand of shade might not work on another.
– Editor

I clean spots on our day/night shades with a solution of OxiClean and water (according to directions on the container). I use a cotton-tip swab or a small brush.

ELEANOR NORBIE,
SIOUX FALLS, SOUTH DAKOTA

For cleaning food spots off of day/night shades, I think I have found the solution. It consists of: 1 teaspoon water softener (Calgon or White King) and 4 cups water. Place a terry towel behind the spot. Dab a small amount of the solution on the spot with a washcloth. Dry as much as possible with the towel. It has not left any spots on my shades.

It also works well on carpet spots, leaving no soap residue in your carpet.

ELVA KOHTZ, KENTWOOD, MICHIGAN

I have dealt with many stained day/night shades during 12 years of professionally cleaning homes. This is the method I use:

First, lightly dab the spot with a clean, barely damp rag, and dry (cotton T-shirts work wonderfully). If the water does not leave a stain, a gentle cleaner can be used.

Dab a bit of Ivory Liquid on the food spot with a cotton-tip swab. (Use only Ivory; other dish detergents do stain.) Wait 30 minutes, then gently blot with a damp cloth and let dry. Repeat if necessary.

I've also had excellent luck with foaming shaving cream. Most contain three kinds of alcohol that prove effective at removing stains (test an inconspicuous spot first).

To dust day/night shades, head to Home Depot for a yellow sponge used to clean tile after it has been grouted. Use it dry to wipe over the shade. Wash and reuse it. Remember to keep day/night shades pulled up several hours a day to keep the pleats well-formed.

MARY FINDLEY,
MARY MOPPINS CLEANING SYSTEM,
EUGENE, OREGON

A Little Dab Will Do It

LYNDA CASTORINO-MILLER, SHANOMG, NEW JERSEY

▶ After finding splatters of dried spaghetti sauce on one of our white day/night shades, I found an easy way to remove the stain. I use a cotton-tipped ear swab dipped in a little Resolve carpet cleaner.

As I dab the stain with the wet cotton swab, I hold a white towel or rag behind the section of shade to help soak up the spot. After the cleaned area dries, you can't tell where the stained area was located.

For colored shades, check for color-fastness before attempting to clean.

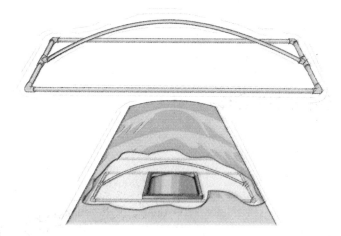

No Poolin'!

STEVE PHELPS, VACAVILLE, CALIFORNIA

▶ To prevent water from pooling on top of my motorhome when the cover is being used, I made an arch from PVC pipe. A rectangular frame held together by 90-degree elbows and two tees supports it. The center pipe is 6 to 10 inches longer than the sides (depending on the width needed) to create the requisite bow.

The arches hold the cover off the top by about a foot and allow the water and leaves to fall off naturally. I can also open the roof vents in the summer to allow the hot air to escape.

Large and Odd

LOU EINUNG, SANTA MARIA, CALIFORNIA

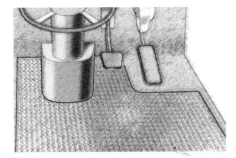

▶ The floor area under the steering wheel of most motorhomes is large and rather oddly shaped and, as a result, most readily available floor mats just won't fit. Also, there is the problem of finding something to match the coach-carpet color.

Our solution? We bought one of those transparent floor protectors that are used under desk chairs. They generally come in very large sizes and are constructed of heavy-duty plastic, designed to take a lot of abuse. They also have built-in carpet-grippers to keep the mat in place.

In our case, we needed a mat that was at least 36 × 32 inches, overall. We went to a local office-supply store and found that its least-expensive mat was larger and cost only $14.

We carefully measured the area to be covered, including necessary cutouts for the steering column and the gas pedal, and managed to get it nicely trimmed on the first try.

It looks really good, mainly because it doesn't look like much at all, which is OK, since the primary idea was to avoid ending up with something ugly. Also, it provides a totally seamless surface in all the driver's underfoot areas, thus eliminating the possibility of getting wadded up (like conventional floor mats), and it's a breeze to clean.

Tie One On

BOB FRANZ, JOPPA, MARYLAND

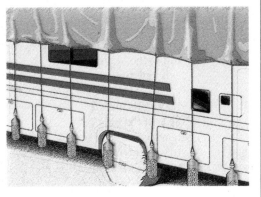

▶ I dislike cleaning leaves, twigs, sap and bird droppings from my motorhome's rubber roof, so I have been using a "poor man's RV cover" to protect everything.

At a hardware store, I purchased a plastic tarp big enough to fit over the motorhome and tied a series of two-liter bottles (filled with sand or gravel), to the tarp's edges. Make sure that the bottles hang below the bottom edge of the motorhome body, but don't touch the ground.

It takes only a few minutes to toss the tarp over the motorhome's roof and to attach the bottles with rope or wire.

I've had no problem with rippling from the wind or wear on the sides of the motorhome.

A CLEAN MACHINE

I have discovered a "must have" for every RV owner. I recently purchased a Mr. Clean Magic Eraser – and was absolutely astounded at the way it cleaned the vinyl dash and seats in our motorhome!

I have used it on almost every surface in my coach and it is the best product to come along in a long time. I had frequently cleaned the dash using products intended for vinyl, but the dirt poured out of the tiny crevices when I used the eraser. I then wiped it away with a wet cloth.

JOY JOHNSON,
HIGHLANDS, NORTH CAROLINA

CREAM THOSE STAINS

Here's a simple (and cheap!) way to clean most dirt and stains from window shades. You will find it also works on most fabrics.

Buy the least-expensive shaving cream you can find and apply the cream to the shade or material; then, brush firmly into the stain (use a soft brush on soft materials and a stiff brush on heavier materials, like carpets), let it set and, once dry, vacuum away the residue. On older stains, a second treatment might be necessary.

HAROLD MORAN,
BLUEFIELD, WEST VIRGINIA

SPOT MOP

Large motorhomes are easy to wash, with products available anywhere, but drying can be a problem. I eased the pain by using a mop that we bought for our Pergo floor. (These mops are available anywhere and are usually used for laminate floors.)

The cloth end attaches by hook-and-loop and can be removed and wrung out just like a chamois. The pole telescopes so I can reach the top of the motorhome without the need of a ladder – I even use it on the windows. Now my motorhome dries perfectly without spots!

GREG GRANDCHAMP,
LA CRESCENTA, CALIFORNIA

cleaning & protecting

A BETTER BRUSH

A whisk broom is handy in the truck or trailer, but I have found that an inexpensive 6-inch paintbrush works even better and lasts much longer than standard straw whisk brooms.

An added benefit is that if the paintbrush gets wet during use, it will dry rapidly without deterioration of the fibers.

ROBERT FRIEDRICH, LOMITA, CALIFORNIA

DON'T BE FOOLED

In regard to refrigerator vent covers turning yellow, the plastic vent cover does not turn yellow.

The pollutants in the air turn the acid rain yellow. The plastic vent is just as white as when it left the factory.

To clean it back to the original white color, spray it with Starbrite Instant Black Streak Remover, and let it sit for 15 minutes. Then, rinse with a hose, being careful not to spray water into the vent holes. If it is not as white as you want, dry it off and repeat the process. Rinse and dry again. Coat with Protect All to keep it white.

MIKE BANISTER, PASADENA, TEXAS

IN THE BAG

We enjoy using an electric casserole in our motorhome, but don't enjoy the cleanup that has to be done in our small sink afterward.

A simple solution is to use an oven bag (such as a Reynolds Oven Bag) inside the electric casserole. Just put the oven bag into the electric casserole, fill with your favorite recipe, and when it's done cooking, remove and dispose of the oven bag.

We find cleanup to be minimal when using this method.

JACQUE COHEN, TROY, MICHIGAN

IT'S THAT EFFERVESCENT ACTION

It may not be exactly what the manufacturer had in mind, but denture-cleaning tablets make short work of stains in the toilet bowl! Just make sure you have enough water in the bowl (a few cups will do it), then drop in one or two tablets, let it sit for about 15 minutes, swish and flush. Denture cleaner also makes cleaning flower vases and coffeepots a breeze.

JOANN WATHEN,
DEARBORN HEIGHTS, MICHIGAN

Register Remedy

KATHY ZIELICKE, FOND DU LAC, WISCONSIN

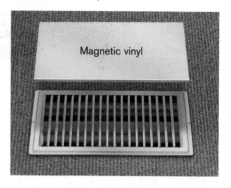

Magnetic vinyl

▶ The in-floor furnace vent grilles in our trailer do not have shutoffs. I know several RVers that have installed the shutoff type vents, but still have the problem of dirt, hair and other debris falling into the ducts.

To help solve this problem, I bought a package of magnetic vinyl from a hardware store. Naturally, this only works if you have the sheet-metal grilles rather than the plastic ones. I used scissors to easily cut the material to fit our registers. Stick the material over the register when the furnace is not in use, and it seals it against debris collection. The vacuum will pass right over without lifting it off the vent.

If you want less heat in an area, simply leave the cover on. We found the magnetic sheet provides a better seal than merely closing the lever.

Got an Old Piece of Carpet?

EDWARD CLARK, PHOENIX, ARIZONA

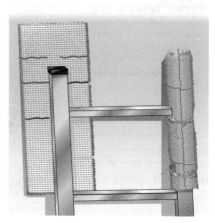

▶ To prevent damage to the finish of my RV when using a ladder to access the roof, I covered the top of the ladder side rails with carpet. The jute backing is placed against the rails, leaving the fiber side to protect the RV.

Cut the carpet twice the width, plus the length of one edge, of the side rail. The length of the piece should be equal to the distance from the top of the second step, over the top, and down to the top step. Cut a notch for the first step, and make four cuts the width of the side rail to allow the carpet to go around and over the top of the ladder rail.

The carpet is secured to the ladder with nylon cord or tape.

Bungee Protection

JERRY KNIGHT, ST. PETERSBURG, FLORIDA

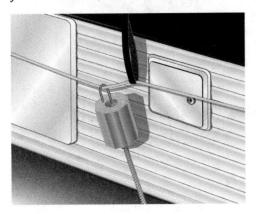

▶ For those who use bungee cords to hold their RV cover in place, there is often the chance that the metal or plastic hooks on the bungee cords will mar the finish on the RV exterior. I solved that problem by buying a swim noodle. They are available at most superstores, especially in the summertime. I selected one that had a hole lengthwise through the center of the noodle. I cut the noodle into 6-inch lengths and threaded the bungee cords through the hole. I now have a built-in bumper that helps keep the hooks away from the finish.

Spout Too Short

FALK BREITMANN, MARTINEZ, GEORGIA

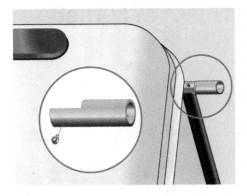

▶ To help fight the dreaded black-streak problem on my fifth-wheel, the trailer is equipped with rain gutters on both sides. At both ends of the gutters, there are spouts designed to divert the runoff from the sides of the trailer.

The only problem with the spouts is that they are too short to do the job. Instead of having black streaks down the entire side of the trailer, there are four concentrated streaks at the four corners of the trailer. In order to correct this, I extended the gutter spouts.

At the hardware store I purchased a two-foot section of 1¼-inch OD clear vinyl hose.

I cut four pieces, each about 6 inches long, and notched one end of each section in order to slip over the existing drain spouts. These spout extensions are then fastened with two painted sheet-metal screws.

Because the hose extensions are constructed of clear vinyl, they are hardly noticeable.

A LITTLE HOUSEKEEPING

Here are a couple of my tried-and-true housekeeping tips:

1. The wood surfaces in my RV sometimes suffer dings and scuffs. An easy, inexpensive fix to the inevitable is Kiwi brown shoe-polishing wax.

Simply pick up a small dab of the wax on a paper towel or cloth. Rub the spot to be covered in the direction of the wood grain. Wipe away the excess and polish with a soft cloth. This procedure even works on most photo-engraved oak-grained wood paneling.

2. For the occasional water ring or stain, wipe real mayonnaise on the affected area; rub it in, clean off the excess, and polish with a clean cloth.

JOE WHITE, DENISON, KANSAS

PROTECT THE FINISH

There are times when you might have to lean a metal extension ladder against the side of your RV for cleaning, maintenance or whatever. No matter how careful you try to be, there is the strong possibility you are going to mar the finish.

To prevent (or at least minimize) this, take some duct tape and apply it to the ladder surfaces which could come in contact with the RV.

DAN DOLAN, LAYTON, UTAH

CLEAN YOUR CEILING

When you have a water stain on your ceiling, it can be a real problem to remove the stain. The following solution will remove any water stain regardless of how long the stain has been on the ceiling.

1 tablespoon Clorox
16 ounces water

Mix the Clorox and water in a spray bottle. Using a white sponge, spray the stain with the solution and keep patting with the white sponge until the stain disappears. You may have to spray several times to remove the stain. It made our ceiling look brand new.

DIANE PRESTEBAK,
EVERETT, WASHINGTON

Editor's note: *You might want to try this on an out-of-the-way spot, to see exactly how your ceiling reacts. Yes, it will remove the water stain, but what other dirt might it also remove? It might even – gasp, shudder – make a clean spot!*

cleaning & protecting

A PINCH OF SALT

I've heard of using club soda to dilute a red-wine or red-soda stain, but all three of my sons were bartenders in college and told me to use regular table salt. Once you see the salt absorbing the color – it will turn the salt red – clean that up and then use a carpet spotter to remove any residue left by the salt. Reapply if necessary.

BETTY TLECKER,
PENSACOLA, FLORIDA

KEEPING IT CLEAN

Keeping the RV clean can be a real chore for full-timers, but there is a way to make it easier.

Whenever we stop for fuel, I get out my one-gallon container that's already filled with water and a measured amount of Protect All's Quick And Easy Wash No Rinsing solution. I keep two Miracle Cloths with the container (one to wash, one to dry).

By the time my husband has paid for the fuel, I usually have at least 90 percent of the truck washed, or the bugs off of the front of the fifth-wheel and the lower sides wiped down.

When we pull into a campsite, before we un-hitch, I use my truck bed as a platform to wash the bugs off of the front of the RV. This is so much easier because the bugs have not "dried out" as they do if you wait several days before cleaning.

After the supper dishes have been washed, I wash the container and Miracle Cloths, refill the container and put it back in the truck for its next use.

SUE McGARTLAND,
STAFFORD, VIRGINIA

Editor's note: *Knock it off! You're spoiling it for the rest of us!*

SAVE THAT BUMPER

The rear bumper on our RV was in need of a new coat of paint because it was chipped and showing rust spots in several places. Instead of having it repainted, however, we opted to have it sprayed with truck bedliner material (after having the chips and rust removed, of course). The bedliner material comes in several colors and we were advised to use the smoothest finish because it is easier to clean.

This has protected against the stone chips and rust spots. We are happy with the result.

BEN RUSNELL, IONIA, MICHIGAN

A Great Idea

WILLIAM ROBERTS, HANOVER, MARYLAND

▶ I found a foam rubber dish-washing brush at the dollar store that does a super job of cleaning cast wheels. I'm sure that anyone would find this tool helpful when cleaning the wheels on a truck, a trailer or a motorhome.

Beat the Dew

CHUCK BOYLE, VENTURA, CALIFORNIA

▶ The frequent heavy dew in our coastal community settles on the roof of our motorhome, mixes with the accumulated dust and dirt, and drips from the front ends of the roofline gutters. The gutters came from the factory with small not-very-effective spouts, angled outward and downward, intended to direct the drainage away from the side walls. We clearly needed downspouts, so I wouldn't have to wash the mess off the windows and sides every time we left the driveway.

I made some simple downspouts, which are easily removed for traveling, out of ½-inch PVC pipe and a few fittings. A 45-degree ½-inch PVC elbow slips nicely over each gutter end, and a short horizontal section rests on the mirror arms, holding it in place. The downward angle of the factory spout helps keep the downspout in place; it sort of snaps into position and stays there.

cleaning & protecting

A Holly Jolly Handle

BERT KALET, WINSTON-SALEM, NORTH CAROLINA

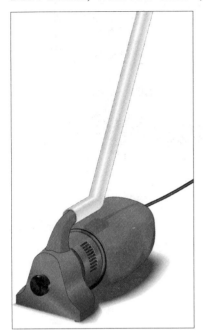

▶ For many of us, bending over or getting on our hands or knees is tough to do, so I put a handle on my Dirt Devil so it can be used just like a regular upright vacuum cleaner.

I took the Dirt Devil to the hardware store and bought a piece of PVC pipe that snugly slid onto the Dirt Devil's handle. I then heated the PVC pipe over a stove burner until the PVC got soft. I then gently bent the pipe to form a 45-degree angle.

I quickly added a crutch tip to the top end, and with two hose clamps, attached the still-soft end to the handle.

Cosseted Covers

CARL R. HARTUP, FORT WAYNE, INDIANA

▶ To protect the tires on our RV from weathering and sun damage, I purchased vinyl tire covers. During high winds, however, the covers would blow off. To solve this problem, I purchased elastic cord and metal S-chain end-links from a hardware store. I measured the front diameter of the wheel and tire, then doubled it to get the cord length. At either end of the cord, I tied an S-link. Now, I simply slip the cord over the rear of the covered tire, then hook the S-links together in front — and the covers stay put.

AND IT SMELLS MINTY FRESH!

Not too long ago, I noticed three small brown stains on our white vinyl recliner. I tried vinyl cleaner and several other cleaning products, but the stains remained.

The trick that worked was a series of applications of Plus White, a five-minute power-bleaching gel that I use on my teeth. I applied it with a cotton swab and wiped it off with a cloth and warm water. By the third application, the stain was gone and the vinyl wasn't harmed in any way.

LORILLA SCHULTZ, BENSON, ARIZONA

Editor's note: *Keep in mind that, if the material is not pure white, any bleaching may cause problems.*

BABY OIL?

I've found I can get a newly polished look on my fiberglass fifth-wheel by applying baby oil.

The RV should be clean before applying the oil. Using a spray bottle, spray the oil onto a small area, wiping down with a folded terry towel. Spray and wipe, spray and wipe, and before you know it, you've completed the job!

The oil puts on a beautiful shine and it also brightens the trim. And, yes, it will collect dust, but just wipe it down with a clean cloth, and the shine reappears. Bugs and those hated black streaks wipe off with ease.

I "oil" my fifth-wheel about every four months; it takes about one hour each time, compared to a full day or two for a conventional wax job.

JOHN KOLBERT, POMONA, CALIFORNIA

Editor's note: *Do not use on rubber roofs, seals or tires, or where petroleum distillates may have a damaging effect.*

WET & MESSY

During inclement weather our slideouts become wet and messy due to the rain and dust in the air.

Retracting the slideout into the RV under these conditions can lead to other problems because the moisture and dampness can ruin carpets, bedding and interior walls.

One solution is to wipe down the wet surfaces. To make that job easier, I use a long-handled Swiffer and blue shop paper towels. I attach one of the paper towels on the bottom of the Swiffer unit and use it to wipe the walls and roof of the slideouts.

DENNIS KALIS, VACAVILLE, CALIFORNIA

NO MORE ACROBATICS

Our trailer has a large picture window at the rear. We enjoy turning our living-room chairs around so we can view the scenery. Unfortunately, after a road trip the windows are usually dirty.

To clean the windows, I use a one-gallon hand-pump weed sprayer (found at any store selling garden supplies) and a window squeegee. Plain water will clean most road dirt.

The spray wand has a long hose that can wet all the windows. By attaching a 5-foot extension handle to the squeegee, I can clean even the high windows on our fifth-wheel's bedroom slide. Now we don't have to perform acrobatics to try to wash the windows with a typical spray bottle and paper towels.

DICK SAMSON,
FORT COLLINS, COLORADO

SOCK IT TO ME

Our RV has a small, dark storage compartment for our power cord. While traveling, I keep an old sock tied onto the plug end. This way, when we arrive at a park, I can easily spot the end of the cord without fumbling around for it. I pull out the cord to plug it in and leave the sock in the compartment.

When we are ready to leave, I wipe the power cord with the sock as I store the cord and then tie the sock on the end of the cord. This helps keep the cord – and the compartment – clean.

PATRICIA BERGEN,
LIVINGSTON, TEXAS

ODOR EATER

How do you get rid of skunk smell on your pet? Contrary to popular opinion, using tomato juice is just a myth. All this does is add the smell of tomato juice to the smell of the spray, or its chemical name, butenyl. In order to fully get the smell off yourself or your pet, use about a quart of 3 percent hydrogen peroxide. Mix this with ¼ cup of sodium bicarbonate, or baking soda, and add a dash of dishwasher detergent. Spray the affected areas. The dishwasher detergent will bring the butenyl to the surface, and the other two chemicals will react with the smell and destroy it.

Wash the areas that have been sprayed with normal soap and water to get the chemicals off your pet – or yourself, for that matter.

KEVIN KEICHENLAU, VIA E-MAIL

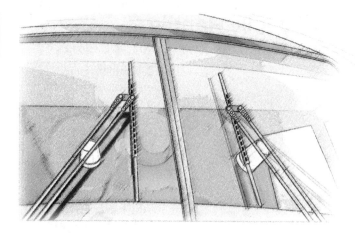

Chocolate Coach Mocha

HARVEY HETRICK, TORRANCE, CALIFORNIA

▶ The next time you enjoy a cup of coffee, hold on to that foam cup — it can be used to help protect those expensive motorhome wiper blades.

Simply place a cup under each wiper arm so that, when you're parked, the blades are raised off of the hot windshield.

Save That Hose

HARVEY HETRICK, TORRANCE, CALIFORNIA

▶ There are many uses for old garden hose. One use around the motorhome is for wiper-blade protectors. Select the parts of that old hose that are not in bad shape. Measure your wiper blades and cut the hose about 2 inches longer. Using a sharp utility knife, slit the hose lengthwise. I 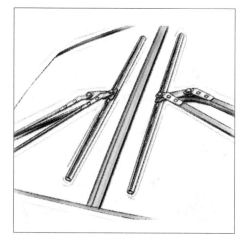 lucked out; my hose had a white line for a guide.

When parked, use two sections of hose to protect the wiper blades from the sun's ultraviolet rays. Remember to remove the hoses before driving away. I have been using them for more than a year and have experienced no adverse interaction between the wiper blades and the hose.

You might even have enough leftover hose to make protectors for your friends.

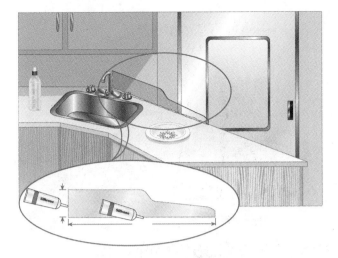

Backsplash Backlash

CARMAN BRUMLEY, HUNTSVILLE, TEXAS

▷ We were having problems with water and other liquids running off the counter in the kitchen area and staining/damaging the wall and cabinet.

To help protect the area near the sink, we had a glass company cut a decorative piece of ¼-inch glass, 18 inches long by 4 inches high, and used silicone to glue it to the countertop and wall. We had the edges of the glass polished to smooth out the sharp, exposed upper edge.

Now, water and other items no longer run off the edge of the countertop.

Chair Care

ARLENE CHIAROLANZIO, FLORHAM PARK, NEW JERSEY

▷ The only chair we have in our coach is a comfortable recliner — and it is used constantly. To keep the arms and headrest clean, I purchased identical material at a fabric store, and made two arm rest covers and a cover that slips over the back of the chair.

The covers keep the chair from being soiled, and are easy to remove and wash!

cleaning & protecting

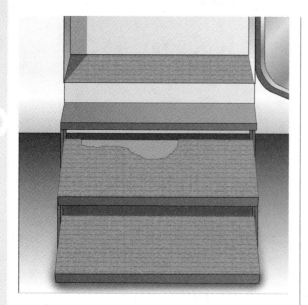

Step Covers

IGNES BARTA, FLATONIA, TEXAS

▶ Cutting pieces from a small AstroTurf mat to fit inside the entry steps helped cut down on dirt being tracked into our motorhome. To clean them, we just pick them up and shake out the dirt.

Also, gluing smaller pieces to the electric steps helped alleviate the "hot steps" when entering barefooted. A cut-out on the second step was needed in our case to clear the electric motor.

DRYING SHORTCUT

After washing my motorhome and rinsing it off, I use a leaf blower to help remove the water. It works great, saves time and keeps water spots to a minimum. Just be careful not to blow the water onto another RV or car.

JIM LEWIS, SOLVANG, CALIFORNIA

GUARDIN' HOSE

I needed to move my satellite dish across a gravel road for better reception, which left a section of the cord susceptible to damage. To protect the cable, I ran it through an old water hose.

RICHARD PREVALLET,
LIVINGSTON, TEXAS

Keeping It Clean

HARVEY HETRICK, TORRANCE, CALIFORNIA

▶ After several years of using aluminum foil as a splash guard around our RV stove, we found an inexpensive and more durable product. Disposable cookie sheets do wonders. We can buy two for about $4, and they will last a very long time. The 15 × 10-inch size works fine. Simply place them around the sides of the stove, and wash them when required. On our stove, no attachment is required. Stow them away in the oven when not in use. Who knows, you might even need them to bake cookies someday!

Protect Yourself

ARLENE CHIAROLANZIO, FLORHAM PARK, NEW JERSEY

▶ When passing the dinette or going down the steps of my motorhome, everyone would hold onto the back of the dinette seat, causing it to get dirty and worn. To fix this problem, I purchased a yard of strong clear vinyl, removed the back cushions, stapled the vinyl over the material and replaced the cushions. It looks good, and the vinyl lasts and lasts!

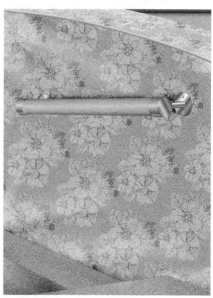

10

minute tech

devices & gadgets

A Boat-Seat TV Mount

A.B. KENNEDY, ETHEL, LOUISIANA

▶ While on a trip this summer, I found that placing the television in a secure travel position became tedious. A search for a permanent travel mount proved to be unsatisfactory, due to high cost and fragility. After I returned home and started to prepare for a fishing trip, the swivel mount under a boat seat caught my attention.

The local Wal-Mart had a seat mount of perfect

height, and some ¼-inch bolts, small eye bolts and a length of hard rubber bungee cord completed the materials list. A small barrel bolt was added later as a travel lock. Some structural reinforcement beneath the chosen shelf location was also required.

Our area provided clearance that allows rotation for different viewing angles.

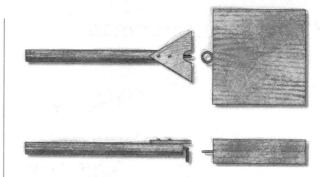

Stop Crawling

JIM HINES, MESA, ARIZONA

▶ I got tired of crawling on my hands and knees to place blocking for the jacks under my motorhome. I tried broom handles, an awning rod, etc., but could not steer the pads into place using these. To solve this problem, I fastened a triangle of plywood to the end of an old broom handle, and inserted an L-screw hook in the handle's end that extends close to the edge of the plywood. This device has become my "pushrod."

My pad blocks are laminated 12-inch squares of ¾-inch plywood. A screw eye in the center of one edge of each block provides a spot to attach the broom-handle pushrod. The plywood triangle keeps the pad from flopping sideways as it's pushed into place, and the hook is easy to hang on the screw eye when I want to pull the pads out for storage.

Removable Flag Bracket

SANDRA REED, ERIE, PENNSYLVANIA

▶ We wanted to fly a flag from our motorhome, but didn't like the idea of mounting a permanent bracket on our coach.

A visit to a boating-supply store provided the answer. We bought a fishing-rod holder sized to clamp to 1-inch vertical tubing.

The holder itself can be tilted forward or back to put the pole at an angle, and is large enough to easily accommodate a wood flagpole. We mount our bracket on the vertical rail near the top of our ladder. Now, in just a few minutes, we can be ready to fly the flag without permanent modification to our coach.

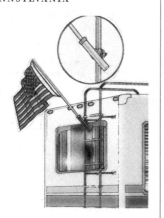

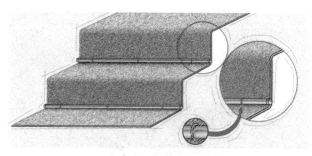

Á Stairway to Heaven

MARLENE ENDECOTT, BOISE, IDAHO

▶ Keeping our motorhome entry steps clean is always a challenge. I find a rug runner, secured by two curtain-rod tension bars mounted against the stair risers, allows me to easily remove the rug for cleaning.

To keep the top edge of the carpet from slipping out of the doorway, I have sewn hook-and-loop fastener to the underside of the top edge, with the other part stapled to the floor.

Control Your Thermos

ROBERT HICKEY, OXFORD, OHIO

▶ When we drive off early in the morning, we like to have a thermos of coffee available for that first "stay awake" cup. The only problem we had was keeping the thermos under control some place other than between the copilot's knees. I devised a setup using two watchbands (continuous type) purchased at Wal-Mart. Strips of hook-and-loop fasteners would work also.

I wrapped and secured the first band (tan band in drawing) around the nonflexible part of the seat-belt anchor arm, then inserted a second band (black band in drawing) at a right angle inside the first. Taking the open ends of the hook-and-loop band, I wrapped it around the thermos under the handle and stuck the hooks and loops together.

On rough roads and even during quick stops, the thermos has not come rolling forward around the pedals, but has remained secure and unspilled. When the seat belt is used the thermos position may need to be adjusted to remain upright, but the setup is still usable.

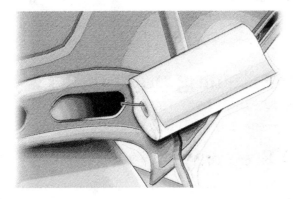

Handy Wipes

DARRYL FOREMAN, LAFAYETTE, LOUISIANA

▶ It may not be high-tech, but a roll of paper towels, hung inside the trunk lid of your towed vehicle using a bungee cord, keeps the roll out of the way and ready to be used when needed.

SOUND MACHINE

Like many motorhome owners, I upgraded to a satellite dish and receiver. In addition to the 130 video channels, my system also has 50 channels of digital stereo sound — unfortunately, the satellite system is attached to my 19-inch television set, a unit with small, poor-quality speakers.

Since replacing the television was out of the question, I added a Sound Feeder from Arkon Resources Inc. (arkon.com) that enabled me to transmit high-quality, line-level stereo audio short distances (6 feet) to the FM stereo radio in the dash of my coach. The system consists of the relatively inexpensive ($10-$20) Sound Feeder and an adapter cable (a ⅛-inch stereo plug and two RCA plugs), available at many places including RadioShack and Wal-Mart.

The unit works by finding and utilizing a blank frequency on your motorhome's FM stereo receiver. With everything plugged in properly, you simply sweep across the FM frequency dial until the television sound is received on your stereo.

As you drive into different parts of the country you will probably have to find a different blank channel on the radio, as the old channel might be active in the new area.

DON DEJARNETTE, NORTHPORT, ALABAMA

TENNIS, ANYONE?

After motorhoming for many years, we have found used tennis balls to be almost as useful as bungee straps on or around our motorhome.

Placed under the wiper arms, they keep the expensive wiper blades from "cooking" on the hot windshield when the motorhome is in storage. Cut an X in them, and they cover the tow ball when not in use. Slide them over the ends of tent stakes to protect people walking by. Slide them over the handles of bicycles on the storage rack to keep them from poking holes in the cover. I'm sure that you can find many other uses for those free worn-out balls that can be picked up around any tennis court.

KENNETH ORR, JENSEN BEACH, FLORIDA

PULL THE RUBBER SEAL OUT

I noticed that when extending the slideouts on my fifth-wheel, the outer rubber seal always has at least one area which stays rolled under. To correct this, I use a vinyl-siding unlatching tool, which is a one-inch wide, thin steel blade with a ⅛-inch long hook bent in one end, to reposition the rubber seal. The tool, available wherever residential vinyl siding is sold, costs less than $5.

RICHARD WIEBE, TUCSON, ARIZONA

devices & gadgets

QUIT RUBBER-NECKING

At one time or another, we have all experienced situations while driving that resulted in a crash, bang or slam noise inside the rear of the coach. Without a windshield-mounted rearview mirror, it is difficult to see how serious the problem is – and to compound the problem, traffic or road conditions may not allow one to pull over, or the copilot to investigate.

My solution was to purchase an inexpensive, suction-cup-mounted mirror, which I found at Wal-Mart. Its original purpose was to allow the driver to view children in a rear car seat. It is convex in shape, pivotal and can be easily removed and reapplied. I can now see the inside of the coach without rubber-necking – and plan a safe stop, if needed.

PAT CRAWFORD,
SAN LUIS OBISPO, CALIFORNIA

VERY REMOTE CONTROL

Did you know that your satellite receiver can be controlled by your system's remote from another room? This comes in handy if you have only one satellite receiver and use a signal splitter for two televisions, such as in a living room and a bedroom.

You can accomplish this by purchasing a set of wireless remote-control extenders. The set we purchased at an electronics store cost about $50. They are less than 5 inches tall and are in the shape of small pyramids. Both require access to an electrical outlet.

Place one in the room in which your second television is located, and place the other so that it is in the line of sight of your satellite receiver's infrared remote sensor. These extenders work very well and are not affected by obstructions such as walls or doors.

CARL PULLUM, ROGERS, ARKANSAS

ANOTHER ROLL STOP

Like most RVers, one of the first things we installed in our motorhome was a paper-towel holder. However, it wasn't too far down the road and not many breezy days later when we found ourselves continually rerolling the towels.

We soon put a stop to that by clamping a bicycle pants clip around the roll. We had an old one handy, but new ones are very inexpensive. If you want to do your own thing, shape a flexible piece of aluminum. The device is easily attached and unattached, and when we want to, we roll.

MARGARET CODA-MESSERLE,
LONG BEACH, CALIFORNIA

Have a Ball

RICHARD NORRIS, SNELLVILLE, GEORGIA

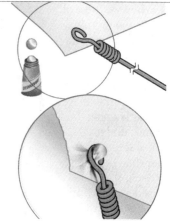

▶ Don't throw away that old deodorant bottle before you remove the plastic ball. The ball serves as a handy movable grommet on plastic sheeting, with the advantage of being able to place it exactly where you want, and then to be able to move it as necessary to adjust your tie-downs.

To secure a tarp or plastic sheeting, first press the ball up from the underside and gather the sheeting around the ball. Next, slip the hook end of a bungee cord or nylon cord under the ball on the top side of the sheeting.

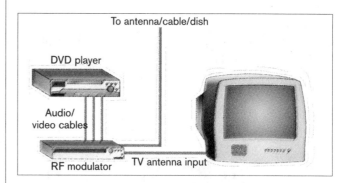

Entertaining Upgrade

STUART TODD, LOUISVILLE, COLORADO

▶ I recently upgraded my motorhome from a VCR to a new DVD player. Not wanting to rip apart the trim and upholstery to route the three-wire cable needed for connecting the new DVD player to the television — and not having the necessary three input jacks on my television — I purchased a nifty and inexpensive gadget at Wal-Mart.

For less than $18, I bought a Philips RF modulator (model No. PH61159) that connected where the old VCR used to be. The modulator's operation is automatic; it "sees" when you turn on the DVD player and puts out a signal on channel 3 or 4, just as the VCR would. The only additional work is plugging in a small power module (part of the PH61159 package) to provide power to the modulator.

Another Filter Holder

JOE BARTOK, HIGHLAND, INDIANA

▶ An effective water-filter holder can be easily made from a highway safety cone. They can be purchased at various locations, including home-improvement centers.

Cut the pointed top off far enough down so that your filter will slip inside, and will be supported by the incoming and outgoing hoses. In addition, you could cut a notch on each side to allow for the hoses, increasing the stability of the complete unit.

The safety-cone holder will also protect the filter from the sun and the bright color will make it very visible.

Fetching Little Cords

TRACY GORDON, BARSTOW, CALIFORNIA

▶ Rather than spend money on those fetching little bungee cords with the plastic ball ends, I cobbled up my own, using paired ¾- to 1-inch-wide strips of old bicycle inner tubes. A length of about 18 inches is ideal for taming a 25-foot water hose, but strips may be cut to any length to suit

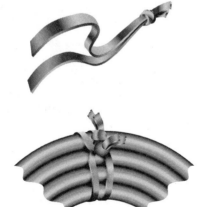

any purpose. Simply tie the strip ends together in a large knot, which acts as the bungee cord's ball end. The knotted ball ends overlap and lock together.

Fifth-Wheel Tailgate

CLYDE WILSON, RENO, NEVADA

▶ I needed a fifth-wheel tailgate to keep objects from falling out of the back of the truck bed. So, for less than $12, I made this one.

From the hardware store, I bought a wire closet shelf and a piece of angle iron with holes (normally used to hang garage-door openers). I cut the shelf to length and mounted a piece of the angle iron to the bed on each side. I cut slots in the angle-iron web so that the end of the shelf frame will slip right in or out. It looks good when finished with a coat of black paint.

Totally Tubular

LARRY BONHAM,
ELLSINORE, MISSOURI

▶ I'm constantly having to dig around in the bottom of the toolbox to find the nozzle tube for the spray can of WD-40. Once I use it, I can never get it back under that piece of tape on the side of the can.

So, I took a short piece of a plastic straw, heated and mashed it flat on one end, then duct-taped it to the side of the can. Now, I just slip the nozzle tube in the straw.

Ladder Lugger

JEFF ADAMS, SANTEE, CALIFORNIA

▶ I purchased a 6-foot collapsible ladder to take with us on the road. The ladder had to be transported inside the trailer and dragged out of the way at every campground and then dragged back in when we were ready to leave. I came up with the following solution:

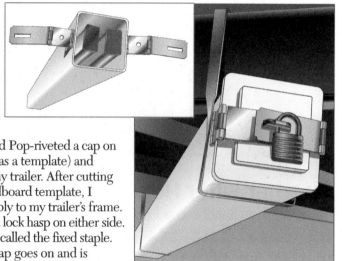

At a home-improvement center, I found a 5-inch-square × 8-foot vinyl tube, used to conceal deck posts. I also purchased two end caps, some 1 × ⅛-inch-thick steel strap, two lock hasps and some ⅛-inch steel Pop rivets.

I cut the tube about 2 inches longer than the ladder and Pop-riveted a cap on one end. I then took some 1-inch-wide cardboard (to use as a template) and made dummy straps to attach the tube to the bottom of my trailer. After cutting and bending the steel strap to match the shape of the cardboard template, I riveted them to the tube. Then I riveted the whole assembly to my trailer's frame.

At the open end of the tube, I riveted the hinge part of a lock hasp on either side. To the remaining cap end, I riveted the part of the hasp set called the fixed staple.

The ladder folds and slides neatly into the tube. The cap goes on and is locked. The ladder stays in place until needed.

Make sure the location for the tube you have chosen won't cause the tube to hang too low and possibly hit high-profile obstructions on the road.

Utility Player

DON UNGER, COLDWATER, MICHIGAN

▶ One piece of ¾-inch PVC pipe, 42 inches long, with a line at 37 inches and a ⅜ × ⅜-inch notch in one end, plus a United States quarter glued to the other end can be used for the following purposes.

•Turn the slide's light switches, (mounted on our 8-foot ceiling) on and off.

•Turn the bathroom-vent-fan switch on and off.

•The notch is used to fit over the crank handle to open and close the ceiling vents.

•The 37-inch line on the stick is used to measure the clearance needed for our slideouts at a parking site (your measurement will vary).

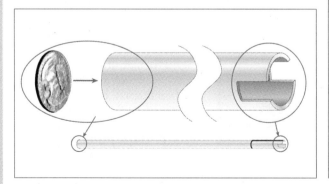

Entryway Shoe Rack

EVE HUPPERT, LIVINGSTON, TEXAS

▶ In an attempt to keep the inside of our new fifth-wheel clean, my husband and I have gotten into the habit of taking our shoes off when we enter. The shoes sitting on our steps looked messy and they could be a hazard. After a bit of planning, we finally came up with a solution.

There is a 3-inch ledge next to our door. We purchased a piece of ³⁄₁₆-inch-thick Plexiglas measuring 12 × 28 inches to protect the wall, and a 2½-inch adjustable shirring rod meant for a curtain valence. We mounted the rod so that the bottom was 3½ inches above the floor. This holds four pairs of shoes by the door, inside the RV and out of the way.

Is There Anything They Can't Do?

PAUL FOREST, ROCHESTER, NEW YORK

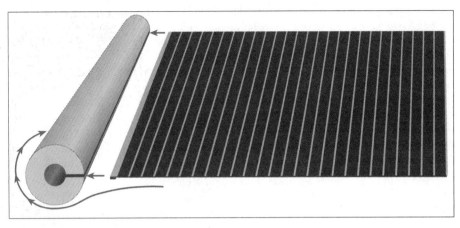

▶ The tonneau cover on my truck does not have "snaps," but instead utilizes a rib-lock-track system to secure it to the truck's bed-rail system. Without assistance, it is very difficult to roll up the cover neatly.

To make it easier, I use a swimming noodle. It is exactly the correct length to match the width of the tonneau cover. Begin with a noodle that contains an inner hole, and then cut all the way down the length of the noodle into the center hole.

Now, insert the end of the tonneau cover into the slit you have cut. The cover's locking rib will help prevent the cover from slipping out of the noodle. Then begin rolling up the cover. The noodle will help maintain an even roll to the cover and, since the noodle is soft, it will not damage the cover.

Cheap Chocks

KIM TINNES, GROVEVILLE, NEW JERSEY

▶ Here's how I made a set of cheap chocks: I took a pressure-treated 2 × 8-inch board and cut eight wedges that fit between the trailer's tandem tires. I used a piece of cardboard to make a cutting pattern for the wood wedges.

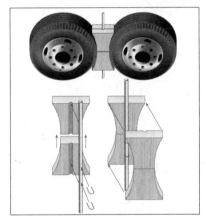

I then sandwiched a piece of ⅜-inch threaded rod between four of the wedges. (I screwed two pieces together and bored a hole down the length of the wedge to allow the passage of the rod.)

I anchored one end of the rod with finishing nails before screwing one set together, so only one wrench was needed. I topped the assembly with a fender washer and a nut.

Once the rod was placed between the tires, I tightened the top nut. This draws the wedges together and stops excessive movement.

Keep the Cord Clean

JOHN McCULLOUGH,
WASHINGTON COURT HOUSE, OHIO

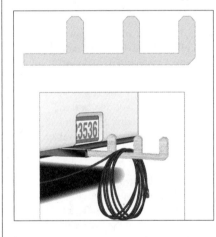

▶ The power cord on our fifth-wheel is quite bulky and heavy. We had tried several different ways of keeping the power cord off the ground, such as a laundry basket. That kept the cord off the ground, but water and dirt would accumulate inside the basket, defeating the purpose of keeping the cord clean and dry.

I designed a holder that fits into the hitch receiver at the back of the fifth-wheel when we are parked. I used a 1-inch-thick wooden board cut to an 18-inch length. Then, I made the section that goes into the receiver 4½ inches long and cut two cavities from which I hang the power cord and the satellite-TV cable.

This works quite well, keeping the cords clean, dry and neatly stored while camping.

devices & gadgets

BEAUTIFUL NOISE

To enhance the sound from a television, MP3, CD, DVD player, PDA, laptop or PC that has an earphone outlet plug, RadioShack has a very simple wireless adapter, the irock! Beamit model 400FM.

The size of a PC mouse, it comes with a short pigtail to plug into the earphone outlet of the device you want to play through a FM-tuned sound system. It is powered by two AAA batteries or accessory plug adapter, has an on/off switch and a range of up to 30 feet. Just plug it in and tune the FM receiver. No extra wires or connections.

JOE TURNER, CLOVIS, NEW MEXICO

UPSIDE-DOWN PRIVACY

My wife and I don't like to close our motorhome blinds. We enjoy the sunlight streaming through our windows in daytime and seeing star-filled skies and visitations from night critters from our bed at night.

Unfortunately this means that nearby campers have a clear view into our bed, which is unsettling to me, though unquestionably boring to my neighbors.

In order to get the privacy we need in the lower half of the window, the shades must be drawn down their whole length from the top, cutting off all view to the outside.

To solve this dilemma, I mounted an ordinary window shade along the bottom of both bedroom side windows. I bent the slotted roller bracket closed with a pair of pliers so the roller won't fall out (because it is mounted upside-down). I drilled a hole through the center of the shade's wooden batten that stiffens the lower (my upper) edge to which I tied a string. The string leads upward to a cleat mounted in the center of the wall just above the window.

To use, I pull up the shade to give the desired amount of privacy that I need and wrap the string around the cleat. I then pull the shade upward to activate the internal spring, and release it slowly until it lowers the end of the string, where the shade remains tight in its final position.

The infinite height-adjustment possibilities of the upside-down shade system allow me to adjust for whatever amount of privacy I desire.

When the shade is not in use, I allow the roller to roll up the entire shade – where it remains out of the way at the bottom of the window.

BOB DIFLEY, WEST LINN, OREGON

Ohm, My!

WILTON DICKERSON, DURHAM, NORTH CAROLINA

▶ In our motorhome, we could never figure out a good place to put our toothbrushes. One day, we were in the hardware store and I found some wire guides, (used to hold down electrical wires), with adhesive on the back. I stuck several up inside the medicine cabinet and our toothbrushes slide right in the holder and do not fall out, even while we are driving down the road. You can buy a package of six of these holders for about $1.50.

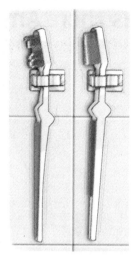

Water Wand

CHRIS HOBBS, RANCHO MURRIETA, CALIFORNIA

▶ I bought a water wand, with a stiff tip, at Wal-Mart for about $2. I wanted to use it to fill the water tank on my RV. I had recently purchased another one that had a flexible tip, but the weight of the attached hose would bend it, stopping the flow.

I cut off the head with a tubing cutter (if your RV's filler spout is curved, be sure to leave the curve in). The brass part fits snugly in the inlet and doesn't back out with pressure. I also added a quick-disconnect, just like all the other hoses in the RV.

Neat Cord Holder

REBA LEWIS, MACON, MISSOURI

▶ To keep electric cords out of the way but accessible, I use the center cardboard from toilet-tissue rolls.

I cover them with colored tape, which makes them a very sturdy holder. I fold the cord and put it in so I can pull the length needed.

This works great for all appliances and keeps the cords from tangling around other things.

Get a Handle on It

F R A N K   M A R E L L I,
L I V I N G S T O N,   T E X A S

▶ When the plastic T-handle on my sewer-drain valve broke, I had difficulty locating a new one. While at the hardware store, I discovered that the metal handle used on outside water faucets was a suitable replacement. I used two thin nuts to secure it to the sewer valve shaft.

Interestingly, I later found the original plastic handle at a camping supply store, selling for $4.39. The garden-hose faucet handle sells for about a buck!

He Saved the Day

A R L E N E   C H I A R O L A N Z I O,
F L O R H A M   P A R K,   N E W   J E R S E Y

▶ When backing into my driveway, I have to back onto a pull-off and up to a chain-link fence. Invariably, I would be either up against the fence or too far away due to the amount of overhang behind the rear axle.

My husband saved the day by putting a low white concrete block exactly where each rear tire should stop. The blocks work especially well at night and can be seen in the side mirrors to line up the motorhome.

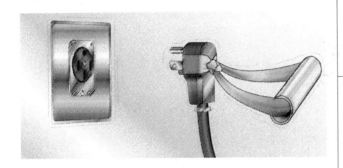

Power Play

R O B E R T   H O L T O N,   S O U T H A V E N,   M I S S I S S I P P I

▶ Due to arthritis in my hands, I sometimes have trouble pulling out the 50-amp power plug from the electrical service when breaking camp.

To make it easier for myself, I took a length of nylon strap and marked the position of the power plug's two prongs on the strap. I then heated the end of an old screwdriver and, at each mark, pushed the heated screwdriver end through the nylon strap. The heat will seal the webbing so it will not fray.

I slipped the webbing over the two prongs and tied a square knot tight against the back of the plug, then slipped a piece of ¾-inch PVC pipe over one side of the webbing and tied the two ends together; remaining ends were trimmed off. With the PVC pipe over the knot, the handle centered itself.

Now, by pulling the handle, I can easily remove the plug from the socket.

Hand Saver

J A C K   F O X,   C A R T H A G E,   T E X A S

▶ While raising the landing gear of my fifth-wheel, after unpinning it, I found it very awkward to get my hand beneath it.

So I took an old bicycle handle bar, cut the end off to length, flattened the cut end and drilled a hole in it.

I bolted it to the landing gear plate to make a very convenient handle with which to raise the plate.

Editor's note: *A countersunk screw would allow the entire plate surface to be used evenly.*

SILENCE IS GOLDEN

Cordless RF (radio frequency) headphones are wonderful in the confined quarters of an RV.

As opposed to the infrared type, this transmitter headphone system will not only allow you to roam inside, but also works up to about 100 feet outside your rig. This is accomplished with no wires and without interruption of the audio signal.

You can watch television while your spouse reads in peace. If one of you is hard of hearing, he or she can use the headphones to increase the volume, while the other watches and listens at a normal sound level. The neighbors will be happy, too.

Another bonus is using the headphones outside while setting up the satellite dish. I select the dish-pointing channel on the television, but instead of opening the RV windows and cranking the TV volume to hear the audio signal, or having my wife relay instructions to me, I simply put on my headphones to hear the audio pitch changes as the dish signal is captured and fine-tuned.

These headphones are not expensive and are available at major electronic outlets.

THOMAS WINTER, PENSACOLA, FLORIDA

RUG CARRIER

Here's an idea for carrying your outdoor rug(s). Get a piece of 4-inch PVC pipe (and two end caps) to fit the length of your pickup's bed. Attach the end caps to both ends. To use, uncap one end, slide the rug in and replace the cap. A smaller rug could use a shorter length of pipe. If you get caught in the rain with a wet rug, you can put it in the pipe and unroll it at your next stop to dry, and not get anything in your rig wet or dirty.

LARRY KILLEBREW, CAULFIELD, MISSOURI

THAT'S THE BRAKES!

I have managed to break two of the yellow knobs (used on many coaches) for setting and releasing the parking brake of my motorhome.

Then an idea hit me. I carry a spare gray-and-black holding-tank valve handle with me. Guess what? The ¼ × 20 threads of the valve handle matched perfectly with the parking knob shaft.

In short order, I had a durable handle that worked even more easily than the OEM knob – and, at just $12, it was cheaper, too! Just be sure to buy the metal valve handle.

CHUCK RICHARDS, SEQUIM, WASHINGTON

The Detangler

TONY HARE, PERU, INDIANA

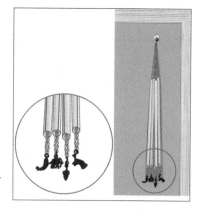

▶ My wife likes to travel with several necklaces that have pendants. While the trailer is moving, the necklaces always seem to wrap themselves around each other and into knots. Tired of being the official "necklace-knot untier," I came up with a way to keep the necklaces from getting tangled: I put each one in a soda straw to keep them separated.

Now my wife is happy with her jewelry and I am happy I don't have to untangle those fine knots.

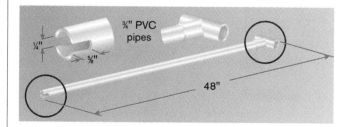

¾" PVC pipes

¼"

⅝"

48"

Valve-Turning Tool

PENN SCHLOEMANN, MIDLAND, MICHIGAN

▶ On some motorhomes, the freshwater storage tank is located in the middle of the coach with the drain valve directly in back of the tank. To open or close the valve it is necessary to open the side storage compartment and lean inside the compartment to reach the valve handle. When the storage compartment is full, it is even more difficult to reach the valve to open or close it.

A simple valve-turning tool can be made using PVC pipe. Make a cutout in one end of a 4-foot length of ¾-inch PVC pipe, so that the pipe fits snugly over the center of the valve handle. The cutout should be about ¼-inch wide and ⅝-inch long. The inside diameter and length of the pipe and the dimensions of the cutout can be changed to fit any valve and motorhome. Glue a ¾-inch PVC tee to the other end of the pipe to aid in turning the pipe and valve. Mark arrows with a black felt marker on the end of the pipe, near the tee, to indicate the direction it must be turned to either open or close the valve.

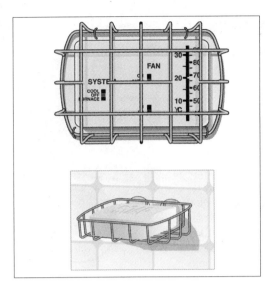

Soapy Security

JIM SABOURIN, MARSTONS MILLS, MASSACHUSETTS

▶ After a season of banging my shoulders into the heat/air conditioning control unit in the narrow hallway of my RV, I knew I had to do something to prevent an expensive repair. The solution had to "deflect bumps" without visually covering the control unit or blocking the air flow to it.

For about $1, I found the answer at Wal-Mart. It is called a suction soap dish (part no. 08380). It's metal and chrome and was perfect for the size I needed.

First I removed the suction cups. Fitting the dish over the control unit was easy, but two of its metal bars blocked the switches on the control unit. I cut them out and filed the edges. I mounted the wire dish upside down against the wall, and it covers the control unit. I pre-drilled the holes for four "U" shaped nails I had on my workbench and pressed them in carefully.

Awkward to Coil

WENDELL SIEWERT, ENID, OKLAHOMA

▶ We have a detached 50-amp shore line on our motorhome. Its 25-foot length is awkward to coil and carry, in addition to its weight.

I took a 5-gallon plastic paint bucket with the lid on. I cut a large hole in the lid with my sabre saw, leaving a lip of 1½ inches around the inside edge. I cut another hole in the side of the bucket, at the bottom below one of the bail ends, large enough to allow the male plug end to be pulled through.

I pull about 2 feet of the male plug end through the bottom hole, and then coil the remainder of the line inside the bucket from the top. The 1½-inch lip around the top keeps the line from popping out, and the entire line is easy to carry with the male end protruding outside, but clipped inside the bail.

When hooking up, I pull the female end out of the top, plug it into the motorhome, carry the bucket to the power post and connect. Should it rain, any water easily drains out of the bottom hole, and you never uncoil any more shore line than you need.

This concept could easily be adapted to 30-amp cords and lines permanently wired to the coach, as long as there is room to store the bucket where the power cord begins.

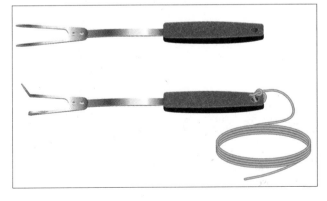

Valve First Aid

MELVILLE KITTILSEN, ARCADIA, CALIFORNIA

▶ Here's a solution for getting that wad of toilet paper out of the rubber seal in the gate valve of your toilet. Buy a barbecue fork (one of those that have two prongs). Bend one of the prongs flat and the other prong at 90 degrees about ⅝- to ¾-inch long. This will work perfectly inside the seal and go over the gate valve. Be sure to get a length of cord and tie it to the handle. Make it long enough, with a loop in the end, that you can fasten it to a nearby faucet, so you won't have to go fishing in case you drop it.

devices & gadgets

Hold That Cargo

ANNETTE O'DONNELL, MESA, ARIZONA

▶ We have a side-by-side closet, which came with a very large shelf. In order to prevent items from toppling out, we purchased an elastic cargo net, which can be found at most auto-parts stores. Just screw in some hooks (around the shelf area) and, when traveling, loop the ends of the netting over the hooks.

Just a Thought

JIM KING,
COLORADO SPRINGS,
COLORADO

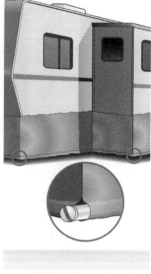

▶ I had a vinyl skirt made for my trailer with pockets sewn along the bottom edge to hold pipes. The skirt snaps in place, and the 2-inch PVC pipes (which are filled with sand for weight) slip into the pockets to anchor the skirt. I built a carrier that bolts under the trailer to hold the pipes when the skirt is not in use. In the summer, the pipes are used to hold down the screen room.

10 minute tech

doors, handles & hatches

Bolt Action

STEVE GARRETT, PENSACOLA, FLORIDA

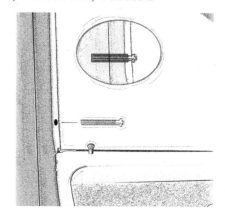

▶ I wanted more security for my driver's side door, especially when my coach is parked in strange surroundings.

The standard lock and latch are not very strong — anyone with a screwdriver could quickly gain entry.

I solved this problem by drilling a ¼-inch hole through the driver's door (on the inside of the coach) and into the door jam. The hole is on the latch side of the door and extends one inch through the doorframe and one inch into the door jam.

I can now insert a 2½ × ¼-inch bolt into the hole, which acts like a deadbolt to secure the door. When inserted, the bolt sticks out about ½-inch so it can easily be removed from inside the coach.

Poodle Protection

MARY COEN, ELKHART, KANSAS

▶ On our last outing, we took our poodle along for the ride. He decided to put a hole in our screen door. Here is how we fixed our problem — without buying a $57-plus door protector.

We headed to our nearby home center, where we found gutter covers, with screening, for about $2 each. All we had to do was cut them to fit and screw them to the screen door frame. The problem is fixed, and the door is stronger — not to mention "poodle proof."

Discourage Them Critters

JAMES GORMAN, COOS BAY, OREGON

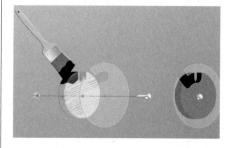

▶ After we bought our new motorhome, I discovered that the compartments that stored the electrical cord and water hose had 4-inch access holes (with threaded plugs to close them when not needed). This is way more room than is needed to pass a hose or an electrical cord through.

I came up with the following idea:

From a piece of ½-inch treated plywood, use a 4-inch hole saw to make a 3¾-inch disk. Then cut a ⅞-inch notch on the edge of the disk (as shown). Notch the plastic lid from a 2-pound coffee can; plastic or wood veneer could also be used. Use a ¼ × 1-inch bolt and wing nut to attach the two sections together until finger-tight. The plug fits snugly in the hole, and the notched plastic lid helps lock the cord in place and keep critters out. It can be used at the campsite and for long-term storage.

Grab Handle

FRANK WOYTHAL, ANDOVER, NEW YORK

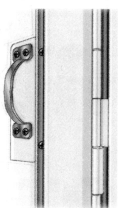

▶ Whenever my wife or I enter our motorhome, we prefer to grip both sides of the doorway, especially on the way in.

Our coach had a standard assist bar on one side, which really helps, but there was nothing on the opposite door frame lip.

I attached a simple metal handle to a piece of angle iron, then mounted the angle iron near the door edge. How high you will want to mount this assembly will depend on how high you want to reach and your level of comfort.

For a clean look, I cut off the ends of the mounting bolts (inside the angle iron) one thread above the securing nuts; the bolt heads attaching the angle iron to the door frame are concealed by the weatherstrip for the door (a second pair have their heads hidden under a vertical vinyl trim piece).

Rubber-Ringing the Rattle

ROSS OWENS, NAVAN, ONTARIO

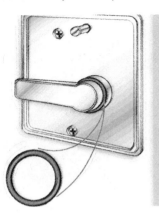

▶ On every trip, I was annoyed by a continual rattle caused by the loose inside door handle on the entry door to our coach. After trying several temporary solutions to the problem that neither worked well nor were eye appealing, I hit upon the idea of using a 1-inch O-ring (available at any plumbing supply store) and stretched it around the door handle.

The O-ring is held in place by the groove between the handle and the faceplate and provides enough pressure between the two pieces to eliminate the rattle. To ensure that the handle can return freely, using only the force of the internal spring, I coated the O-ring with a little silicone grease.

Vertically Challenged

BRUCE DAVIS, NORWICH, ONTARIO

▶ Many of today's trailers have high ceilings, and many people cannot reach the roof vents and fan controls without a step ladder.

I have devised a 30-inch pole that will allow one to open regular vents and open and operate the speed control of those hard-to-reach fans.

It is made from a section of 1-inch plastic pipe with a wooden insert with a hole drilled in it to fit regular vent handles. There is also a short piece of rubber hose on the same end to change the speed of the fan.

The other end has two finger-like pieces of aluminum to open and close the fan cover.

A MOUSE IN THE HOUSE?

After the second year in which mice and chipmunks had gotten into our motorhome, we started another inspection of the coach. Using a flashlight under the back area while a partner was looking into the rear storage compartments, we found an area where the frame and compartments did not quite meet. That left hidden, but animal-accessible, holes. Once inside the storage compartment, the animals could also gain entrance to the living area through the heating duct located in the middle of the compartment.

To solve the problem, add an extension tube to a can of spray foam (minimum expanding). Start with the end of the tube far up in the space and slowly pull it out, while continuing to spray. You'll need to fill the hole at the frame, not fill the entire compartment — so you have to be careful with the "trigger." And to prevent animals from entering the living area through the heating duct, we placed craft wire in the duct end.

LINDA MYERS, LaVALE, MARYLAND

A NEW USE

As you are probably aware, it is not too difficult to open most vehicle doors with a slim jim or, in many cases, a coat hanger. Being concerned with the security of my Class C motorhome while it was parked in storage, I came up with the following inexpensive idea.

To make it more difficult for someone to get into the cab, I purchased a Pro-Grip cargo strap with ratchet (part no. 85084) at Ace Hardware for less than $10. I run the strap through both inside door handles, hook the strap ends together and tighten the ratchet.

Although this is not foolproof, it will slow entry into the coach. Even though my aim was for security while in storage, it could also be used on the road or in a campground. In addition, it never hurts to have the strap to secure something in or on your coach or at the campsite.

KENNETH SCHWENKE,
WILDWOOD, NEW JERSEY

BEE, BE GONE

Between trips, our Sunline trailer's rooftop air conditioner attracted yellow jackets, and they built hives inside the condenser housing.

Our solution was to buy a 48 × 48-inch baby carriage mosquito net. No alterations were necessary; just pull it over the housing and you're done.

J. PETERSEN,
BEARSVILLE, NEW YORK

ANYBODY HOME?

Have you ever had someone tell you that they came over and knocked on the door of your RV and got no answer? Usually it's because you are in the bedroom and couldn't hear them.

I solved this problem by purchasing a wireless doorbell. The doorbell button was attached beside the door and the doorbell receiver was mounted in the bedroom. They are attached with double-face tape that is included. Both the button and receiver use batteries.

The doorbell is available at any home-improvement store.

ELAINE SHELTON,
LIVINGSTON, TEXAS

BOUNCE THOSE CRITTERS

Rodent intrusion is a problem when a motorhome has to be stored for an extended period. Mothballs keep them at bay, but they leave a distinctive odor that seems to last forever.

Fabric-softener sheets, used in clothes dryers, do as good a job, if not better, at keeping unwanted critters out. I place them in all the cabinets, drawers, closets, outside compartments and any area that has a concentration of electrical wiring. My coach is stored five months a year in a farmer's machine shed; undoubtedly there is a large population of mice around, but they keep their distance.

A very pleasant fringe benefit of the fabric-softener sheets is that our RV always smells fresh and clean.

JACK NOSBUSCH,
MINNEAPOLIS, MINNESOTA

SCREEN GEMS

I had a problem with debris getting on my vent screens by blowing underneath my MaxxAir vent covers. Cleaning the screens involved removing the screens from the inside or, on the roof, removing the MaxxAir vent covers. I eliminated the problem by removing the MaxxAir covers, applying self-adhesive weatherstripping to the bottom lip and reattaching them.

LAWRENCE NOGGLE,
VINITA, OKLAHOMA

Keep Out the Bugs

BILL JONES, SALOME, ARIZONA

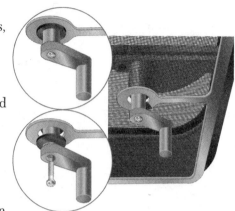

▶ When looking for places where small bugs, such as mosquitoes, might be able to enter my RV, I noticed some space between the overhead-vent crank and the vent screening. Although small, it was nevertheless a possible entry point.

To completely seal the opening, I used a rubber grommet with an inside diameter that is slightly smaller than the outside diameter of the crank mechanism. By sliding the grommet up close to the screen, so that the grommet very lightly brushes the screen, I was able to completely seal the opening, yet not affect the operation of the vent-crank mechanism.

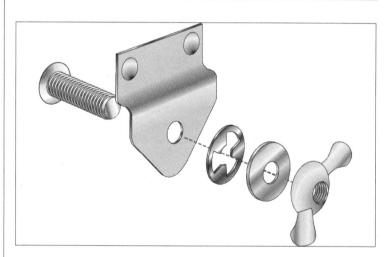

Door Prize

FRED L. TIMM, MILWAUKEE, OREGON

▶ Recently the closure on the door of my RV's water heater broke off in my hand. There was no way to keep the door closed once this happened, so I came up with this solution.

I slid a $\frac{3}{16} \times \frac{3}{4}$-inch bolt through the old closure hole and held it in place with a $\frac{3}{16}$-inch push-on retainer.

Closing the water-heater door, I then slipped a $\frac{5}{16}$-inch flat washer over the bolt and installed a $\frac{5}{16}$-inch wing nut to hold the door closed. I had to slightly enlarge the existing hole to accommodate the bolt with a few strokes of a small round file.

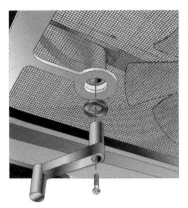 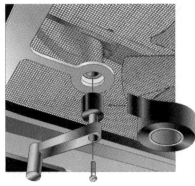

Keep the Bugs Out

DAN HILL, TILLAMOOK, OREGON

▶ Small bugs can be a real nuisance, and any opening in the RV can be a welcome mat to let them in. I found two obscure (but present in most RVs) openings that are big enough to let in the pests, so I had to find a way to seal them off.

Both openings are at the roof vent-door-crank handles, but each needs a different solution to seal the opening. Neither fix interferes with the operation of the vent-door handle.

The first was fixed with a simple washer and the second with electrical tape. The base of the crank handle on the first vent was almost flush with the screen and had the largest opening. I simply unscrewed the handle, inserted a ¼-inch flat washer above the handle and screwed the handle back on. A simple 5-cent solution.

The base of the second vent's handle was positioned too far into the vent-screen hole, so I unscrewed the handle and wrapped electrical tape around the barrel of the handle until the diameter was almost as large as the diameter of hole in the screen. Another simple solution, and no more bugs!

No More Flapping

JIM MERLONE, TRAVERSE CITY, MICHIGAN

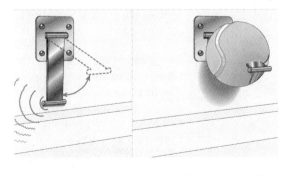

▶ The door latches on the side of our RV used to hang down against the rig.

I poked the latch through a tennis ball, keeping the latch horizontal. This stops the latch from flapping against the side wall as you drive down the road, and when you open the door, you don't have to go out to latch the door open.

Batting Cleanup

CHET PEACHEY, GOSHEN, INDIANA

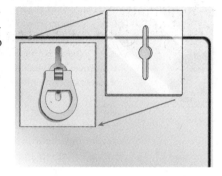

▶ Rust around the water-heater-door retainer clip is a common problem on RVs.

To eliminate this problem, I asked our local Ziebart vehicle-care dealer for a piece of Zglaze, which is a very tough plastic that had been placed on the front part of the hood of our pickup to eliminate chips caused by stones and other debris.

To apply the Zglaze, open the water-heater cover and place a 2 × 2-inch piece of the Zglaze on the outside of the water-heater-cover clip hole. Slit the Zglaze so that the clip can protrude through the hole. Pull the clip through the clip hole and latch properly.

There is now protection from rusting where the clip comes in contact with the metal of the cover.

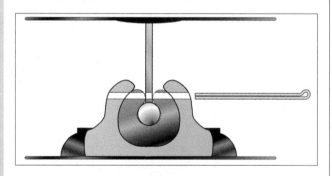

Slammer Jammer

ERIC & MARIA MAYA, HUNTSVILLE, ONTARIO

▶ My husband and I camp by the ocean all winter. The strong winds were continually making our RV's door slam shut, and we were afraid that the door's glass would break. The factory door catch consisting of a rod with a ball on the end that snaps into a rubber socket on the side wall wasn't up to the task.

Our solution cost only pennies. We drilled a ⅛-inch hole through the metal surround holding the rubber socket and also in the middle of the ball shaft. We next slid a cotter pin, anchored to the trailer body by a string, through the hole to lock the door in place.

Going Strapless

DONALD RHOADS, CLARENDON, NEW YORK

▶ My fifth-wheel has seen about 24,000 miles. With all the wiggles on the highways, the plastic straps that kept the doors to the bedroom and the bathroom from closing broke.

I replaced them by installing ordinary window-sash locks, which are available at hardware stores.

There are now no more straps to break and the appearance is more attractive. They can be used on sliding or pocket doors and the installation will vary with each RV.

Double Door Trouble

JUDY BRENHOLT, CUSHING, WISCONSIN

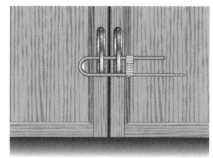

▶ I use child locks on all double doors in our RV to prevent doors from coming open when we travel. They are available at all hardware stores.

JANET WILDER, LIVINGSTON, TEXAS

▶ We live in a large fifth-wheel, and we love to travel on rural scenic byways. Sometimes the curves in the road unleash the trailer gremlins, who throw things against the cupboard doors, causing them to open.

One particular door was causing me problems. So I went to the discount department store and purchased a child-proof cabinet lock.

When we are parked, I leave one side attached so I don't misplace the lock. It takes only seconds to thread the other strap into the lock. Goodbye gremlins!

Short People

DAN GOULD, WORCESTER, MASSACHUSETTS

▶ As with most little kids, my 4- and 6-year old boys could not safely or easily open the screen door to our fifth-wheel.

To reach the door handle, they would have to climb to the top of the steps, grab the handle, and then step down backward, while swinging the door open. This was difficult and dangerous.

Our screen door needs only light pressure on the door itself to open or close. A simple pull (or push, from the inside) on the door frame opens it. You do not need to operate the latch.

I installed a small drawer knob that can be easily reached from ground level in the bottom corner of the screen door. This allows them to swing the door open, and then climb the stairs as adults do.

Make sure that the knob is small enough so that it will not interfere with the closing of the main door.

One note of caution to further protect the little ones: The corners of the screen door are very sharp, so file them and sand them smooth.

Keep 'Em Closed

STEVEN VIERRA, HAYWARD, CALIFORNIA

▶ I solved the problem of our fifth-wheel's kitchen drawers bouncing open while driving down the highway.

I simply dropped a wooden dowel rod tipped with a rubber screw bumper on the bottom, through the drawer pulls. I carved a shallow groove near the top of the dowel rod to keep a bungee cord in place while traveling.

A small eye screw secured to the backsplash holds the bungee's other hook. Now the drawers — and their contents — stay in place, even on the roughest roads.

Get a Handle on It

JAMES THOMAS, WINDSOR, CALIFORNIA

▶ Closing the screen door on our RV was always a real problem. For the cure, I purchased a cabinet/drawer handle, two No. 8 one-inch screws and washers.

I drilled two small pilot holes through the metal strip above the screen door slide. Then I installed the handle on the inside of the door and the screws and washers on the outside. I then touched up the screws with white paint to match the door.

Keep 'Em Closed II

K.P. MOREAU, LIVINGSTON, TEXAS

▶ The illustration shows an inexpensive, easy way to secure drawers while in transit. The dowel rods are held in place by a cup hook placed in the fixed cabinet surface between any two drawers, and another hook, installed lower, further secures the drawers. Use of two hooks also works when the drawers don't have loop-type handles. When not in use, the dowel rods are stored in our clothes closet.

doors, handles & hatches

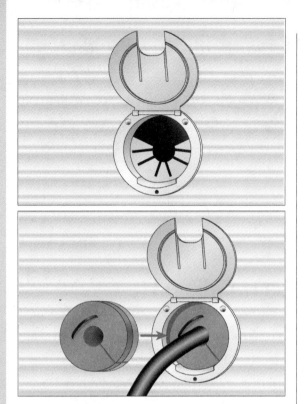

Batten Up the Hatches

W. STEVE SHEPARD JR.,
NORTHPORT, ALABAMA

▶ To prevent cold weather from penetrating the shorepower-cord hatch, a removable insulating plug can be easily fabricated.

First, find a fairly rigid piece of foam that will support the weight of the power cord. I used a piece of an old pool raft made of 1-inch-thick foam, similar to that of a swimming noodle.

Using a sharp blade, cut the outer diameter a little larger than the inside diameter of the hole, so the plug will fit snugly. Likewise, the inner hole (for the power cord) should be a little smaller than the power cord. Next, add a cut between the two circles so that the plug can be slipped over the cord.

Finally, use a long cable tie to penetrate the foam, creating a loop that serves as a handle to remove the plug.

The exterior door won't close all the way because the cord is now in the center of the hole. However, the insulation plug creates a much better weather barrier and also helps keep out critters.

When used in the winter, this plug helps keep the interior cavity and the nearby water pipes a little warmer.

No More Freeloaders

HORACE SEARICE, CINCINNATI, OHIO

▶ In my coach, the bays containing the AC generator and spare tire are open to the ground. When dry camping in really out-of-the-way places, my concern is about uninvited "guests." To avoid surprises upon opening these compartments, I covered the open bottoms with ¼-inch wire mesh.

Measure the square footage of the open bottoms, and at a hardware store, buy an appropriate amount of wire and other needed supplies. Measure the bay being enclosed, cut the wire, and mark the places (along the bottom edges of the bay) where the wire will be attached.

Using sheet metal screws and ¼-inch washers, drill holes and attach the wire mesh. You're now safe from mice, snakes and other vermin.

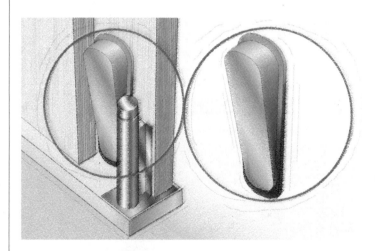

Who's That Knocking?

F. JUANITO TERWILLIGER, LIVINGSTON, TEXAS

▶ The pocket door on our motorhome made quite a racket when we were on the road. To stop the clatter, we purchased a doorstop wedge (available at any hardware store or department) and wedged it between the floor lock and the door. This fix is simple, inexpensive — and quiet!

Clear & Cool

PAM BERRIAN, EUGENE, OREGON

▶ Whenever we stop during our travels for any length of time, I prefer to use the screen door so our RV is open to view the surrounding area. Unfortunately, this wonderful view causes the loss of cool (or heated) air.

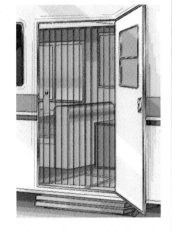

I found that a "screen" can be made using lengths of clear, heavy plastic strips similar to those you might see protecting the doorway to a walk-in cooler at a grocery store. Such a screen can be easily assembled and hung above the doorway of a motorhome, and can be rolled up and stored when not in use.

The walk-through is easy, the inside climate of the coach is maintained, and the view stays wonderful.

Add a Switch

DONALD BULL, REDONDO BEACH, CALIFORNIA

▶ Our motorhome has a Fan-Tastic fan mounted in the ceiling vent over the galley. The fan switch (speed selector) is mounted at ceiling height, which is above the reach of my wife. In order to allow her to operate the fan, I added a separate wall-mounted switch on the side wall of the nearby microwave-oven cabinet.

I temporarily removed the microwave oven and the fan switch panel to gain access to the wiring. I rerouted the 12-volt DC ground wire from the fan switch and attached it to one terminal of the new wall switch.

I then ran a new wire from the other terminal of the new switch to the ground connection.

We leave the speed-control switch on the fan at a preselected level. Now the fan may be operated whenever desired by turning on the easily reachable new switch. When it becomes necessary to run the fan at a different speed, I can reach up and reset it, as desired.

Air It Out

PAUL SLATER, BEAVERCREEK, OHIO

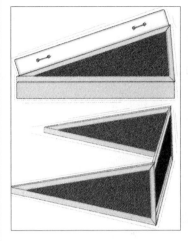

▶ Our diesel motorhome has spent a few summers standing in our driveway, and I discovered that leaving some windows open to keep air circulating and cool the coach subjected the interior to rain damage.

So, I raised the engine cover up by a foot and made a wedge-shaped screen enclosure to keep out nature's visitors. This allows relatively cooler air to flow up through the engine well and push warmer air out of the coach through the bath and kitchen vents.

The simple screen enclosure was made using plastic fly screening, stapled to a 1 × 2-inch wood frame. I made it in three pieces (one rectangular end and two wedge-shaped sides) and hinged them together so the apparatus can be folded and stored when not in use.

Just Hangin' Around

TOM HELM, DURANGO, COLORADO

▶ I don't care for the way conventional coat hooks stick out from the wall — it's too easy for someone to back into them. Instead, I installed the chrome metal door latches normally used to hold RV compartment doors open. These latches are ideal hooks, since when not in use they fold out of harm's way. They can be placed at any height, and can be used to hang coats, towels, washcloths, etc. Just be sure to mount them on a stud.

doors, handles & hatches

Automatic Closet Light

DON MALETTE, SAN DIEGO, CALIFORNIA

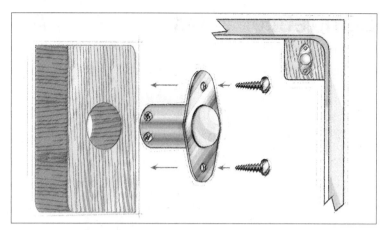

▶ My wife isn't tall enough to reach the ceiling-light switch in the wardrobe closet. To eliminate the problem, I went to our local home-supply center and purchased a small pressure-sensitive switch. I cut a small block of oak and drilled a hole in it to snugly hold the switch, then ran a pair of wires from the original light switch to my new switch. I then glued the block into the upper corner of the door frame. Now when the door is opened the light automatically turns on.

Chicken Bar

HARVEY HETRICK, TORRANCE, CALIFORNIA

▶ After we had owned our motorhome for almost a year, my wife told me she would feel more comfortable if she had something to hang onto around curves and over hills. At a local RV dealership, I found what I think was a good solution to her problem.

I bought a wooden bar that was originally manufactured as an entry aid, but now, when mounted with metal screws onto the window frame of our vehicle, serves as a "chicken bar." Now, no matter who is driving, one of us can hang onto the steering wheel and the other has the handy chicken bar.

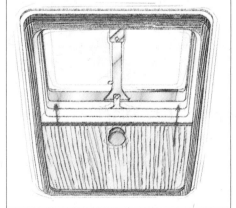

Á Sliding Cover

ROSS OWENS, NAVAN, ONTARIO

▶ We wanted to cover our roof vents to keep out the morning light and the winter cold. None of the standard products, such as bubble-pack covers, foam-rubber plugs or cloth covers, seemed to be appropriate, so I designed my own.

I used four strips of ¾ × ¾-inch wood for my frame, with the two longer sides twice the size of the vent and the shorter pieces the size of the vent. With a bench saw, I cut ⅜-inch-deep slots the length of the longer pieces to form a channel for the sliding cover. The sliding cover is made from a piece of ⅛-inch plywood, and I sanded the edges to allow it to slide easily, but not so much that it would rattle when traveling.

The frame is assembled by attaching one shorter piece to the end of the two longer pieces with wood glue and screws, so the slots in the two longer pieces face inward, toward each other. The cover slides into the slots, and the last piece is placed on the open end to hold the assembly together. I also put a knob on the cover for convenience. I rounded the frame corners with sandpaper and finished the wood with stain and urethane to match the décor of our motorhome. The frame is fastened to the ceiling with small wood screws.

Completely Baffled

DANIEL LANDRY, EAST DUMMERSTON, VERMONT

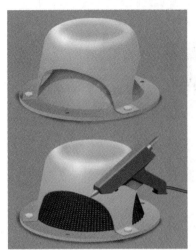

▶ My wife and I were completely baffled as to why the sewer odor around our motorhome seemed to get worse each day. We tried everything from draining and flushing to using different treatments. After a week or so, the odor was as bad as ever.

One day, while sitting outside, we noticed a large number of wasps buzzing around our black-water roof vent. Further investigation revealed that the wasps had built a large thick nest, almost entirely blocking the vent tube!

After getting rid of the wasps and their nest, we modified our roof vent caps as shown. A little hot glue and some small pieces of screening completed the cure.

Simple Door Latch

JOHN SCHERR, POWHATAN, VIRGINIA

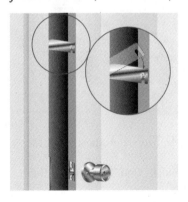

▶ To keep the RV bathroom from getting too hot and to keep the bathroom door from swinging open, I came up with a simple door latch. Here's how to do it:

Find a thin piece of metal plate. Drill a hole in one end and a slot in the other. The length will depend on how far you want the door held open. With a small screw through the hole in the plate, attach the plate to the inside of the doorjamb with enough slack that the bracket moves freely. Make sure the door will close and not hit the screw. Drive a screw into the edge of the door for the notched end of the metal plate to hook onto. When the door is closed, the latch hangs out of sight.

ELIMINATE THE FLEXING

Going in and out of our trailer and opening and closing the screen door several times a day, we noticed that the door was getting bent. Taking note of the lightweight material that the door frame was made of, we could see why it was bending so easily. To eliminate this flexing, I bought (from a home center) a length of ½-inch, U-shaped aluminum channel that fit tightly on the door frame. I had enough clearance so the extra U-channel thickness didn't interfere with the door closing all the way.

This has strengthened the frame and keeps it from bending.

DUANE VAN DYKE,
OAK HARBOR, WASHINGTON

LOCKDOWN

The sliding bathroom door in my RV did not have a lock. Obviously, a lock is a desirable feature when you have guests camping with you. The sliding screen on our home patio door provided the answer.

A locking plastic knob (from the hardware store) for a sliding screen door was attached to the inside frame of the bathroom door. With the door fully closed, I marked the spot where the pocket for the locking point needs to be cut. After cutting the small pocket with a wood chisel, it was finished with a faceplate from a household door lock.

The result is a simple, inexpensive lock for a sliding bathroom door.

JIM COPPINS, ATTICA, MICHIGAN

LET'S HAVE SOME QUIET

After installing the doghouse-insulation kit featured in the October 2001 issue, the noise reduction was so dramatic that a lot of other rattles were audible. Most were from the cabinet doors. There are 24 cabinet doors, and I found 14 needed quieting because the little round pads that came with the doors do not stay in place. The adhesive never dries, allowing the pads to keep moving around until they no longer serve their purpose.

I took some nonslip material (usually used to keep dishes from sliding around) and cut some strips about ⅝-inch wide. By tapping on each door with my fingers, I found which ones were rattling. I then inserted about ½ inch of the end of the nonslip material between the door and the cabinet, and by tapping and moving the nonslip around, I found the best location to stop the rattle. I fastened a small square of nonslip with a dab of clear silicone adhesive at that point.

Things have quieted down now to the point that I can even hear my tinnitus!

LUTHER STRUVE, POCATELLO, IDAHO

"C" Me, Fix Me

REAL GAUTREAU, COPPERAS COVE, TEXAS

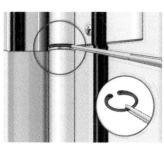

▶ The entry door on our 4-year-old motorhome was getting harder and harder to open and close. The weight of the door had worn its way down over the friction washer enough to cause a misalignment between the door-latch assembly and the locking pin on the door frame.

At my local hardware store, for 19 cents each, I found "C" clips, which are normally used to secure things like automotive interior window cranks onto cylindrical mounts. I bought several of the right size and, using needle-nosed pliers, inserted them under the washer and around the door-hinge pin. In my case, the thickness of two washers solved the problem.

Screening Out Unwelcome Visitors

LEE NELSON, HASLETT, MICHIGAN

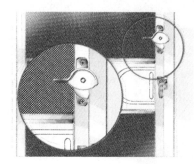

▶ We wanted a little added security when the main door of our motorhome is open and we're using just the screen door to keep bugs at bay, so we installed a sash lock (designed for house windows).

For swing-out doors, simply mount the moving half of the lock to the screen door of the motorhome. In the locked position, the lock is across the doorjamb frame and prevents it from opening; in the unlocked position, the lock is vertical with the screen-door frame.

Secure Sliding Doors

RICH PAYNE, TILLAMOOK, OREGON

▶ At the rear of our motorhome, we have a closet with large mirrored sliding doors. The motorhome manufacturer installed plastic locks to keep these doors secure while traveling. Unfortunately, the weight of these glass doors, combined with rough roads, snapped the plastic locks and the doors slid open.

After replacing the locks twice, I cut two wooden blocks (each 5 × ¾ × ½-inches) to fit the door frame. I then drilled two ¼-inch holes on the bottom of each block (3 inches apart), and one ¼-inch hole centered on the top. I glued 1-inch-long dowels in all three holes, then attached a small knob to the top dowel.

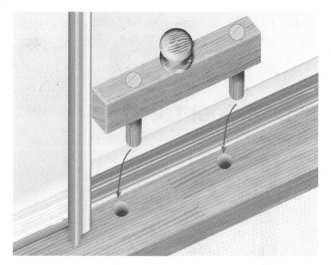

After positioning a sliding door against the side of the closet, I wedged one of the blocks against the door at the center of the closet, then drilled ⁵⁄₁₆-inch holes in the frame directly beneath the two dowels. I repeated these steps for the second door.

Before traveling, we insert the dowels into the holes in each door frame, securing the blocks, and then remove them at our destination. The doors have stopped sliding around since switching to this device.

10 minute tech in camp

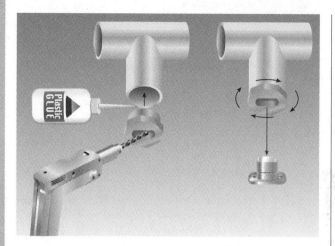

A Helping Hand

PHILLIP UHAS, MAGALIA, CALIFORNIA

▶ I have difficulty working the small metal twist-locks to secure my outside window coverings because my hands don't work like they used to, so I purchased a 1¾-inch plastic tee and a plug from the hardware store.

I glued the plug into the bottom of the tee, and drilled (in the surface of the plug) the proper-size holes to match the locks that hold my window coverings in place. It is now a snap to secure and unsecure my window coverings.

Knee Savers

DERALD McCONNELL, YAKIMA, WASHINGTON

▶ I use knee pads that are made for gardening, laying tile and other hands-and-knees jobs when I need to get down under our motorhome to hook up hoses, power cords and the like. They are available at hardware stores, home centers and mass merchandisers. They are foam-padded for protection, easy-on and easy-off, and they take very little storage space.

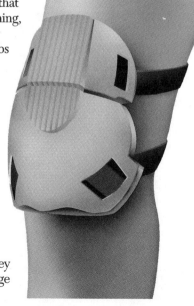

Avoid the Birds

CAROL WALTERMYER, ANNVILLE, PENNSYLVANIA

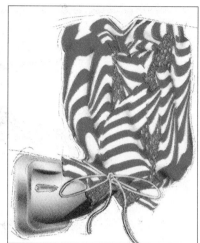

▶ While camping, we often would encounter birds that like to peck at our side mirrors, so we would cover the mirrors with a plastic grocery bag. I decided I wanted a more attractive look, so I made bags out of a patriotic print fabric and tied a cord around the bottom. No more plastic bags. To avoid losing the cord, you could also add a pocket to store the cord.

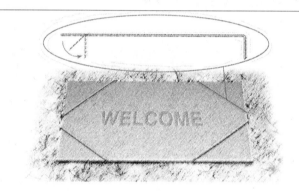

Stapled to the Ground

HARVEY HETRICK, TORRANCE, CALIFORNIA

▶ While wind has little effect on our comfort while inside our motorhome, the same can't be said of our outdoor mat. No matter what I used, the mat would not stay in place. I decided to make some large staples to hold down the mat. To create the staples, I used four ¼-inch-diameter steel rods, each 2 feet long. I put a 90-degree bend several inches up on the ends of each rod, then ground a blunt point on the ends. I position a staple across each corner of the mat and pound them into the ground; a claw hammer easily removes them when we are ready to leave.

With this method, you never have to put a hole in the mat — and, because the rods are pounded flush with the ground, you will never trip or stumble over them.

in camp

Clever Table

John MacDonald, Youngsville, North Carolina

▶ I use a piece of cut conduit (as pictured) to act as a support of one of my motorhome's basement doors, which enables me to use the door as a table. A precut piece of cardboard is also brought along and placed on top of the "table" to protect the finish.

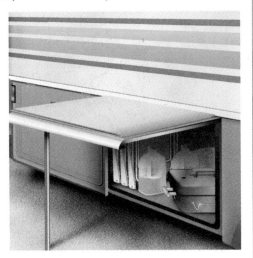

Foolproof Funnel

Alonzo Kelly, Kountze, Texas

▶ Many of the Forest Service campgrounds we like to visit provide water at faucets and pitcher pumps. Seldom, however, is there a faucet to which we can connect a water hose to fill our motorhome tank.

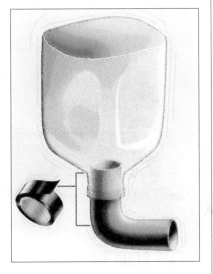

Our motorhome has a freshwater fill port where we pour in the water we have carried from the nearest faucet, but most funnels are difficult to hold while pouring in the water — plus, the angle of the funnel when placed into the fill port usually means that we spill more than we store.

I cut the bottom from a one-gallon plastic milk container, and then purchased a pre-molded, 45-degree, ⅞ × 1⅛-inch automobile heater-hose fitting. After cutting the hose on each side of the 45-degree curve, this hose fits snugly into the milk-container top opening (I secured it to the container with electrical tape).

We remove the fill cap on the side of the motorhome, press the hose into the line, and then twist the funnel assembly until the funnel is facing upward. This funnel stays firmly in place. We store this funnel in a plastic bag marked water only.

A YARD OF ADVICE

As a campground manager, I find that more than 50 percent of RVs have slides — but, for whatever reason, most owners imagine that their slides stick out from the side of the RV from 4 to 6 feet! When parking, they allow for unneeded space that could be better utilized on the side of their rigs.

A simple solution is to take a yardstick (or any thin piece of wood or PVC pipe) and, when the slide is open, cut this to match how far the slide projects from the side of the RV. When parking, the person outside, who is assisting with the parking chores, can use it to determine the needed distance.

Troy Wenzel, Jasper, Arkansas

ROAD WISE

Here are a couple of ideas we have found useful while RVing:

1). When camping with pets, here is a temporary identification tag that works great: Use a 1-inch split-ring disposal key tag, which are available at any office supply store. When parking at a campground, write on the tag your cell phone number and campsite number. Don't forget to make a new tag every time you change campsites or campgrounds.

2). Many times after emptying my holding tanks, it's not practical to wash my hands with soap and water. The solution? Waterless hand sanitizer.

I choose to mount a small 2-ounce bottle, using hook-and-loop fastener, near the dump valves. When empty, I use a larger bottle of the cleaner to refill. It's quick, practical and it won't get lost.

Gary Metcalfe,
Orange, California

LET THERE BE LIGHT

In a perfect world, everyone would always arrive at his or her campsite with plenty of time left to set up before night settled in. Unfortunately, it rarely happens that way. When arriving at your destination at night — in the dark — and it's a site with hookups, plug in a string of rope lights and place them along the edge of the camping pad. This not only lights up the pad to help you guide the motorhome in, but illuminates the side of the coach, as well.

Carroll Burgus, Oskaloosa, Iowa

CANNED YARN

Since I do a lot of knitting outside, I use a 5-pound coffee can to dispense and protect the yarn. Make a small hole in the center of the plastic lid, put the yarn in the can and bring the loose end out through the hole. With this simple arrangement, you can knit or crochet anywhere without getting the yarn dirty.

DOROTHY HESS, KILLEEN, TEXAS

FIDO TO THE RESCUE

While shopping for a sun shade for my awning to make the late afternoon a little more comfortable, I was put off by the high cost.

Then, while looking through a hunting catalog, I came across dog kennel sun shades, which came in just the right size, at about half the price.

I found that it works great, and saving money is always an added bonus.

DON PEDERSON,
FARGO, NORTH DAKOTA

HOLD THAT COVER

The cover over the electric controls for the front jacks on our fifth-wheel would not stay up while operating the system. I did not want to put on the catches that require screws, so to solve this annoying problem, I super-glued a small magnet on the body of the trailer at the spot where the lock on the cover touches the side of the fifth-wheel.

If you want the magnet to be less noticeable, paint it to match your trailer.

JOY BEARD, HENDERSON, KENTUCKY

RED, GREEN, YELLOW

In regard to the external power cord from the RV to the AC power supply, this tip has saved wear and tear on my cord, anchor and/or internal electrical connection.

On the power cord, with it fully extended, I put a ring of red vinyl tape around the cord, approximately 6 inches from the wall opening of my RV. Then I put a ring of yellow tape about 12 inches from the red ring. Finally, I add a ring of green tape 12 inches from the yellow ring.

Now I know when to slow down and stop pulling out the power cord.

JIM HOLMES,
NOLENSVILLE, TENNESSEE

Easier Chocks

BOB BRANSON, BASTROP, TEXAS

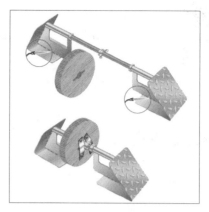

▶ For those who use the type of wheel chocks that fit on the ground between the tandem tires and expand out by turning a wing nut, I have an improvement. I cut a disc from ¾-inch plywood, drilled a hole in the center and cut a couple of slots from the center hole, to fit over the "wings" of the wing nut. Removing one of the chock wedges enabled me to slide the wood wheel down the threaded shaft and over the wing nut. The other end of the chock is then attached. If it wobbles, you can stabilize it with a couple of strips of metal screwed over the wings. I marked arrows on each side with a felt-tip pen to indicate turn direction and chock-movement direction.

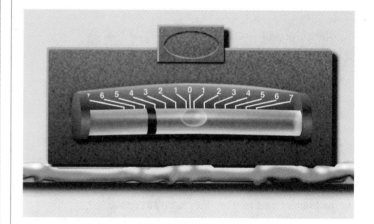

On the Level

GERRY WILLARD, CARIBOU, MAINE

▶ When unhitching my fifth-wheel at the campground, I lower the landing gear just enough to take the pressure off the tow vehicle. Then, before unhooking, I make a mark on a level, at the end of the bubble, with a Magic Marker. Then I unhook and level the fifth-wheel.

When I reconnect, all I have to do is raise or lower my landing gear until the bubble is at the mark, and I am ready to back in, with little or no guesswork. When I'm done, I erase the mark and I'm ready for next time.

in camp

Barbecue Tool Carrier

ALBERT MOSS, ZAVALLA, TEXAS

▶ This is a handy way to carry all the equipment for your grill.

Buy a 3-foot section of 4-inch PVC, two 4-inch end caps and two handles. With PVC cement, glue one end cap to the end of the 4-inch pipe. Attach one handle to the top of the other end cap, and the other handle to the side of the pipe. The end cap with the handle is used as the pipe cover, and with the assistance of the attached handle, can be slipped on and off as needed. The stand for the grill, long-handled forks, tongs and even a spatula will all fit in your carrier. Additionally, an automotive-oil drain pan is a handy item for catching ashes that fall from the grill.

These Rocks Won't Roll

ED REKOLA, LYNNWOOD, WASHINGTON

▶ We enjoy outdoor cooking, but because of storage space limitations we use an inexpensive, low-profile propane grill. Our grill came equipped with lava rocks that cover the burners and retain heat for cooking, but when stored (while traveling) the rocks move around. Before

we can use the grill, the rocks have to be repositioned over the burner — a messy task. In addition, the nature of their design requires that the rocks be turned frequently to burn off all the grease.

I found that by encasing the rocks in chicken wire, the task of flipping them is a snap — and the rocks always stay put, even when on the road.

Old Glory

RICH VEDDER,
TREMONT, ILLINOIS

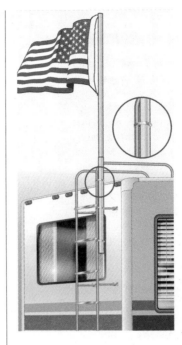

▶ After Sept. 11, as a permanent RVer, I wanted a way to fly my flag that was easy to disassemble for travel. I made this flag pole out of varying diameters of PVC pipe for less than $20. When I travel, I just lift the 10-foot section and flag out of the holder, and store it in the trailer.

I leave the 30-inch section of PVC secured to the ladder, where it is ready for the next flag raising.

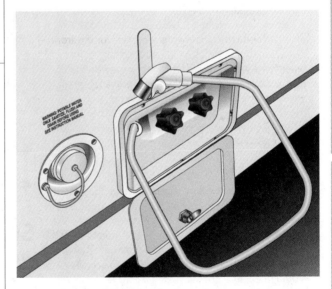

She's Hooked

BILL COOK, DULUTH, GEORGIA

▶ On trips to the beach, we use the outside spray nozzle often. My wife complained about having to coil the hose back each time she used it.

So she picked up a plastic hook, with adhesive backing, at a kitchen supply store. Its color matches the outside of our RV and has stayed on securely for more than two years.

in camp

IMPROVE YOUR RECLINER

I recently bought two multiple-position outdoor recliners. They provide a comfortable way to relax outside, but if you're tall, your legs are going to extend over the crossbar at the end of the footrest.

In order to make this as comfortable as the rest of the chair, I bought a length of foam insulation normally used to cover water pipes (it looks like a swimming noodle, except it's smaller in diameter).

I cut a piece the exact width of the footrest end bar, pulled the fabric chair cover back and slipped the piece of insulation around the metal crossbar. Then I pulled the fabric over the insulation, giving me a very comfortable area to relax my legs.

PAT PULLUM, ROGERS, ARKANSAS

INSULATED COVER

As a full-timer, this winter I found myself in some below-freezing weather. With the rig's water-connection inlet facing the cold north wind, I had to be creative in order to keep the connection from freezing during the night when the hose was removed.

My solution was a disposable insulated cover made up of three components: a margarine tub, a 6- to 8-inch square of pink insulation and duct tape. Simply put the insulation square inside the plastic tub and duct tape the tub over the water-collection inlet.

BRENDA BOYD,
SAND SPRINGS, OKLAHOMA

HOW LOW CAN YOU GO?

RVers constantly worry about the clearance at the top of their rigs, especially in campgrounds. I have a solution.

Buy two (any size diameter) PVC pipes at a hardware store. Cut them so that you have two pieces, each half the height of your rig (to simplify storage). Be sure to measure the height to the top of the roof air conditioners.

Take one of the PVC sections and cement a connector coupling to it with PVC cement. Upon arrival at the campsite, take the second pipe section and slide it into the other end of the connector coupling (do not glue). You can now check any questionable clearance areas at the site to make sure your unit will safely fit.

GEORGE PANOS,
LEESBURG, VIRGINIA

Locking Wheel Chocks

GARY SCHULTZ, WINNIPEG, MANITOBA

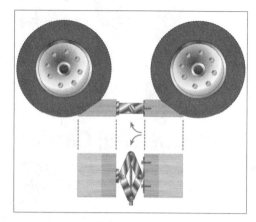

▶ I find this approach to stabilizing my trailer both effective and economical. Go to an auto wrecking yard and purchase a used scissor jack from a compact car. Using blocks of wood (at least 4 × 4 inches), cut one end into a wedge to fit against the tire. Fasten the scissor-jack base to the square end of one of the blocks. Dimensions of the parts will vary from one trailer to another. When parking, slip the chocks and jack in place, turn the jack handle and you're set.

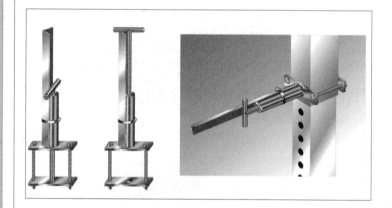

Snap to It

BILL MILLER, MEEKER, COLORADO

▶ I purchased a set of "snaps" to replace the pins in the landing gear of my fifth-wheel. They worked great, except that it was awkward to hold out the spring-loaded pin with one hand while raising the leg with the other.

To remedy this, I attached a 6½-inch piece of ¾-inch aluminum angle to the barrel of each snap with a hose clamp (grind or file the sharp corners of the angle so you won't gouge yourself).

When raising or lowering your landing gear, pull the pin out and twist it so the T-handle rests on the edge of the angle. When the leg is close to where you want it, slip the T off the end of the angle, and the pin will snap into the nearest hole as you raise or lower the leg.

Store Your Bars — Twice

LEONARD FURLOTTE, TRENTON, ONTARIO

▶ I have a simple, cheap and virtually invisible spring-bar storage system that I use.

1. Secure a length of 36- × 1½-inch diameter black PVC pipe to each side of the trailer frame, using heavy-duty black wire ties. Measure the length and width of your spring bars for proper sizing.

2. When parked, insert one bar into the PVC pipe on each side, then padlock the chain ends together in front of the A-frame jack.

RICHARD DIXON, SALISBURY, NORTH CAROLINA

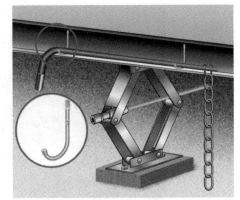

▶ I wanted to find an easy way to store my equalizer bars, without having to go to a lot of trouble. I bought 6-inch J-brackets for about $1, and they were just what I needed.

I positioned two brackets against the trailer frame, 24 inches apart, underneath the trailer body near the front of the trailer. I marked where the holes in the bracket were, then drilled and tapped the holes with a 10-24 tap and drill set. Each bracket was mounted to the frame with two, 10-24 × 1-inch machine screws. The same steps were done on the other side.

The equalizer bars are placed on the brackets for storage when at a campsite.

My trailer has a slideout, so the frame has two members welded together on top of each other for strength. On one side of the trailer I have added two more brackets on the top frame member, above the equalizer bar brackets, so I can also store my sway bar.

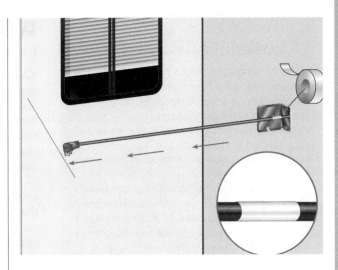

Slideout-Clearance Gauge

JOSEPH RICE, O'FALLON, MISSOURI

▶ A handy gauge to make sure that your slideout has ample clearance is something which already exists in most of our RVs — the AC power cord.

When the slideout is fully deployed, pull the AC cord out until it is extended the same distance as the slideout. Using white paint or tape, mark the spot where the cord just emerges from the side of the RV. You can now use the cable to measure the distance to an obstruction and verify that your slideout has enough room.

Reel Genius

RICHARD CARTWRIGHT, ARLINGTON, NEBRASKA

▶ I made a water-hose holder from a reel that's generally used to wind up electric cords. The reels are sold at all types of stores, including Wal-Mart. Mine holds 25 feet of hose.

When I roll the hose I start at the male (RV) end and leave about 2 feet unwound (or the length you need to reach the city-water hookup from the ground), then I roll up the rest of the hose.

At the campground, when we are ready to hook up, I take the 2-foot section and hook it to the RV. Then, with the reel on the ground, I unroll only as much hose as needed to reach the water spigot.

in camp

A LONG-REACH SOLUTION

Some campsites require a long reach for the placement of an RV's rear stabilizer jacks, so I had started carrying wooden blocks to increase the reach of our pedestal stabilizers.

Later, while assisting a fellow motorist who had a flat tire, it occurred to me that the bumper jack we were using would solve the long reach problem of many campsites.

Since they could be used in conjunction with the pedestal jacks and can be stored in a long, narrow space, their usefulness offsets the extra weight. A piece of angle iron can be welded to the hook for a more-versatile placement capability.

ARCH KENNEDY, CLINTON, LOUISIANA

ROLLING IN THE WIND

Our roll of paper towels was always being blown or knocked off picnic tables, getting dirty and/or unrolling. My husband solved this by taking two metal tablecloth clamps and drilling two holes to match the position and size of the holes in a plastic paper-towel holder. He then screwed the clamps to the holder and now clamps the whole assembly to the edge of the picnic table. It holds both the paper-towel roll and the tablecloth in place.

SANDRA ROEDDING,
BELLEVILLE, MICHIGAN

RUG ROLLER

I prefer a rug spread out under my awning, but don't like the hassle of folding it up and trying to stuff it neatly into a compartment for storage.

The carpet that I use for ground cover is 6 feet wide. To help store it away, I cut an old broom handle to a length of 40 inches. Folding the carpet in half lengthwise leaves a 36-inch-wide section. I lay the broom handle across that section at one end.

The broom handle sticks out 2 inches on each side of the folded carpet, so it can be used as a handle when the carpet is rolled around it. The next step is to roll up the carpet with the broom handle inside.

Now I have a neat roll of carpet that is easy to handle and store. Best of all, laying the carpet out is a simple matter of holding both ends of the broom handle and unrolling.

DAVID LLEWELLYN,
SAN DIEGO, CALIFORNIA

A Bright Reminder

RICHARD SMITH, MASON CITY, IOWA

▶ After some camping neighbors complained about my accidentally leaving the outside light on all night, causing it to shine into their bedroom, I devised a solution.

I purchased a neon lamp and installed it on the light side of the ON/OFF switch, with the small bulb in plain view.

Now, when the outside light is on, the bulb glows brightly as a reminder.

Shake, Rattle and Roll

WARREN PETKOVSEK, LUMBERTON, TEXAS

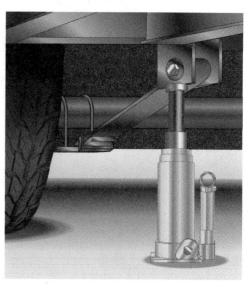

▶ In order to eliminate trailer movement and greatly increase stability while set up at a campsite, I obtained two small 2-ton-capacity hydraulic bottle jacks.

After leveling the trailer, but before lowering its stabilizer jacks, I place a bottle jack under the leaf-spring mounting bracket at each corner of the trailer suspension (example: left rear and right front). I then pump up each jack 1 to 2 inches at each corner. The wheels do not leave the ground; the bottle jacks only take some weight off the suspension. After this operation, I lower and set the trailer's stabilizer jacks as normal.

It is amazing how much more stable the trailer has become, and I didn't have to spend money on expensive devices that immobilize the trailer wheels. The jacks can also serve double-duty for tire changing, per the trailer manufacturers' instructions for safe jacking and lifting, and other roadside repairs.

No Picnic Table

HOWARD SIMPSON, STEWART, OHIO

▶ We solved the problem of campsites without picnic tables by bringing along a lightweight aluminum folding table. We store it under a bunk-bed mattress when traveling. It's handy and out of the way when not needed.

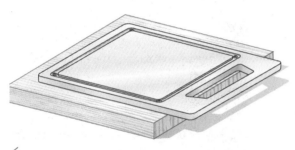

Slip 'n Slide

THOMAS WINTER, PENSACOLA, FLORIDA

▶ I have always used a couple of square pieces of 2 × 10s under the standard metal pads of the front jacks of our fifth-wheel. It helps to distribute the trailer's weight, which is critical on soft ground and asphalt.

With the trailer wheels chocked, the legs would flex and then hop when retracted as the trailer was being hitched to the truck. Even painting the wooden pads did not reduce the friction enough to allow the legs to slide freely.

My answer was to add a cheap slippery plastic cutting board on top of each pad. Just fasten it to the wooden board with a couple countersunk screws or use a ready-made recess like the juice groove around the edge to keep the screws below the surface.

Now the legs relax smoothly as they retract and I even have a handle on my footpads.

TOTALLY SEPARATE

Like many RVers, I had a problem when using an electric heater, which tripped a circuit breaker if I used other heavy-draw appliances at the same time. I came up with a way to provide a totally separate circuit for the heater from the extra 20-amp circuit on the power pole.

I removed the cushion from the bottom of one side of the booth and cut a hole large enough for a normal 120-volt AC receptacle in the front of the booth bottom. Directly below the spot at which the receptacle would be mounted, I drilled a ½-inch hole for the wire to go through, after making sure that there was nothing under the floor that could be damaged.

I then ran a wire with a male plug on the end through the hole, with the plug hanging down a couple of inches on the underside of the RV. I sealed around the wire with silicone. The wires on the other end were stripped and connected to the receptacle, just as normal 120-volt AC wiring.

Now when I pull into an RV location and hook up the electric, I use a short extension cord to go from the extra 20-amp plug at the 30-amp service and plug it into the male plug hanging down.

Anytime I want to use the electric heater in the RV, I plug it into the 120-volt AC receptacle.

ROY MATHIS, VAN BUREN, ARKANSAS

Editor's note: *Be sure to inform the campground host that you will be using both power receptacles, so you can be charged accordingly, and also that the extension cord is properly rated for the task.*

TAKE THIS STEP

I have found a new use for a Reebok five-position exercise step. This step's height can be adjusted, and it can also be leveled from side to side. We glued some carpet to the top of the step to match our outside carpet, and use it to help enter and exit the trailer. This works extremely well with our rear-entrance fifth-wheel, and should work with other high-profile RVs. It also works great for washing windows.

CHARLES RAMP, ODESSA, NEW YORK

WRONG IS RIGHT

I've been putting the "Y" hose connector on the wrong end of my water hose. Installed at the trailer end of the hose (instead of at the water source), it accomplishes three things:

1. It's easier to reach than the park-provided water spigot.
2. It acts as a hose-strain relief.
3. It can be used to relieve the water pressure while disconnecting the hose.

ROLAND ROBINSON,
SUN CITY WEST, ARIZONA

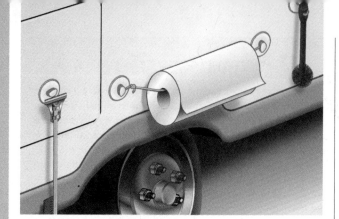

Handy Hangers

WAYNE LAMPHERE, MELROSE, NEW YORK

▶ Two suction-cup snap hooks and a piece of rope tied into a loop make an ideal temporary paper-towel holder that can be mounted to the exterior fiberglass of your RV.

I also use these handy hangers to hang my outdoor cooking utensils.

These suction cup snap hooks are available at Camping World and other stores for about $1.25 each.

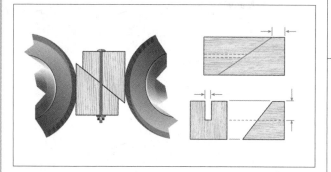

No More Rockin'

ROBERT WYBLE, CALEDONIA, NEW YORK

▶ You can stop the rocking in your tandem-axle trailer or fifth-wheel in a very economic way.

Take a 7-inch piece of 4 × 4-inch lumber and slice it diagonally, as shown in the illustration. Drill a ⅜-inch hole in the center of the top block. Cut a ⅜-inch-wide slot in the bottom block. Assemble the blocks together as shown with a 7-inch carriage bolt, using a washer and nut. Make two assemblies.

Place the assembly between the tires as shown, and tighten the nut.

This will help eliminate the rocking when you walk in the unit.

Wash 'n Drive

EDWIN COLE, RED DEER, ALBERTA

▶ No matter how large the RV, there never seems to be enough room to hang the wet towels and cloths. Treble that with three young children and campgrounds that generally frown on hanging clotheslines on their trees, and you have a dilemma.

Here is what we do, and so far, none of the campgrounds seem to have a problem with it.

By attaching four brass cup-holder style hooks to each corner of the RV and running a clean piece of line to the luggage rack of my tow vehicle, I have a handy clothesline that can be adjusted by simply parking the tow vehicle farther from the trailer.

Riding the Pine

MEL KITTKSEN, ARCADIA, CALIFORNIA

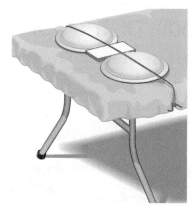

▶ We camp a lot in areas that get windy in the afternoon, and setting the outdoor table often becomes a battleground to keep everything in its place.

I purchased some bulk elastic cord from the hardware store. I measured the length of cord to go around the table and then crimped the ends together to form a loop. (You could also just tie the ends together.)

Now, when setting the table, the plates, napkins, etc., go under the cord and stay in place.

Holder's Broken

JOE CAMPBELL, GOODWATER, ALABAMA

▶ Having had wind and negligence in storage break some of the plastic holders for my outside lights, I found a neat way to still be able to use that string of lights.

I took some old scratched or unplayed CDs and some sample discs I got in the mail and used them as reflectors.

The center holes are just the right size for the C7 bulbs to fit in. Just unscrew the bulb from the existing holder, place the disc with the shiny side down and replace the bulb. The reflective surface illuminates great.

Yankee Doodle Distributor

LARRY HALL, PUEBLO WEST, COLORADO

▶ Wanting to fly several small flags, I picked up a junk engine distributor cap. These caps are available anywhere they work on cars, and I turned mine into a flag holder.

I drilled a hole through the center post and attached it to the front of my travel trailer.

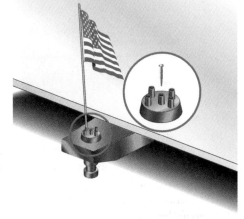

BREAKER, BREAKER

You can use two hand-held walkie-talkies to help you tune your satellite dish.

Turn on your television as usual. Put a rubber band around one radio to hold the microphone button open. Lay this radio next to the television so that it will pick up the sound.

Turn on the second radio and put it in your pocket so you can listen to the sound that is transmitted by the first one. That way, as the sound changes, you will be able to tell what the signal strength is.

This method eliminates having a second person inside relaying the signal strength information or turning up the volume very loud.

CHARLIE MOOMAW,
WILMINGTON, OHIO

WATER, WATER EVERY-WHERE

I needed a water outlet on the door side of my camper and didn't want to run back and forth turning the hose off at a distant hose bib, so I came up with this idea.

Many catalogs, such as Whatever Works and other mail-order operations, feature a faucet attached to an aluminum stake with a 5- or 6-foot hose. Simply attach this faucet to another longer hose and run it under your RV to the water connection.

This way, you have water access where you want it.

JOE CAMPBELL, GOODWATER, ALABAMA

PURRFECT DISPOSAL

If you travel with a cat — or know someone who does — save those large, rectangular plastic kitty litter containers. They are perfect for disposing of used motor oil from engines or AC generators, and diesel fuel from changing fuel filters.

The mouth of the container is wide enough to take a drain hose or large funnel, and the screw cap seals the container securely. Be careful, of course, about pouring in hot liquids.

Actually, it's a good idea to have some kitty litter on board even if you don't have a cat. It will absorb spills and can be swept up when it dries. The same principle is at work in the Oil Dri used in auto-repair shops to soak up oil and radiator spills.

NANCY MILLS,
ALDERSON, WEST VIRGINIA

in camp

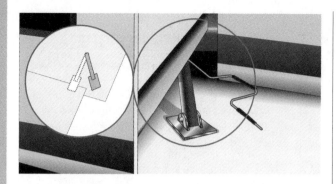

Do the Twist

BRUCE TRUDGEN, WILLIAMSBURG, MICHIGAN

▶ With our dinette slideout fully deployed, one of our stabilizing jacks was very difficult to reach. So, with no weight on the jacks, I removed all but one of its attaching screws, rotated it about 45 degrees and reinstalled the screws in newly drilled holes.

Now we can operate the jack with the slideout fully out.

From Dusk 'til Dawn

JIM HINTON, NORTH AUGUSTA, SOUTH CAROLINA

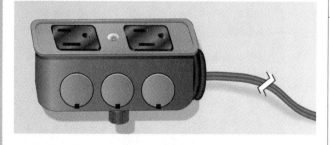

▶ We like to come back to our RV after a night hike or a campfire program with some kind of illumination at our site. This allows us to not only identify our home, but also helps when it is time to unlock the door.

We already have rope lights on the edge of the awning but did not want to turn these on while it was still daylight.

I decided to use an automatic dusk-to-dawn sensor to control the lights. I picked up the metal electrical box, duplex outlet, cover plate and dusk-to-dawn sensor at the hardware store. I completed the unit with an appliance cord.

I plug the unit into an outside RV electrical outlet and the rope light cord into the switch-box outlet. After returning, if I do not want the lights to remain on — which might annoy our neighbors — I simply unplug the unit.

Padding the Pad

CHARLES HAXTER, NEW HUDSON, MICHIGAN

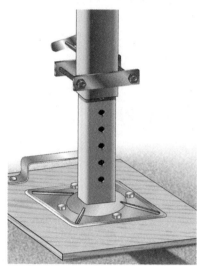

▶ With heavier vehicles these days, it is becoming more important to put blocks under the jacks and support legs of our RVs. The tiny pads the manufacturers mount on their jacks are too small to evenly spread the RV's weight and keep them from punching through parking-spot surfaces.

I have bolted a $12 \times 12 \times \frac{3}{4}$-inch piece of treated plywood to the front and rear legs of my fifth-wheel under the metal foot pad. I also bolted a handle on the front two pads, large enough to insert my gloved hand. Pulling the quick snaps and then lifting with the handle makes for fast-and-easy setups and take-downs.

Level With Me

DOROTHY SEMTANA, SALEM, OREGON

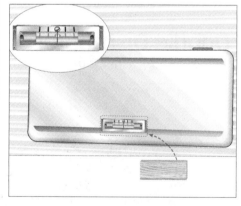

▶ I'm a solo RVer. When I was new to towing a trailer, in order to help me park level, I bought a large level to install on the front trailer-window cover. The level was centered and fastened to the window cover with a piece of wood on the cover's underside.

It's a great help when conditions require me to park in a parking lot. I drive around until I find a level spot.

This is my third travel trailer, and I'd be lost without my large level that I can see from the driver's seat.

The Flow Was Slow

LEE JUNGKANS, WAUWATOSA, WISCONSIN

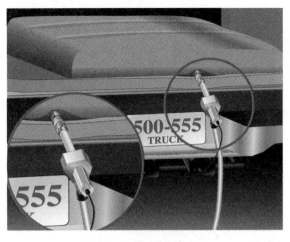

▶ I have found that using a water-mattress-style water tank for transporting water works great while boondocking. Usually, the difficulty in dry-camping lies in transporting the water on the roof and trying not to lose any while the vehicle is in motion. Additionally, the water-fill inlet on my trailer is about chest-high, making the gravity flow painfully slow.

My solution was to incorporate an aerator pump. The unit was fitted with pipe-thread to garden-hose adapters on the suction and discharge fittings. The pump draws 1.7 amps at 12 volts DC and the electrical supply is provided by a connection on my truck.

The pump moves about 2 to 3 gallons per minute from up to about 50 feet away, and requires no lifting of heavy water jugs for refilling the RV. The mattress holds about 35 gallons. Also, by placing the mattress in the bed of the truck, you can drive at highway speeds without worrying about spilling water.

Prevent Corrosion

FORREST McCLURE, AURORA, COLORADO

▶ The common trailer-stabilizing jack can mar the underside of your trailer because the top is a round, zinc-coated metal plate.

As the screw is extended to contact the underside of the trailer, the plate can chip or scratch away the paint from the trailer's frame, which could allow rust and corrosion to accumulate.

To keep this from happening, I hot-glued pliable furniture-caster cups to the top of each stabilizing jack. The caster cups are designed to prevent furniture from scratching the floor in houses, but work equally well to prevent damage to the underside of trailers.

The 1¾-inch cups fit the jacks perfectly, and are available at hardware stores.

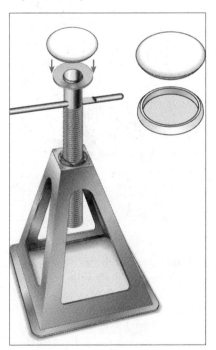

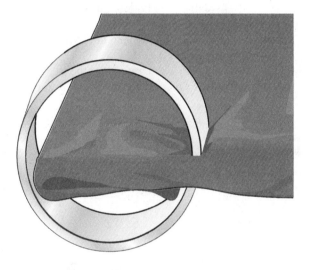

Hold Tight

ROBERT WHITE, FRANKLIN, KENTUCKY

▶ Outdoor tablecloths often fly up in the wind. Commercial hold-down springs are too small for the thick concrete or very thick wooden tables found in a lot of parks.

At the hardware store, I bought a couple of feet of 6-inch PVC pipe and sliced it into 2-inch-wide circular sections. Then I made a cut across each circle to allow it to spring open.

After the cutting, I sanded the edges smooth. These rings spring open to fit virtually any table thickness, and always hold tightly.

in camp

Why Bend or Kneel?

GARY LOUGREN, VERONA, NORTH DAKOTA

▶ We always had to kneel or bend over to lift our jack stands on our fifth-wheel. This usually meant kneeling in gravel, mud or other wet conditions.

I bought two ½-inch × 18-inch eyebolts, and then drilled ½-inch holes in the front edge of the jack stand plate. I put the threaded end of the eyebolts into the holes in the plate with a nut on each side, and tightened the nuts.

Now you can grab the eyebolts to lift the stands without kneeling or bending.

If the eyebolts end up too close to the fifth-wheel, just bend them forward as needed.

This system makes it a lot easier to lift the jacks — especially if you are an older camper.

Doggy Dilemma

DANNY LINDSTROM, CASTROVILLE, CALIFORNIA

▶ My wife and I have been RVing with two dogs since 1998.

The constant concern is where to securely tie them up without being in the sun or bothering the neighbors — one of them is an 85-pound Labrador retriever that can move picnic tables, when he spots someone who might pet him!

We solved this by mounting eyebolts under the coach. The eyebolts were affixed at solid points, and sealed.

You can tether the dog to the eyebolts using whatever length leash you find offers decent roaming room without inadvertently allowing the animal to hurt himself; even the shortest tether still lets him relax under the RV, in the shade.

Secure Your Jack

STANLEY FREDRICK, TUCSON, ARIZONA

▶ I have always worried about somebody messing with the controls for my electric A-frame jack when the trailer was set up in the campground, and I was even more worried about somebody dropping the jack partway down when we stopped en route.

My solution was to purchase a weatherproof in-line fuse holder. I wired the fuse holder into the jack's power-supply line.

Now, when I want to use the jack, I insert a 30-amp fuse (max rating for the unit) into the fuse holder. When I remove the fuse, all is secure.

Hang On

NEIL JOHNSON, PENSACOLA, FLORIDA

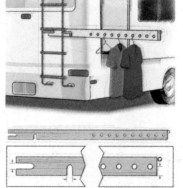

▶ While many RV parks have rules against clotheslines at their sites, none of them seem to mind if you hang things from your RV. To facilitate this, I built a portable hanging board that attaches to the ladder mounts at the rear of my motorhome.

The board is made from a 7-foot-long length of 2 × 4, with a one-inch-wide slot (about 8 inches long) cut in one end of the board and a 11¼-inch-wide slot cut in one side of the board (about 16 inches in from the end where the other slot was cut).

These two slots allow the hanging board to slide onto the inner ladder mount, then slip down on the outer mount at the point of the most convenient height for hanging clothes. The slots also allow for quick removal when breaking camp.

Along the length of the board, I've drilled a series of 1¼-inch-diameter holes, spaced 3 to 4 inches apart, to accommodate plastic hangers on which the clothes are hung to dry.

"Home" Decorating

BEVERLY MICHALEK, GALLATIN, TENNESSEE

▶ Most of us like to give our motorhomes that cozy, comfortable atmosphere. Many opt for a steering wheel table, so an extra lamp can illuminate the surroundings. We found an easier and quite attractive way to add table space in our coach.

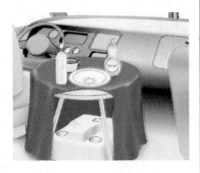

We bought a three-legged decorator table (which can be found in stores like Wal-Mart/Kmart) and placed it between the driver and passenger seat. It covers the console and cup holders between the seats.

Because the table legs are made of wood, they can be easily cut and trimmed to the height needed so that the table will be level. When parked, we can keep items underneath the table. To cover the table, I bought a cloth to match the coach interior and added a crocheted overlay to dress it up.

When ready to travel, the table easily comes apart and is stored until we reach the next campsite.

The Disappearing Shelf

HARVEY HETRICK, TORRANCE, CALIFORNIA

▶ Since our overhead entertainment center was already full (satellite receiver, VCR, switch boxes, etc.), there was no room to add our new DVD player. The overhead storage area was likewise

full of tapes and movies, and would require additional hookup cables if we put the DVD there. What to do?

My wife suggested that I lower the sun visor, use it as a shelf and temporarily stow the DVD player on it. Sure enough, the lowered visor is strong — and solid — enough to hold our lightweight DVD player, and the hook-up cables reach the television. Even the electric cord is long enough to reach a nearby outlet.

As I stated, it's only temporary and is not utilized while on the road.

BAG IT

We have always enjoyed a campfire in the evening. Since you never know if the firewood available at the campground is seasoned and/or wet, we carry some of our own.

Carrying firewood in our trailer or SUV always created a mess. We solved that problem by using empty 40-pound dog-food bags to transport the wood. They hold about an armload of wood. If each bag is filled with some kindling and a few logs, you have a perfect campfire in each bag.

Each fire lasts a couple of hours and will produce enough hot coals to get even wet wood burning if you want a longer-lasting fire.

We take one bag for each evening. If we don't use it, we carry it back home to our seasoned pile. The bag can be reused if you keep it dry.

MARK BOARDMAN,
LOUISVILLE, KENTUCKY

LINE IT UP

A telescoping golf-ball retriever (the longer the better) has proven to be a great tool in parking my RV at a campsite. Using a colored felt-tip marker, I mark important measurements along the length of the retriever.

For example, to determine height, a mark at 12 feet allows me to carry the extended pole through the campsite to verify that my 12-foot-high rig will clear any overhanging limbs.

You can also use it to determine such things as how far the slides will extend (and the distance from the slide bottom to the ground, to clear electrical pedestals, etc.); awning length; and overhang beyond the rear wheels.

Now I can avoid many of the scratches and dents that have resulted from trial and error. In its collapsed state, the stick takes up very little room.

ROY CORBETT, PROSPER, TEXAS

ROPE-A-DOPE

Concerned about safely entering and exiting the steps on my RV, in dimly lit or dark camp areas, I came up with this "bright" idea that is both easy and inexpensive.

At a home-center store, I bought a 2-foot-long rope light and mounted it above the pullout steps. Since the cord unscrews from the length of rope light, I leave the light strip permanently attached, but remove the cord when traveling.

I plug it into a timer that is plugged into my AC outlet.

JOE CAMPBELL, GOODWATER, ALABAMA

Store the Cord

TERRY NANCE, NIXON, TEXAS

▶ I have a 50-foot-long 50-amp electrical cord for my fifth-wheel. It is very hard to pick up and very hard to coil.

Here is an idea to make that job simple: Store the entire cord in a plastic milk crate. Get the milk crate (or similar crate) where containers are sold. Cut a hole in one side at the very bottom of the crate, large enough to allow the trailer end of the cord to pass through. Feed enough cable through the hole so that the cord can connect to your rig. Coil the rest of the cord inside the crate.

For travel, coil all the cord that has the campsite (male) end of the plug in the crate first. Then coil the RV (female) end of the cord into the crate. The crate has built-in handles. Now, you can store the cord in any convenient storage area.

When you get to your campsite, pull out the female end and plug it into your RV. Then pull out the other end of the cord just far enough to reach the campsite electrical outlet.

A Helpful Step

DOREEN ALFANO, WINDSOR LOCKS, CONNECTICUT

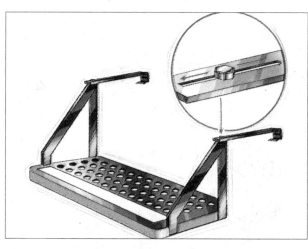

▶ Being a short person with arthritis, I used to find it very difficult to reach that first high step to get into my motorhome. I found a great product, called Add-A-Step, that attaches to the first step, providing lower entry into my motorhome. I paid $115.

Once you are at your campsite, it attaches quickly and easily. When not in use, it's portable and foldable. It's made of steel, perforated for rain drainage, and comes with a hanger arm that adjusts to the width of your existing RV steps. It has a high-gloss finish.

The company is All Trails Inc. of Utica, Michigan; (586) 731-2340; e-mail: alltrailsinc@yahoo.com. Just tell the staff what motorhome you own, and they will fix you up with the correct step. It's as easy as that.

Twice the Table

ED REKOLA, LYNNWOOD, WASHINGTON

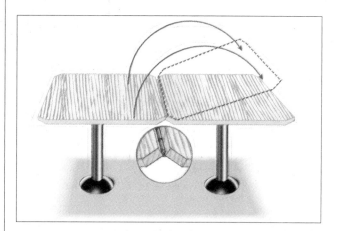

▶ Our motorhome came with a 2-foot-round table in the dining area, plus an additional 4-foot-long table to replace the smaller one when more surface area is needed. The larger table comes in handy, but when not in use it has to be stored.

I resolved the storage problem after visiting a home-supply center, where I bought a 2 × 4-foot sheet of laminated oak and a 24-inch brass piano hinge. By using the hardware from our 4-foot table and modifying the length of its legs, we now have a table that folds out to 4 feet when we are parked and retracts to 2 feet when we are on the road.

We no longer need to store our 4-foot table, and the portable table leg fits beneath the table while we are underway. We put nonskid place mats between the table halves and the portable leg.

Cat House

JERRY ZERBE, FLUSHING, MICHIGAN

▶ My wife wanted an attached area for our cat, in our motorhome. I had seen examples, but all required either legs outside or window-frame attachments, which did not allow closing the window when not in use.

I found that attaching the frame of the cat house to the RV's window frame with hook-and-loop fastener and hanging the outside of the cat house to the window's awning roller bar with plastic pipe hangers worked well.

I can put it in place or take it down in five minutes.

The frame is made of 1 × 2-inch boards, covered with nylon insect screening stapled to the wood frame. All components are hardware store items. A lightweight blanket covers the floor.

The cat found it within minutes after we opened the window.

So Proudly It Waves

JOE CAMPBELL, GOODWATER, ALABAMA

▶ To proudly display my American flag, I attached the bracket to a block of wood and attached screw hooks on each side. Depending on the diameter of a handy tree at the campsite, I select appropriate-length bungee cords and secure the wood block at the top and bottom. This way, there are no screws or nails in the tree and the flag is easily put up or taken down.

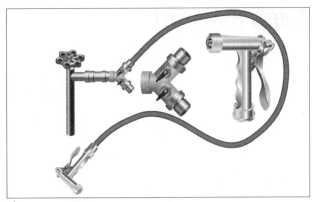

Outside Shower

JOHN CRITTENDEN, POWDER SPRINGS, GEORGIA

▶ My motorhome does not have an outside shower. I didn't want the kids to track dirt and sand into the motorhome, so I came up with a solution.

I attached the water-pressure regulator to the water faucet, then screwed on a Y-splitter. On one side of the splitter I put the water line to the motorhome. To the other side I attached a short length of garden hose with a sprayer on the end. It works great.

Portable Solar Light

ANNA VAN ETTEN, MAPLECREST, NEW YORK

▶ Individual solar-lamp assemblies are available at many hardware stores and home centers. They make nice light sources while camping. And in order to be able to place your solar light in the sun, for charging, make it portable.

Cover or paint a 13- to 16-ounce coffee can or a one-gallon paint can. Cut a hole in the cover the diameter of the solar-light stem. Insert the light fixture through the hole into the empty can. Fill the can with sand, stones, plaster of paris or cement to add weight.

During the day, place the can in full sun, and at night, move the light to show the way to your entrance door. Simply store in a compartment between uses.

in camp

Tag & Release

HARVEY HETRICK, TORRANCE, CALIFORNIA

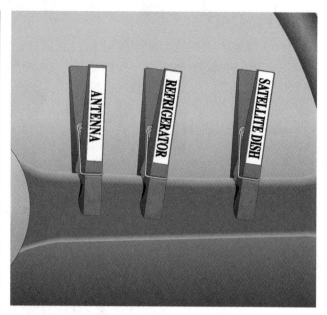

▶ Entering many of our national and state parks requires the purchase of a pass, which then is required to be displayed on the windshield so it can be checked, if need be, by a passing ranger or guard. After several days of bright sunshine, or after a rain or dew, the taped pass is a mess — and the tape glue is stuck to the windshield.

A no-more-tape-to-scrape solution can be purchased anywhere office supplies are sold: an inexpensive plastic picture frame with a molded stand. Just ask the ranger to hand you the pass so you can place it in the frame, then place the self-standing frame inside the windshield where it can be seen.

Memory Jogger

PAUL LINDSTROM, GRAND JUNCTION, COLORADO

▶ Needing some method to help remind me to stow and/or secure certain items, I came up with this solution. I painted some spring-loaded clothespins red and put on some labels so I could write the name of the item I wanted to remember to stow securely for traveling.

You can make as many as required and name them to suit your needs. Where to put them is up to you, but I put them on the steering wheel as we use the item, and when we get ready to hit the road, the various clothespins are placed back on the items they are labeled to match.

YES, YOU CAN-CAN

Want the "luxury" of an outside trash can at your campsite without having to haul around a smelly, full-size receptacle? Buy a pop-up gardening container. You can find these containers in the garden section of most hardware and home-center stores. The name comes from the fact that they fold into a nice flat circle for storage, then pop up when needed. They are made in different sizes, too; ours uses 39-gallon-size garbage bags, which is perfect when traveling with large groups.

BRENDA GUETTHOFF,
ELBURN, ILLINOIS

STOP THE CURL

After using a plastic-turf entrance mat for awhile, we noticed the corners had a tendency to curl up and become a tripping hazard. To stop this from happening, I screwed the mat to a piece of ½-inch-thick plywood. For longevity, I used treated wood (you also can paint the wood to repel moisture). When ready to pack up, we just knock off the dirt and put it in one of the outside compartments.

JOHN KASDORF,
WHITE PIGEON, MICHIGAN

STOP LOSING

After misplacing several 15- to 30-amp electrical adapters for shorepower hookups, I decided to stop the losses by bolting a dummy 15-amp outlet inside the motorhome's electrical compartment. When it's not needed, I plug the adapter into this dummy outlet, ready for use.

JOHN FAW,
FALLBROOK, CALIFORNIA

10
minute tech
livability

MAKE FRIENDS WITH YOUR FLOOR VENTS

If you have ever dropped anything down the RV floor-duct vents, you will appreciate this simple retrieval solution. Remove the grille and cut a piece of Precisionaire filter (available at Wal-Mart) to fit the underside of the grille. As a bonus, these filters are antimicrobial to control bacteria, mildew, germs and mold, and they are washable.

JOHN KOUDELKA, DELTONA, FLORIDA

NO SLIP

Motorhome beds are often comprised of a lightweight mattress atop a piece of plywood. Not surprisingly, the top flat sheet is continually pulling out.

The cure? I put a foot-square piece of Non-Slip Line It (available at Camping World) at the foot of the bed at each corner.

I stapled them on and covered the staples with clear packing tape. Now, the top sheet never comes out!

FRANK BERENTSEN,
NEW BERLIN, WISCONSIN

SHOWER CURTAIN CAPERS

When a shower curtain is made of see-through material, it can be quite difficult to keep clean.

Rather than expend unnecessary energy, I purchased a spring-loaded (or fixed-mount) extension rod to fit the opening and fit it with a light-colored, but opaque, shower curtain. This brightens up the motorhome, is easily replaced and is an inexpensive remedy.

FAY LAUVER, ANCHORAGE, ALASKA

ONE CD IS WORTH A MILLION WORDS

My husband and I are preparing to start full-timing soon.

For the past few years, I have been preparing for motorhome living by scanning and saving (on CDs) all the information I can. I have done recipes, photos and yes, even "Quick Tips" and other articles from *MotorHome Magazine.*

I made about 10 CDs, with different states as file folders, and have places to visit all scanned and within easy reach while traveling.

Why go to all this trouble? I started cutting this information out of the magazines and found the notebooks I saved them in grew too big, too heavy and took up too much space!

ALICIA SHOOK, STANWOOD, IOWA

SOCK IT TO ME

Besides keeping your tootsies toasty, here are a few more uses for your tube socks:

■ A sock makes a great place to gather up the long cord from an electric hair dryer or a curling iron.

■ A sock makes a great pouch for your hot-glue gun and glue sticks.

■ A long sock makes a good place to stow a ratchet tie down, or that hank of rope that keeps getting tangled up in things.

■ A sock over the WD-40 can will keep the cap, nozzle and can together, in one place.

■ Socks make great applicators for polishing compound, car wax, Rain-X window coating and other rag-tag jobs. A small sponge, inside the sock, gives just a little more grip to the applicator.

■ Baggy, worn-out socks pulled over your dress shoes will protect the shine.

MARK KUYKENDALL, LIVINGSTON, TEXAS

STOP SLIDING CLOTHES HANGERS

If your clothes hangers tend to slide on the clothes rod when traveling, you can slip a piece of swimming-pool vacuum hose over the rod. This type of hose has ridges that allow it to flex without breaking, so it will keep the hangers in place. It can be purchased anywhere basic swimming-pool supplies are sold.

ROBERT CURRY, PETERSBURG, INDIANA

TWO "JARRING" IDEAS

Most RVers carry assortments of nuts, bolts, screws, nails and other small items. The problem is organizing these things so that you can find what you need.

I use the plastic jars most brands of peanut butter come in. These jars are clear, making it easy to see the contents, and they won't break. These same type jars can be used to store food items also.

Clean the empty plastic jar, and remove the label. Keep the jars in a small peck basket with a collapsible handle (like the kind fruit comes in). The basket is easy to store and, with the handle, easy to retrieve.

WALT WILL, WESTERVILLE, OHIO

When using empty jars for storage, paint a matching number or design on the jar and the lid. That takes the guesswork out of which lid goes with which jar.

CATHY UMBLE, FORT MYERS, FLORIDA

livability

A Bit Too High

D E N N I S J O H N S O N , P H I L A D E L P H I A , P E N N S Y L V A N I A

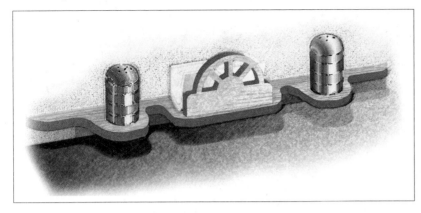

▶ In our motorhome, we found that the dinette tabletop was a bit too high for our taste, and I set out to lower it. I relocated the wall track and cut the leg to lower the top about 2 inches, which now makes it very comfortable. This left me with five unsightly screw holes in the wall at the old track location. I looked for some brass studs or something to cover these holes, then had a better idea.

I designed and built a napkin and salt-and-pepper rack, long enough to cover the old holes. The new holder is of walnut, finished to match the coach cabinets. Napkins stay put while traveling, and it eliminates the need to get up for salt, pepper or napkins after siting down for a meal. Under the salt and pepper shakers, I cut circular pieces of nonslip mat to keep them from dancing around. The holder has enough clearance under it to allow removal of the tabletop for conversion to a bed when needed. And if you like popcorn in bed, salt and napkins are right at hand!

Pantry Quick Fix

F R A N K W O Y T H A L , A N D O V E R , N E W Y O R K

▶ The slide-out wire rack in our motorhome's pantry had adequate shelf space, but it did not slide out even one-half its depth. That forced us to reach into the back for a large portion of the groceries stored on the rack. My quick fix was to replace the rack's hardware with 24-inch ball-bearing drawer slides I purchased at Home Depot.

No special fasteners were needed in this transformation, and the job took about an hour. Now the 24-inch wire rack slides out to its full length.

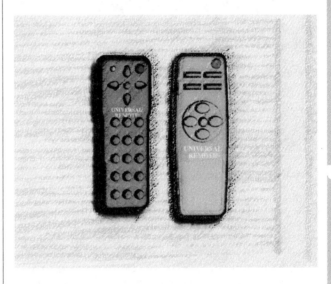

Where'd You Put It?

E L I Z A B E T H B E A T T I E , P E N S A C O L A , F L O R I D A

▶ In our travels, we kept misplacing the remote controls for the television and VCR. We put a strip of hook-and-loop fastener on the back of each remote and the other part of the fastener strip on the area above the RV sofa. This way, we can use the remote and easily hang it up in its place. Since I'm notorious for setting one of them down wherever I happen to be, my husband just has to look and ask, "Where is it? Please put it back."

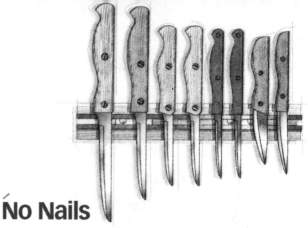

A RECENT DISCOVERY

I recently discovered an industrial-strength adhesive, E6000 from Eclectic Products Inc., (800) 767-4667, that is clear, flexible, waterproof and paintable with easy cleanup. It's available from Wal-Mart and some hobby/craft stores and costs about $3. I've used it satisfactorily on numerous repair projects in my coach and home. I keep a tube in each.

DON HOWER,
GRAND JUNCTION, COLORADO

THEY RATTLE A LOT

The day/night shades in our motorhome used to rattle a lot while we were driving. To eliminate the problem, I bought some gum-rubber erasers at an office store and cut them diagonally to form two wedges. I simply push them between the bottom bar of the shade and the window frame. Now I have a nice quiet ride.

GARY CHRISTENSEN, KENOSHA, WISCONSIN

HANG UP THE PHONE

We found that a vertical soap-holder, found in the shower accessories section of many stores, makes a great hanger/holder for our cell phone, keeping it accessible, yet out of the way. These soap-holders are usually sold with a suction cup attached to the back; we removed the cup and altered the suction-cup attachment hole so it would slide over a raised screw head. Now, with different holders mounted at various locations, our phone is handy from the bed, copilot's seat or the "office."

CLAIRE ROGERS, TUCSON, ARIZONA

BOOTS AND BEANS

My wife and I travel in our RV a lot with our two dogs, Boots and Beans. Until recently, the pups would hesitate before entering or exiting the trailer when they were called – even at chow time. The reason was that their toenails kept getting caught in the holes in the fold-away steps of our travel trailer.

To remedy the situation, I bought a piece of indoor/outdoor carpet and cut pieces for the steps, allowing approximately 3 inches of overlap for each. Next, I wrapped the carpet pieces around each step, and used hook-and-loop fasteners to secure each piece in place. This padded the steps so that the dogs now have no difficulty entering and exiting the trailer. I can even leave the carpet in place when I fold the steps away.

RICK FOWLER, CHANDLER, ARIZONA

No Nails

SARA WARDLOW, LIVINGSTON, TEXAS

▶ Over the years, we have had many different RVs and I never have used nails or screws to hang things on the walls. I use industrial-strength hook-and-loop fastener. One of our bigger hanging jobs was to mount my 12-inch magnetic knife holder in the galley. It's been up for two years and has never come loose.

The Greenhouse Effect

LARRY BLACK, SNELLVILLE, GEORGIA

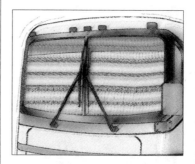

▶ Anyone who owns a Class A motorhome knows about the greenhouse effect in the driver's area, due to the large windshield and side windows that collect heat from the sun. I went looking for a solution and found a product called Reflectix. It's an aluminized plastic material that looks like bubble pack and is used to insulate heating and cooling ductwork. I found rolls 4 feet wide and in lengths of 25, 50 and 125 feet. It is available in many home-improvement centers or heating-supply stores. It is manufactured by Reflectix Inc. of Markleville, Indiana; (800) 879-3645, reflectixinc.com.

The material is about 5/16-inch thick and is stiff enough to stand up in most applications. If necessary, foil tape can be used to attach 1/2-inch dowel rods to stiffen the material. It can be cut with scissors to match the shape of your windshield and side windows. The front-window curtain gives extra support.

Now, when we park for a period of time, the driver's area stays cool with this insulation material in place. It can be rolled up and stored easily when not in use.

livability

Three Quickies

DAVID LITOGOT, LARGO, FLORIDA

▶ We find that coffee filters make the best and cheapest way to cushion bowls in the RV cabinet so they don't rattle. Camping-supply stores sell "industrial strength" nonslip pads, but filters work just fine.

▶ We have a coffee maker mounted over the dinette. To keep the empty pot from falling out, we drilled two small holes to accept a small bungee cord. The bottom of the pot is cushioned with a rubber pad.

▶ When washing clothes on the road, we sometimes need to hang shirts up to dry completely. A plastic towel rod, attached to the ceiling, does the trick. A clothespin/ hook works well with towels. We have one rod in the bedroom for drying while driving, and one over the front seats in our Class C to dry items at night.

Limp Connections

DEE POPE, HENDERSON, NEVADA

▶ Back when they were new, the seat-belt connectors for the driver and copilot seats in our motorhome stayed upright and out of the way — but after a few years, they began sagging outward and, when not in use, obstructed our pathway. At a fabric store, I found some upholstery trim in a color that matched our seats perfectly. I sized two pieces of the trim to fit the side of the seat bottom, then hand-stitched each end of the trim piece to the seat while leaving the middle open so the connectors could slide back-and-forth. This allows seat movement while keeping the seat-belt support connector in place.

PUNCH THREE HOLES

My husband and I always look forward to reading *10-Minute Tech*. We have tried many of the ideas and, when camping, friends see the results of some of these tips and always ask how we did it. So, I started assembling a book of *10-Minute Tech:* Every month I remove this section from the magazine, punch three holes along the side and insert them into a three-ring binder. I keep this binder in the motorhome. I bring it out for friends who are just starting out in the motorhome world — they love it!

DEBBIE HALE, GOODLETTSVILLE, TENNESSEE

PLACE MATS

We laminate the brochures RV parks give incoming campers. The unfolded brochures usually measure 11 × 17 inches and make neat place mats for the dinette. We can relive pleasant times spent at the various parks and read the information about the park. In addition, they often have a local city map, plus interesting facts about the surrounding area. To keep the mats from slipping around, we use Slip Stop under them.

RICHARD WALTHER, LOS ALAMOS, NEW MEXICO

SIMPLE AND QUICK

Here is a simple, quick and inexpensive way to keep out sunlight, heat and bright lights at night and also to keep your shades, curtains, etc. from fading. Cut a piece of black felt to fit the window. Put the sticky-backed piece of hook-and-loop fasteners on the wall on each side of the window and sew the other part onto the felt. Slip the felt under the shade over the window. If you use black, it doesn't look bad from the outside and the amount of heat it keeps out is unbelievable!

LINDA CLARKSON, MELBOURNE, FLORIDA

TWO FOR THE ROAD

1. If you say, "Plastic, please," at the store, you have an unlimited supply of trash bags that also are great for carrying items to and from the campground shower.

2. A ring cut out of a 2-liter plastic bottle will keep your paper towels from unrolling when you travel; the top will make a great funnel; and the bottom can be used as a flower pot or a candy/condiment dish.

BARRY HOUSEKNECHT, APOPKA, FLORIDA

livability

Bigger Is Better

ALICE BROWN, VIRGINIA BEACH, VIRGINIA

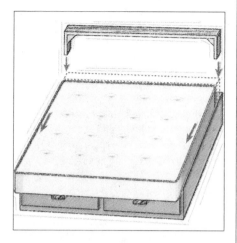

▶ My husband is 6 feet, 4 inches tall, but the mattress in our motorhome is nowhere near that! To make him more comfortable, I built an extension to match the width of our mattress, but not its height. That allowed me to pad the extension with an elongated pillow which acts as a mattress extension (and is flush with the existing mattress). This extension is put in place after the slide is out. The extra 10 inches makes a world of difference!

Weatherizing the Dinette

ARLENE CHIAROLANZIO,
FLORHAM PARK, NEW JERSEY

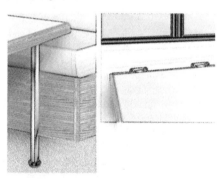

▶ The dinette table in our motorhome has been the source of many loud squeaks and groans. I have used sticky tabs, wadded paper, foam wedges — all of which fell out or didn't work.

After putting new weatherstrip around the door, though, I had several pieces leftover — and it occurred to me to try them to quiet the table.

I lowered the table and put the weatherstripping along the edge of the table that touched the wall, which made the table snug.

Next came the unsteady table leg. A rubber circular furniture cup was slipped under the leg, and now that doesn't move or make noises, either!

Takes a Ribbing

JIM COMMONS, HENDERSON, TEXAS

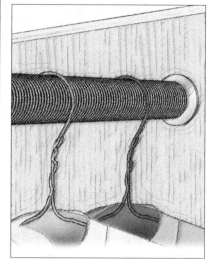

▶ To keep clothes from sliding on the closet rod inside our motorhome, I purchased a ribbed hose from a pool/spa store and slipped it over the rod.

This is a ribbed hose instead of a spiral, which makes it easy to cut to length — plus, the hangers fit well and stay in place.

Hang It Up

EDWARD SOMMERFIELD,
POUGHKEEPSIE, NEW YORK

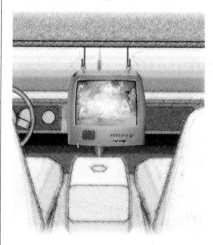

▶ For on-the-road stability in our Class C coach, we try to store as many of the heavy items as low to the floor as possible. When we set up at a campground, this requires lifting a somewhat heavy 13-inch television up onto the bunk-over-cab, a difficult task for senior citizens.

The bottom of the center-section of this cabover bed is made of ¾-inch plywood. After drilling two ⅜-inch holes, we fastened a pair of ⅜-inch threaded hooks with washers and nuts. Two threaded loops were then installed on the top of the television.

Now, when setting up, all we have to do is lift the television from the dinette seat and hang it on the hooks. The hooks can be protected with slip-on covers made from scrap rubber tubing to avoid catching anyone's head or other body parts.

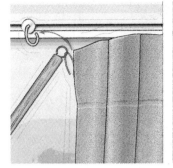 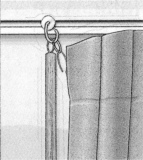

A Real Curtain Rod

JERROLD REIMER, MILTON, WISCONSIN

▶ Are you tired of climbing over seats and dash to spread the curtain around your RV's front window at night? I was — so I made a rod to guide the curtains along the track and across the windows.

At the hardware store, I purchased two dowel rods, each about 24 inches long, and two screw eyes. Screw the eyes into one end of each dowel (first drilling a small pilot hole).

To install, unhook the first hanger on your curtain, pass the screw eye over the hanger wire and re-hook the hanger.

The wand hangs down alongside the curtains when not in use. It can be sanded and painted to make it more appealing.

A Sip in Time

ARLENE CHIAROLANZIO,
FLORHAM PARK, NEW JERSEY

▶ Being left-handed, the cup-holder in the center console of my motorhome wasn't the handiest place to rest my drink.

So, I mounted a plastic cup-holder (available at various places, including Wal-Mart, for about $3) to the window channel frame near the driver's seat of my  coach. I used an existing molding screw already there, so no holes had to be drilled.

ANOTHER USE

A large plastic lid from a coffee can could also be used as a chopping block or slicing board. The lid hardly takes up any storage space, and is easier to use than a large board. The lid can conveniently be packed in a lunch container, and after use can either be cleaned or discarded.

DONNA MANN,
HAVERTOWN, PENNSYLVANIA

SILLY STRINGS

A common failure of day/night shades is that one of the cord retainers (string anchors) comes loose at the bottom end – and those strings disappear into the bottom rail.

Retrieving the proper strings and re-anchoring can be an extensive project. Most larger blinds actually have two strings (as a loop) exiting through an end cap on each side of the bottom rail.

To prevent this from happening, insert a medium-size safety pin around one string in the loop and let it hang at the bottom of the loop; if an anchor comes loose, the loop will not retreat into the rail. You now only have to pull the loop down and reattach the cord-retaining anchor.

CLIFFORD LOEHR,
ELIZABETH, PENNSYLVANIA

BETTER BAKING

I used to hate to try to bake anything in my RV oven. It always seemed to burn on the bottom. At a kitchen shop, I found a "simmer ring" for less than $5. Just place it under your baking pan. No more burned bottoms.

PAT RICHARD, JONESBORO, LOUISIANA

SINGING IN THE RAIN, ER, SHOWER

If you've ever been camping and gotten caught in the rain, you know how hard it can be to dry your clothes inside a motorhome if your coach isn't equipped with laundry facilities.

After this happened to us, we hit on the idea of installing a movable spring-tension-mounted rod in the shower. We placed the wet clothes on hangers and hung them on the tension rod, then put a small electric heater – set on low – in the corner of the shower, away from the dripping clothes.

The heat from the heater turns the shower into a dryer. Our jeans and sweatshirts were completely dry by the next morning.

LINDA TAILEUR, MOUNT VERNON, NEW YORK

(FABRIC) TAPE IT

We installed an under-shelf coffee maker in our motorhome, which required that we store the glass pot elsewhere when preparing for a trip.

To avoid this, my wife made a 44-inch-long piece of fabric tape, about an inch wide, with hook-and-loop fastener sewn on each end. Now we leave the coffeepot in the coffee maker — but secure it with the fabric tape. Be sure to wrap the tape through the pot's handle and around the coffee maker (to prevent the tape from slipping off the coffeepot), then attach the ends together.

EDWIN HATHAWAY,
NEW BERN, NORTH CAROLINA

PUMP SOLUTION

I wanted a pump-type soap dispenser at my RV sink, like the one I had at home. My husband was agreeable and easily installed it. However, with hot and cold temperatures and some noticeable changes in altitude, the pump dribbles out soap on its own.

My husband came up with the cure; he drilled a small air hole near the top of the plastic soap reservoir. That fixed the problem.

Now, when we fill the dispenser with liquid soap, we leave air space at the top for expansion.

HARRIET BADESHEIM, BOISE, IDAHO

PUZZLING DEVELOPMENTS

Like to do jigsaw puzzles, but don't have the space in your motorhome to leave them until you are done? I went to a glass supplier and had a piece of ⅜-inch-thick Plexiglas cut to the size of our tabletop.

Now, when I'm working a puzzle and my wife wants to put dinner on the table, I lay the sheet of Plexiglas over the puzzle and she sets the table – right on the Plexiglas. If we are going to travel before I'm finished with the puzzle, I just clamp the Plexiglas to the table using spring clamps.

RICHARD RICE,
PORT HURON, MICHIGAN

STICK IT

There have been more than a few tips published on how to keep paper towels from unrolling when you're driving down bumpy roads. I think I have the simplest and easiest method of all. Just stick a straight pin through the roll of towels. I use a pin with a large colored head to make removal easy.

DEMRIS STARR, OXFORD, ALABAMA

Table With a View

JUDY KIRK, MEDFORD, OREGON

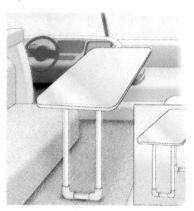

▶ It seems like there's never enough room in our coach, especially when we sit down to eat. I changed that by creating a movable dinette table.

I purchased some 2-inch PVC pipe, four 2-inch PVC caps, two 90-degree/2-inch fittings and some screws.

I first screwed the caps to the underside of the table — making sure the screws did not go through the tabletop — then fitted two long sections of the 2-inch PVC pipe into the caps at one end of the table and two shorter pieces into the other end. The shorter pieces fit into the drink-holders on the doghouse engine cover.

The two 90-degree fittings go on the ends of the long legs and are connected at the bottom by a short piece of the 2-inch pipe.

I also made two additional long legs so that the table could be used outside if we wanted. The table can still be used as per the original manufacturer's intent.

Shake, Rattle and Roll

WILLIAM POWELL JR., WARREN, OHIO

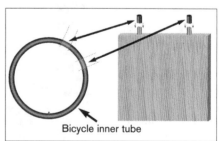

Bicycle inner tube

▶ My trailer features a dinette that folds down to make a bed. However, the table was not completely stable when it was in the dining table position. While my family and I were eating, or just sitting at the table, the slightest movement would make the table shift.

To fix this problem I took a bicycle inner tube, cut two pieces about two inches long, and slid them over the metal tabs on the back of the table (it was a tight fit). This worked like magic — the table was stable instantly, and has been for almost three years!

He's Hooked

PAUL DIEHL JR., SPRING GROVE, PENNSYLVANIA

▶ I am always on the lookout for ways to hang wet clothes and towels. I purchased a 10-pack of self-adhesive hooks (the kind you moisten and rub to activate the glue before application) for about $5.

I placed them around the top edge of the shower stall. Now I can hang items so they will dry quickly before being added to the rest of the laundry.

Take Their Pictures

BONNIE BLUNK, GRAND JUNCTION, COLORADO

▶ When we retired and started RVing, we began spending winters in Arizona. We soon discovered that we missed our kids terribly, so I decided that if we couldn't bring our children with us, at least we could take their pictures along.

With double-sided tape, I positioned about 45 photographs of our family on top of the camper's kitchen table. We had a piece of Plexiglas cut to fit the tabletop, and then placed it over the photos. The edges of the Plexiglas are secured to the tabletop using double-sided tape.

Now, when we sit down at the table, our family is right there in front of us. The memories evoked by these photos give us so much pleasure and help keep us from getting too homesick for our kids.

Editor's note: *Be careful how you clean the Plexiglas tabletop. Too much scrubbing or excessively harsh treatment could cause your memories to disappear in a fog of scratches.*

BOLSTER CUSHIONS

I live in a cold climate, so there are some nights when I hang curtains over the doors to hold in heat and reduce drafts.

I had a pair of quilted curtains for this purpose, but no place to store them. When I bought my trailer, there were no bolster cushions for the sofa. I made two bags, making sure that one end was round, and the other end closed with a drawstring. I rolled the curtains, folded them to fit the length of the bag, and inserted them into the bags.

Now they are stored, and I have bolsters for the sofa.

DOROTHY WELTER,
AVOCA, PENNSYLVANIA

DOUBLE USE

A scrub pail is an essential item to have along while traveling, but it can be difficult to store, especially in smaller RVs like ours. I put my scrub pail into daily use by having it double as our wastebasket. The plastic bag that you get at the grocery store is a perfect fit for a liner. When you need the pail for a clean up job, it's readily available.

SHIRLEY KATT, SHEBOYGAN, WISCONSIN

FIX-A-VENT

The louvers on my ceiling air conditioner would not hold a given position. I went to an auto parts store and bought several rubber O-rings. I inserted one on each end of the louvers, taking up the space and restoring the friction fit. No more trouble!

BOB MORRIS, PAHRUMP, NEVADA

THE EASIEST FIX

Many ideas have been published to solve the common problem of paper-towel rolls unrolling while driving down the road. But perhaps the easiest fix is simply the brand choice of paper towel.

An unadvertised feature of Kleenex Viva towels is that they stick slightly to the roll. That means that even if the roll turns while driving, the towels will stay on the roll.

Try it – the only cost is the price of one roll of paper towels!

PATRICK GARZIGLIA, RESTON, VIRGINIA

Editor's note: *He's right. We have been using that brand for years and, in addition, it does a much better job of absorbing spills, etc., than the harder-surfaced cheapo brands.*

livability

Dining Table Extension

TOMMY RYAN, MARBLE FALLS, TEXAS

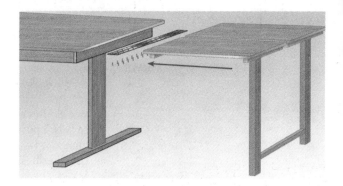

▶ While on the maiden voyage of our new trailer last summer, my wife and I became aware of the necessity of extending the length of our dining table, which is part of a large slideout.

Although the oak table came with four chairs, there was hardly enough room for four adults to sit comfortably and enjoy a meal, let alone play table games.

We had brought along a set of four oak TV trays, and decided to make a table extender out of two of these small tables, which were remarkably close to being the same width, color and grain as the dining table.

First, I removed the scissor legs from two of the small tables, and used parts of the discarded leg assemblies to connect the tabletops together from the underside. Then I purchased a piano hinge (hardware-store item) to connect my new extension top to the original table. The need for legs for the extension was solved by fashioning a removable leg assembly, also from leftover TV-tray parts. Voila!, a table wide and strong enough to accommodate four adults comfortably for a variety of activities.

During travel, the added leg assembly is removed, allowing the extension to drop down via the piano hinge, to hold the chairs in place (since the dining table is part of the slideout, it would be impossible for the leaf to remain up when the slideout is retracted).

Keep Off the Floor

SYLVIA WILLIAMS, ZANESFIELD, OHIO

▶ Our RV has a rear closet. I found that when we traveled over rough roads, by the end of the day, all of my clothes wound up on the floor of the closet.

After a couple of trips where I had to force the closet door open due to the clump of clothes on the floor, I knew I had to find a solution.

I purchased spring-loaded extension curtain rods that fit the closet opening on the double side, and a longer rod for the full-length side. I placed the rods so they just touch the neck of the hangers below the main rods, and now, no more hangers fall off.

They are easy to put in place and remove, and they eliminate all the aggravation of finding the clothes on the floor.

Had a Problem

ARLENE MCCOY, LIGONIER, PENNSYLVANIA

▶ We had a problem in that our golden retriever wanted to ride right up front with us in our motorhome. I was willing to compromise her complete happiness for safety and comfort's sake, but I was able to come up with a solution for keeping both the family and the family pet safe and happy while driving.

I inserted a plain window screen (from an unused storm door) across the center aisle, behind the cab seats. It fits snugly and thus, there is no need for any makeshift mechanism to hold it and it's very easy for us to step over. It not only allows her to see us, but she actually feels more secure in her own "den."

More Bathroom Space

CHIC CANNON, LIVINGSTON, TEXAS

▶ Shelf space in the bathroom is always at a premium, so to make more room, I mounted the tissue box holder on the wall, above the counter. By using two 1½-inch × 1-inch brass hinges, it was an easy project.

The hinges are mounted on the top back edge of the tissue holder and fastened to the wall. Be sure there is enough room for the holder to swing up to get the tissue box in and out without hitting the cabinet above.

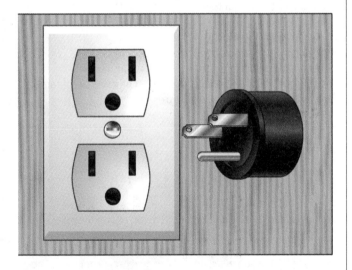

Plug-In Storage

HAROLD NELSON, DENVER, COLORADO

▶ Because I was continually misplacing my electrical-adapter plug, I needed to come up with an ideal spot in which to store it. I cut a hole in the side of a cabinet to fit a 120-volt AC single receptacle. I didn't have to worry about wiring the receptacle, since it would only be used for storage.

When the adapter is not in use, I plug it into the receptacle.

A PAIR FROM PENNSYLVANIA

As snowbirds leaving our home after the Christmas holiday, we invariably have two or three nights of cold weather to contend with before we reach our southern destination. The head of our bed snugs up against the bedroom window, exposing us to cold drafts.

To solve this problem, I took a dressmaker's cardboard folding cutting board, and cut it to match the dimensions we needed. I then stood it up between the mattress and the window wall — no more drafts. Best of all, it folds up and stores right under the mattress.

JANALEE SERWINSKI,
TAYLOR, PENNSYLVANIA

While camping this year, it was quite cold and windy, and there was a draft pouring down from the window over my bed.

To beat the cold, I got a piece of quilted material and cut it to fit over the valance, just long enough to tuck in behind the mattress. I attached a section of hook-and-loop tape to the wall alongside the valance, then attached the other part of the hook-and-loop tape onto the cloth cover. It fits snugly over the valance, covering the entire window and wall behind the mattress, and blocks all of the cold air. It's easy to put up and take down and stores under the mattress.

DOROTHY WELTER,
AVOCA, PENNSYLVANIA

CLOTHES HOOKS

On laundry day, my wife and I never had enough places to hang clothes that needed ironing. I purchased several brass clothes hooks that match the hardware on our cabinets. I mounted them on the walls close to where my wife does the ironing. The hooks match the interior so well that they are almost invisible when not in use.

This was such a success that I purchased more hooks and mounted them above our closet doors and on the walls of the bedroom, for use when we are changing clothes.

SCOTT STEWART,
HAMILTON, MONTANA

NON-SKID

Does the dinette cushion in your RV slip out of place? It's easy to stop it by placing a piece of non-slip, rubberized fabric (available at Camping World and other retail outlets) between the cushion and the wooden seat base.

SUE LEIMER, PENDER, NEBRASKA

livability

SEVERE-WIND PROBLEM

While staying in Colorado, we encountered some severe-wind conditions and saw the tent portions of pop-up trailers, like our Coleman, collapse. The cause seemed to be that the tent portion of the trailers appeared to act as an airfoil and lift the bed platform up from the supports. This allows the extension-rod ends to slip from the retaining holes the support braces to collapse.

Our solution was to purchase four tie-down straps with plastic-coated hooks.

With the platforms extended, hook one side of a strap under each corner of the bed platform, and the other side to a bumper or frame member.

You only have to put enough tension on the straps to keep the bed from lifting.

ARCH KENNEDY, CLINTON, LOUISIANA

THIS IS A STICKUP

Did you get one of those adhesive maps with the stick-on states that allows you to brag about where you've traveled?

Are you afraid, as I was, that you can't install it so that it will look nice on your RV? Or do you not want to mount it permanently because you rent or are planning to trade soon? Here's a tip to resolve these questions.

Obtain a piece of Plexiglas larger than your map that will fit into the space where you want to put the map. Align the map so it suits your line-of-sight and apply it to the Plexiglas per the manufacturer's instructions. You can use standard picture-mounting hardware or adhesive hooks to mount the Plexiglas-and-map assembly to the side of your trailer when your rig is stationary.

DAN DOLAN JR., LAYTON, UTAH

AN A/C FOR THE TV

We only had our television set for three months when it broke down. The repairman told us that our television had overheated, since there was no way for the air to circulate because of the TV cabinet. He said our type of problem was common, especially among RVs.

To avoid this problem in the future, we bought a new television set and an inexpensive 7-inch, clip-on 120-volt AC fan. The fan didn't need to be mounted – we just put it on top of the TV-cabinet vents, face down, so it would blow the heat out of the cabinet.

BETTY HECKER, PENSACOLA, FLORIDA

Hangin' Out

PAUL MALLY, CLINTON TOWNSHIP, MICHIGAN

▶ There are never enough clothes hooks in an RV. My wife and I have discovered that 3M hooks with Command adhesive are an excellent solution to this problem. They come in a variety of sizes, and we've installed them in the bedroom, living room and bathroom.

If you need to relocate or remove them, they are easily peeled off and don't leave any marks.

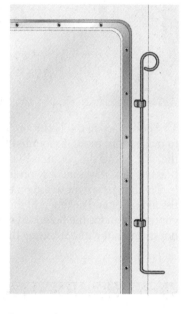

ROGER RIDGWAY,
BIG SPRING, TEXAS

▶ On every rig that I've owned, the awning pull-down rod was supplied with no provision for storage. Here's a solution I've used on my last couple of rigs.

Just inside the door there is almost always a few inches of space where the rod can be stored vertically, and it's a handy to reach from the outside, too.

I bought self-sticking plastic clips, similar to small clothespins, to hold the rod to the wall. They can be obtained at hardware and other types of stores.

INDOOR-OUTDOOR

My wife kept asking me what the temperature is, what it was last night, etc., but all I could do was shrug my shoulders – until I purchased an indoor/outdoor thermometer at our local home center. It has 10 feet of wire to the sensor, but where to put the sensor was a big question. In order to give reasonably accurate readings, the sensor must be kept in the shade, outside the vehicle.

In our case, I fed the sensor wire out through the weep (drain) hole of one of our windows, then up the window edge. I mounted the sensor in the shade just below our awning. I glued the sensor and wire to the window frame with silicone cement.

The thermometer displays indoor and outdoor temperatures, and has a memory of the highest and lowest since being reset.

DON MALETTE, SAN DIEGO, CALIFORNIA

Outta Sight

BRUCE TRUDGEN, WILLIAMSBURG, MICHIGAN

▶ RVers enjoy taking their pets along when they travel, but one problem with having a pet on board is where to put the food and water dishes. We all look for an out-of-sight spot where the dishes won't get kicked or stepped into.

My wife came up with a great idea to address this problem. She asked me to remove the door from the storage compartment below the stove. This provides an area for the pet's dishes, where they are out of the way and virtually out of sight.

Give 'Em the Hook

DICK WRIGHT, BELLINGHAM, WASHINGTON

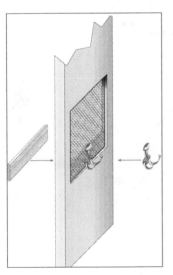

▶ Our RV has an open bathroom with a stool, a sink and a shower, but has no place to hang clothes or a robe.

So, we mounted a clothes hook on the washer/dryer compartment door. Not wanting to screw into the closet-door frame, we mounted the hook by screwing through the screen mesh.

Using a piece of ⅛ × 2-inch wood spanning the full length of the screen mesh as a backing, we screwed the clothes hook through the holes in the mesh into the wood backing. There should still be plenty of space left for ventilation.

If the mounting screws are too long and stick out past the wood, grind the ends flat with the wood surface, to them prevent from catching on and tearing clothes.

CHEAP BAG CLIP

For a very effective and inexpensive bag clip, I use clamp-type paper clips, available anywhere office supplies are sold. They come in five different sizes and will outlast any commercial plastic-bag clips by a wide margin.

JIM LILJA, MIDDLEBURY, VERMONT

THEY TIP OVER

I like to cook when I travel, so I always bring along many of my spices. These small bottles have a tendency to tip over, plus it can be difficult to find a particular spice among all of the bottles. To solve this problem, I wrote the name of each spice on the top of the cap of each bottle, and placed all of my spices in a shoe box (but you could use any size box that will snugly accommodate all of your spices). Now all I have to do is pull the box out of the cabinet and grab the spice I need.

LOIS CARLSON, MANCOS, COLORADO

THREE QUICKIES

Here are some useful tips we have discovered that make our trips easier and more enjoyable.

■ We carry our leveling boards and wheel chocks in a plastic milk crate and mount it on the battery-holder rails, securing it with bungee cords.

■ A good wheel chock can be made from landscape timber or 4 × 4-inch lumber (pressure-treated for longevity). Cut each end at a 45-degree angle and make each board just long enough to fit between the tires and it will keep the trailer from rolling in either direction.

■ We have plastic boxes (similar to shoe boxes) in our pantry to hold jars and cans. Sandwiching the jars between cans eliminates breakage. And if something should break, the box contains the spill. We also have cardboard boxes, with dividers to eliminate glass-to-glass contact.

WARREN THIBEAUX, DEKALB, TEXAS

RUN AND HIDE

For running and hiding wires when I can't get into the walls, (for hooking up speakers, etc.), I found a product available in most home-improvement and hardware stores that works very well. It's called Wiremold On-Wall PVC Channel Conduit Canal, and it's available in white and ivory (it can also be painted) in 60-inch lengths.

One part screws on the wall or ceiling, the wires are placed in the channel and the cover strip snaps into place. Couplers and corner angles are also available.

JOE CAMPBELL, GOODWATER, ALABAMA

livability

BUNGEE BED

My RV has a two-sided pillowtop mattress and the custom-fitted sheets that were shipped with it aren't quite big enough to wrap securely around the corners. The sheets were continuously slipping off the mattress corners, making comfortable sleep a thing of the past.

I now use a pair of long bungee cords with alligator clips attached at both ends. I grip the misbehaving opposite corners of the sheets and run the bungee cord under the mattress.

DINO FIABANE,
CHERRY HILL, NEW JERSEY

BUG OFF!

My mail carrier told me that the United States Postal Service sent a message to all letter carriers to put a sheet of fabric softener in their uniform pockets to help keep yellow jackets away. This is also handy when camping, traveling and while mowing the lawn.

The fabric-softener sheets will also chase away ants, bees and flies at campground potluck dinners. Just lay out some sheets on the tables and between serving stations. It also repels mice. Place sheets in RV basements and vehicles that are just sitting, and it keeps mice from entering.

And all this time you had just been putting fabric-softener sheets in the dryer!

FRED ROSI, VINELAND, NEW JERSEY

PICTURESQUE PLACE MATS

Got any scenic plastic place mats that you are tired of using, but are too pretty to toss out? Cut them to fit inside drawers or as shelf liners. Then, when you look down on the shelf or into a drawer and you see an Arizona cactus, Colorado mountains or even South Dakota buffalo, you will be reminded of trips past.

JUANETTA CONNER,
HOBBS, NEW MEXICO

PIN UPS

To keep all of my pendant necklaces from becoming a tangled mess in the jewelry box, I put straight pins in the padded valance of the bedroom window and hung the pendants on the pins.

They are out of sight as long as they're placed on the valance end facing the closet, where they are readily available to wear.

MARY MADDEN, ROCHESTER, MINNESOTA

Sew What

MARIE HASKINS, DERRY, NEW HAMPSHIRE

▶ In order to protect the microwave plate and stop some of the rattles in the RV, I came up with this idea.

Using rubber-like, non-slip shelf liner, I cut a circle a little larger than the plate and folded it, bringing it about halfway up the front. Another half circle overlapping from the top, like the top of a sock, completely encloses the plate.

I sewed it around the edges (not too tight) with a double thread and a basting stitch. The holder is easy to put aside when we're in camp and to slip on the plate when we're traveling.

It protects the plate and keeps the noise at a minimum.

A Warm, Soft Glow

JOSEPH HOLMES, NEW EGYPT, NEW JERSEY

▶ Our trailer has a 120-volt AC night light in the bathroom. When camping, we use it every night. I was concerned there would be times when we would be camping in areas with no electricity.

I bought a very small 12-volt DC orange truck marker light, and a small switch. I mounted it under one of the bathroom cabinets, near an existing 12-volt DC light. The marker light is far less bright, and draws little power. A marker that uses an LED instead of an incandescent bulb would use even less current, which would help save the battery when dry-camped.

Hang 'Em High

JIMMIE B. BUTLER, OOLOGAH, OKLAHOMA

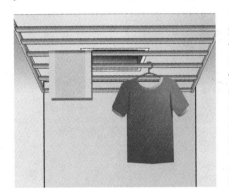

▶ There are never enough towel racks in an RV, especially when on an extended trip. I made a frame the size of the top of my shower stall out of wood-trim scraps, measuring ¾ × ½-inch. I screwed in four ½-inch dowel rods, which extended across the frame, and mounted the unit using hooks, just below the ceiling in the shower. The rack can easily be taken down, and the hanging area is extremely useful for swimsuits and extra towels.

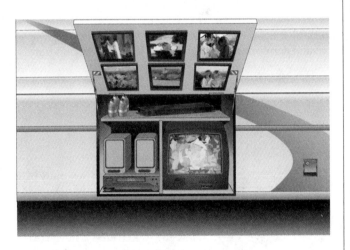

Instant Art Gallery

JIM WILLIAMS, GEGORY, MICHIGAN

▶ When sitting outside the RV, with the storage door open, ever get tired of seeing a boring, blank space? I did, and I wanted to display pictures of family and friends and had only a limited amount of space to use.

I purchased five 8 × 10 picture frames and one 5 × 7 frame. The frames I bought came with shadow boxes in them. The 8 × 10 will hold two 4 × 6 pictures and the 5 × 7 will hold one 4 × 6 picture.

With two small screws per frame, I attached them to the inside of the outside storage door, and they can easily be removed to change pictures when desired.

ALMOST USELESS

Our RV kitchen featured an almost useless flip-up counter extender. We removed it and installed a 24 × 32-inch wooden cutting board with two new larger fold-down brackets for a great counter extender.

KEN RITCHIE, TRUCKEE, CALIFORNIA

THE ABC'S OF RVING

After extended periods of searching high and low for a certain state map or information on an RV park where we have previously stayed, we came up with this solution.

We now keep an alphabetized expandable file in our RV to keep the registration sheets and site maps from the RV parks along with state maps.

We file them by state, and now have immediate information at our fingertips. We also keep articles on things we want to see in our travels.

GALE INGALLS,
SILVERTHORNE, COLORADO

ALLIGATOR KISSES

Instead of using clothespins to divert the water off the four corners of our RV, I fabricated a different design.

I purchased large alligator clips from RadioShack and attached a 2-inch length of white 10-gauge wire to each clip.

The clips secure nicely to the drip gutters and look more professional than clothespins.

PAUL MALLY,
CLINTON TOWNSHIP, MICHIGAN

SUN BLOCKER

Sometimes I have no choice but to position my RV in a spot where the sun shines directly in, so that the afternoon sun becomes a real scorcher. The window blinds don't always keep the heat out, which makes the air conditioner work harder.

One day I came up with the idea of using the windshield sun shade from my pickup. Putting the shade silver-side out between the window and the blinds really keeps things cooler. It fits perfectly in the living-room and dining-area windows.

Another nice thing is that the little groove that goes around the rearview mirror allows you to see out if necessary. The shades fold up easily, and I store them under the couch.

KARI WORM, LINCOLN, NEBRASKA

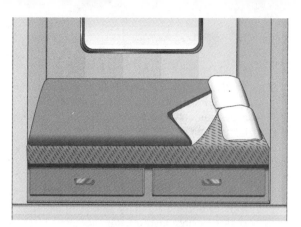
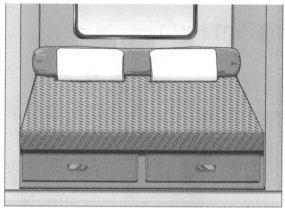

Áre You Ready for Some Futon?

NANCY MILLS, ALDERSON, WEST VIRGINIA

▶ The bed in our RV is surrounded on three sides, which makes putting on standard bedding a bit of a challenge.

In my mind, the logical approach is to go with sleeping bags, or a "bed sack" system, which is what we've done — but with a twist.

We enclosed our full-size mattress in a futon cover. The fabric cover is sturdy — with a choice of many colors and patterns — closes with a zipper and completely covers the mattress.

For our double sleeping bag, we made sheet liners from twin-size flat sheets. They keep the sleeping bag clean, and are easily washed.

In the morning, we smooth the sleeping bag, zip it closed and roll it up into a long bolster along one wall. Our pillows go into shams and prop against the bolster to make an attractive and comfortable lounging area. It's our grandchildren's favorite place to play or read on rainy days.

In Living Color

DANA WILCOX, REPTON, ALABAMA

▶ Our motorhome is an oldie but goodie. However, it came with a tiny 13-inch television. In order to install a larger one, it appeared that I would have to cut away some of our oak cabinets. Instead, I opted to go with a flat-screen, LCD unit.

Since the new unit was larger than the space between

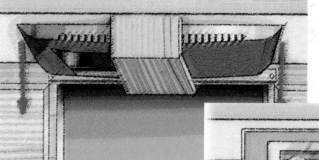

the existing cabinets, I built an oak mount (stained to match the existing cabinetry). The mount is hinged so it is securely latched to the ceiling during travel, and allows

access to the cabinets. A variety of latches are available at hardware stores and home centers.

The space where the original television was located is now used as a bookcase.

Pillow Talk

BOB GAIDO, IRVINE, CALIFORNIA

▶ We have two clothes closets on either side of the island bed in the rear of our trailer. After many unsuccessful attempts at keeping the hangers with clothes in place during transit (e.g. reversing the hangers, special hangers

using bungee cords, etc.) and still finding all the clothes piled on the floor when we parked, we came up with an idea that works for us and is much less time-consuming.

Now, after placing the clothes on the standard hangers in the normal fashion, we simply wedge a foam pillow, placed vertically in the middle of the hangers, to fill the remaining space and absorb the shocks of the road.

We now arrive at our campsite with everything still hanging.

Slide-a-Bed

ROB STRATTON, BRADENTON, FLORIDA

▶ We full-time in a fifth-wheel in which the bed is attached to a slideout. When the slideout runs in and out, part of the bed slides over the floor.

After a number of years of use, the bed

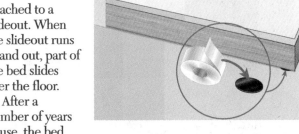

end started dragging on the carpet and actually started to pull the end of the bed off the sides. After reattaching the bed's end panel, I solved the problem by putting oblong sliders that are sold to move furniture on the undersides of the bed supports. I used industrial strength double-sided tape to attach them.

The sliders are available at almost any hardware store. They work perfectly and leave no marks on the carpet.

ALL SPACED OUT

When the weather was cold, I found that the bed pillows and the top of my mattress seemed damp from condensation where they touched the outside wall of the RV.

I took a 2 × 8-inch food-saver dish from my cupboard and put it between the mattress and the wall.

It's hidden from sight, and it holds the pillows and mattress just far enough away from the wall to let air circulate. No more dampness!

SHIRLEY SABLE,
SILVER SPRINGS, FLORIDA

A SECOND USE

We have three square insulating pillows to put in the roof openings of the ceiling fans in our unit. I covered each one in durable fabric with a colorful pattern to match the décor of our unit.

Now they have a second use. We use them to sit on steps, on picnic benches and on coolers. They also make nice backrests at our bench-type table unit. Then, when the cold wind or hot sun invades our RV, back into the ceiling openings they go.

With these multiple uses, we never have to store them, as they are always in use.

VICKY BRITTAIN, LAKE PLACID, FLORIDA

Á CLOSE SHAVE

In the close quarters of a motorhome bathroom, I had a problem with the mirrors steaming up. I found that smearing shaving cream on the mirror, then polishing the glass with a dry paper towel, keeps it from steaming.

If your favorite shaving cream doesn't work, try the Gillette brand.

GERALD UPCHURCH,
METROPOLIS, ILLINOIS

SWITCH THE SWITCH

Our bathroom ceiling-fan switch was hard to reach because it was located in the ceiling mount.

To correct the problem, I removed the switch from the fan housing, then ran two wires from the fan inside of a cabinet and inside an interior wall by fishing it with a coat hanger accessed through a door-striker-plate hole. I then drilled a hole in the wall about three feet off the floor and mounted the switch.

The switch is now easily accessible and readily available.

DON DIROLL, SURPRISE, ARIZONA

livability

A T.P. Tepee

MARY PENNINGTON, FENWICK, WEST VIRGINIA

▶ Our fifth-wheel was delivered with the towel bars and the toilet-paper holder in a package, which the dealer left for us to install. We never did find a satisfactory place to put the T.P. holder, so we devised this fix: We constructed a shelf that fits in the corner to the rear of the toilet.

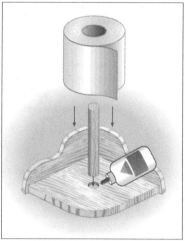

We mounted it using double-sided foam tape, as we didn't want to put any holes in the wall. The main piece of the T.P. ledge is cut from a scrap of ¾-inch-thick shelving. The side pieces are ⅜-inch plywood, and are screwed into the main section. The tape was placed on two sides.

The T.P. tube is dropped over a piece of old broom handle, which has been glued in a cut-to-fit hole.

The T.P. is now easy to reach, and in the narrow confines of our bathroom, we don't have to be concerned about bumping into a holder with our hips or elbows.

Cold Feet

GREGORY EI, WESTMINSTER, MARYLAND

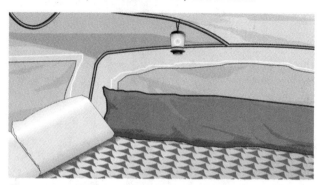

▶ Those with pop-up or hybrid campers with bunk-outs know all too well how cold it gets near the rear end of the bunk. This is due to the metal support rails, and the fact that the canvas folds over the ends and does not make an air-tight seal.

I found a simple solution to this problem. I place a large body pillow along the edge of the bed where my back usually ends up. This provides a soft, comfortable support, and about 10 inches of insulation over the gap. A second body pillow could be placed at the foot of the bunk for those whose feet get cold at night.

These pillows are available at most discount department stores for less than $10, and come in a variety of colors and prints.

Make Your Mark

ARLENE JEKNAVORIAN, DAVENPORT, FLORIDA

▶ I store a number of camping directories and catalogs upright in a magazine basket on the floor.

I was always pulling out the wrong book. I solved this problem by writing the publication's name across the top of the book on the edges of the pages.

Now I always pull out the correct book the first time.

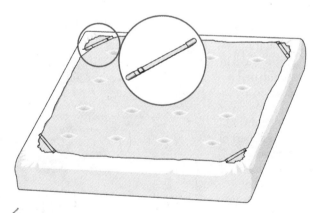

Snug as a Bug

PETE GRAY, LIVINGSTON, TEXAS

▶ My RV's queen-size bed is not quite queen size. Consequently, a standard queen-sized fitted sheet is too loose.

I found Snug Straps in the fabric department of Wal-Mart. They did the trick. Now the sheets are tight and stay in place.

Á Long Winter's Nap

PAIGE BRIDGES, WILLS POINT, TEXAS

▶ During the first night in our new fifth-wheel, I skinned my leg twice on the bare wood edge of the mattress platform while getting into and out of bed. I decided then and there that I would cover the platform with vinyl.

The sharp, bare wood edges are now covered with a nice color-coordinated vinyl fabric, which took only a few minutes to staple to the underside of the platform. The mattress also slides easily from side to side when I'm making the bed. Plus, the vinyl surface saves wear and tear on the mattress fabric. I've noticed on our previous RVs that the mattress cover was worn, not only from people sleeping on it, but from the usual sliding back and forth as the bed was being made as well.

Rusty Towels?

JOHN PETERSEN, BEARSVILLE, NEW YORK

▶ From the first year we've had our trailer, we've been plagued by rust spots on towels and washcloths. They were caused by the metal bars on the bathroom door's towel rack. 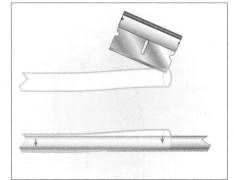 The towel rack looked like brass, but was only low-grade, cheap steel under a thin lacquer finish.

My cure was to go to the hardware store and buy about 5 feet of ¼-inch ID (inside diameter) clear plastic tubing. Using a single-edge razor blade, I split the tubing lengthwise and pressed it over the towel-rack rods. Bye-bye rust stains!

BIGGER IS BETTER

We purchased a motorhome a short while ago. The kitchen area has all the appliances we have at home, but the counter area is obviously smaller than we are used to. Our coach didn't come with a sink cover, so we resolved to fix that.

To increase the counter area, I purchased a ready-made wood cutting board at a home center. It is large enough to completely cover one bowl of the double sink. To the bottom of the cutting board, I attached four wooden cleats so they would fit snugly into the sink bowl, and the board would rest on top of the sink.

Not only did we gain valuable counter area and a cutting board to work on, but the board hides the sponge and other cleaning items in the sink.

RUSSELL GENDOLFE,
NORTH PROVIDENCE, RHODE ISLAND

BOUNCE NO MORE

We bought a travel trailer that has a nice storage area under the bed. But as we traveled through the mountains or along bumpy roads, the bed apparently would bounce up and down, as evidenced by the comforter/sheets strewn about the room.

We went to the hardware store and purchased a couple of latches, originally intended to be used on wooden windows, and installed them on each side of the bed.

Now, when we travel, we no longer worry about the bed bouncing around.

WILLIE MAE MARTIN, RICHMOND, TEXAS

TOPSY-TURVY TABLE

My fifth-wheel has a rear kitchen with a free-standing table and four chairs. After a day's drive, I would frequently find that the table had moved and the chairs were lying in the aisle.

The first thing I fixed was the table. At the hardware store I purchased four small brass hinges with removable pins the same length as the width of the table legs. I positioned the table where I wanted it and fastened the hinges to the table legs and to the floor.

I didn't want the chairs to be fastened down, so I got some bungee cords. When we are ready to hit the road, I fasten the two chairs on each side together.

Haven't had anything move since.

WILLIAM DICK, SAN ANTONIO, TEXAS

Editor's note: *Mark one of the hinges so it will line up properly with the correct table leg when you refasten the table to the floor.*

A TUCK IN TIME

We all know that the mattress in a motorhome always extends beyond the frame, making it almost impossible to tuck the sheets in.

At home I have always made a tuck at the foot on top of the mattress, and then tucked in the remaining sheet. In a motorhome you do not have enough sheet to do this, so I took an old sheet, cut off the hemmed edge about 18 inches long and stitched it to my motorhome's top sheet. This leaves me enough to properly tuck and leave a top tuck.

No matter if the extra piece of sheet matches or not, it doesn't show.

MARTHA ANN DODD,
BROOKS, GEORGIA

GETTING HOOKED UP

Our motorhome, as many others, has no rearview mirror – which is oftentimes used to hang park admission passes – so we added one of those quick-release, pull-tab, adhesive-backed hooks on the inside corner of our windshield.

Now, when the campground clerk or park personnel, says "Hang this on your rearview mirror," we have a place to put it – and it can be seen at all times. (Hanging these tags on the sun visor doesn't work when you close the curtains.)

YVONNE KNOWLES,
FREEHOLD, NEW YORK

QUEEN SHORTY

I was having problems finding fitted sheets for the bed in my RV. As with many other RVs, the mattress is called a "short queen," which is 60 × 75 inches, while a regular queen-size mattress is 60 × 80 inches.

So I decided to take a standard queen-size fitted sheet and shorten it about 4 inches. I folded the right sides together and made about a 2-inch seam across the top of a queen-fitted sheet, and put it on the bed so that the seam is under the pillows.

No one sees or feels the seam there, and now the sheet fits just fine. The regular-size queen sheets are sold in a lot more colors and are less expensive and easier to find than the short queen sheets.

BARBARA RAECK,
SEATTLE, WASHINGTON

Limited Room

LEE EVITTS, GLENDALE, ARIZONA

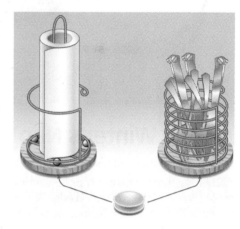

▶ We are traveling in a cabover camper, thus our room is very limited. When we get ready to go back on the road I used to have to place my silverware and paper-towel holders in containers or on the couch so that they didn't fall off the counter.

In order to solve this problem, my husband made wood bases to fit the bottom of each container. Then he purchased small Lazy Susans and mounted them to the bottom of each wood base of each container. Suction cups were mounted to the base of each Lazy Susan.

Now each container is secured to our countertop, and they no longer have to be packed away while we're traveling.

Rack 'Em Up

FRANK WOYTHAL, ANDOVER, NEW YORK

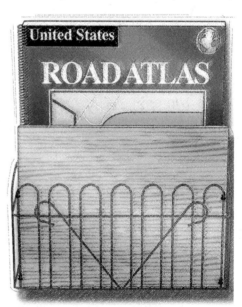

▶ After equipping our motorhome with a much-needed magazine rack, we found it had a huge shortcoming:

Large road maps couldn't be kept there because their height caused them to bend in two!

We remedied the situation by inserting a piece of thin paneling, inside the rack, against the front edge. Secured with tiny black wire ties, the panel supports the road atlas, yet isn't too tall to prevent access to the magazines kept there.

By Hook or by Crook

KAY HILL, LIVINGSTON, TEXAS

▶ I like to use the plastic bags left over after grocery shopping to line the small trash cans we use in our RV. However, they have an annoying habit of sliding to the bottom of the can.

To solve this problem, I attached small adhesive coat hooks on the outside of either side of the can, about four inches from the top. To secure the bag, just simply slip the bag handles over the hooks.

Too Much of a Good Thing

JOHN HIBBARD, ANDOVER, MINNESOTA

▶ Like many trailers, my fifth-wheel has a light fixture in the inside cargo area. After dark, when it was turned on, much of the light shone in my face, practically blinding me. My solution was to line half of the inside of the lens (the half closest to the door) with aluminum foil so the light shines only into the storage compartment. It was easy, and it works great!

BLIND HOLDERS

During travel, our Venetian blinds were held down by plastic brackets with small plastic pins that fit into holes at the base of the blinds. These brackets were always breaking off and were very difficult to find and replace.

The cure was to take a couple of inches of self-sticking hook-and-loop fastener and apply it to the bottom of the blinds and the matching spot on the window frame. We put the loop part on the blind and the smooth part on the window frame. Bigger pieces work on bigger blinds, smaller pieces on smaller blinds.

MARION SCHELL, AYR, ONTARIO

KNOW WHEN TO FOLD 'EM

With a limited amount of drawer space in our motorhome, I fold T-shirts the same way they were folded when purchased – then I unfold the bottom and take one pair of socks, a handkerchief and a pair of underwear, lay them on the T-shirt bottom and fold it back up.

This way, at shower time, everything is together, and space is saved in a drawer.

LAURA DUPE, BUTLER, PENNSYLVANIA

THE GIFT OF GLAD

To temporarily close off small openings that allow air, sand, bugs, etc. to enter the inside of an RV – and even to cover tears in window screens – try Glad Press 'n Seal.

It adheres temporarily to most any surface and shape, and is easily removed without any sticky tape residue.

BEVERLY TOTMAN, SALOME, ARIZONA

TO SLEEP, PERCHANCE TO DREAM

To provide a better night's sleep for our bad backs, we replaced the mattress in our motorhome. The combination that works for us is comprised of two layers of foam: We use a conventional high-density foam, five inches thick, for the bottom layer, and top it with a two-inch-thick slab of isotonic (memory) foam.

We ordered our foam from the JCPenney catalog, but there are many other sources of foam on the Internet if you can't find it locally.

To hold it all together, we use a zippered fabric mattress cover that completely covers both pieces.

NANCY MILLS,
ALDERSON, WEST VIRGINIA

livability

IT'S IN THE AIR

We purchased a small dehumidifier for our motorhome, and it has served many purposes. We no longer have any fogged windows and there are no lingering food smells from cooking or pet smells from our two dogs and cat. It's also a great mini-dryer for wet towels, etc., and, in winter, another heating source. We place it under our dining table, where it's out of the way, yet handy for operation.

DAYNA BREAULT,
FORT BENNING, GEORGIA

LOOKING THROUGH YEL-LOW-COLORED GLASSES

When driving in reduced visibility conditions such as rain or fog, I've found that wearing a pair of tinted shooter's glasses (clip-on's are available) can greatly enhance one's ability to see. They are available in sporting goods stores or at gun shows.

LAWRENCE BLACK,
SEYMOUR, TENNESSEE

NEVER HANDY

Because I never seemed to have an oil rag or a paper towel handy, I hit upon this simple solution.

Above the rear window of our pickup truck I mounted a regular plastic kitchen-towel holder, on which I use the cheapest paper towels available for use in checking the oil, washing windows, etc. To keep the towels from unrolling, I use a bungee cord or stick a pin in the roll.

CLARENCE HALL,
STEPHENS CITY, VIRGINIA

SAVE THE FOAM

Platters and other serving dishes take up a lot of room, especially in an RV, where every inch of space counts. One way to solve this is to save the foam plastic trays on which vegetables are sold. When covered with foil, they make very acceptable dishes, bowls and platters for chips, appetizers or whatever.

If you're bringing an appetizer to a campground happy hour, this eliminates having to remember to get your dish back, and if used in the RV, there's no washing; just discard.

RUTH DUNKEL, MIAMI, FLORIDA

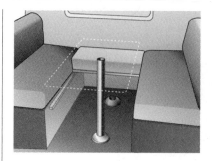

Board-Game Builders

DON WEIR, CUMBERLAND, INDIANA

▶ When camping, we often play board games, and sitting side by side is inconvenient. So, we installed a leg support at the center of our dinette table, so we could move the table away from the wall about 11 inches. We use this new support and the outside floor support, so the table uses only one leg. (The table came from the manufacturer with two legs.)

To make a bench seat to rest against the wall, we took a 14 × 27-inch piece of ¾-inch plywood, and a similar size piece of 4-inch foam and covered this assembly with material. It rests on the bed-support rails of the dinette. We use a stool for the fourth seat.

Now we can play board games more comfortably.

Flower Boxes

EDWARD HESS, KILLEEN, TEXAS

▶ As full-time RVers, my wife and I are on the move a lot. My wife wanted a flower garden, so I came up with the idea to get flower boxes the size of the slideout windows.

I drilled a hole in each corner of the flower box. Then I attached 30-pound fishing line to the box and put an S hook on the end of each fishing line. I opened the window, hung the S hooks over the window crank bar and closed the window.

I glued plastic foam in the box and inserted a selection of artificial flowers. Different kinds of flowers can be purchased to provide a change as the seasons progress.

Holder Helper

BOB GAIDO, IRVINE, CALIFORNIA

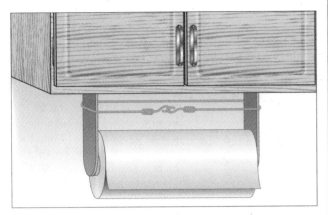

● Our trailer, with minimal counter space, has an under-the-cabinet mounted paper towel holder. It had lost most of the compression in the arms, causing the roll of paper towels to keep falling off.

I attached an 18-inch bungee cord around the arms of the holder to add extra pressure against the roll of paper towels.

No more rolls falling into the sink.

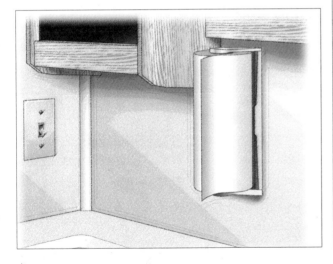

Sideways Works

JAY KOOL, JENISON, MICHIGAN

● Unable to find a suitable place to mount a paper-towel holder, my wife suggested mounting it vertically. We have used it this way for more than five years and it works fine. At the same time, it also solves the problem of the paper towels unrolling while driving down the road!

A HIGH-PITCHED SQUEAK

In a recent issue, someone requested a trap- and poison-free method of controlling mice in an RV.

A farmer friend told me that he kept rodents out of his feed storage area with an electronic device manufactured by Victor (the mousetrap company), which is sold at most co-op stores. The cost is about $20, which is a small price to pay considering the damage the pests can do.

The device is harmless to pets (except hamsters and other rodents) and humans, and works by creating a high-pitched sound that is offensive to the vermin. The only requirement is a constant 120-volt AC power source. For maximum effect in larger RVs that are in long-term storage, leave the cabinet and closet doors open.

A.B. KENNEDY, CLINTON, LOUISIANA

BRIDGING THE GAP

To eliminate items falling in the gap between our RV's couch and the shelf behind it, I purchased some washable, medium-weight material cover at a fabric store. I cut the fabric to match the length of the couch and shelf and made it wide enough to tuck under the back cushions. Then, I sewed hook-and-loop fastener along the edge of the fabric that would lay on the shelf.

Next, I used liquid-silicone glue to attach the other half of the hook-and-loop fastener to the shelf. After the glue had completely dried, I pressed the hook-and-loop fastener on the fabric edge onto the shelf and "presto," no more lost articles behind the couch.

I made matching covers for the seat cushions, too. They add color, keep the seat cushions clean and are easy to launder. A specialized cleaner, such as Goo Gone, will remove the silicone glue on the shelf should you ever want to remove the couch cover.

JO ANN SODEN, PAHRUMP, NEVADA

STUFF 'EM

Like most RVers, I stuff our RV to the max. I kept crushing the boxes for our garbage bags and zippered storage bags.

Watching my son, the potato-chip eater, gave me an idea: Use the round containers that some chips, such as Pringles, come in.

Now I remove the storage bags from their original boxes, roll them up and insert them into the old chip containers after cleaning out any chip residue. These cans can be stored standing or lying down.

MARLENE TRACY,
BRADENTON, FLORIDA

livability

Removable Rack

JIM HICKS, RIVERSIDE, CALIFORNIA

▶ After driving our motorhome for a few hours, I would experience a circulation problem in my right leg. The layout of the motorhome is such that the driver's seat is in front of the dinette. The driver's seat back hits the dinette seat back, preventing it from reclining to a more relaxing position. After considerable thinking, I hit on the idea of making the dinette seat back removable. This is what I did:

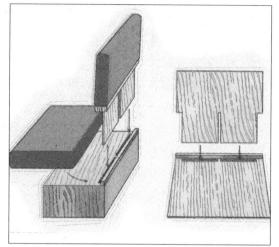

I removed the dinette seat, which was attached by five screws, four in the floor and one into the wall. The seat frame is made of 1 × 1s with a plywood skin. Upholstered panels are then attached with screws and brackets. I removed all the upholstered panels and carefully cut the seat back off the seat, using a circular saw, making sure not to cut the seat.

I then added bracing to the inside and the outside of the seat to provide additional support for the new seat back. I used a 1 × 1 on the inside and a piece of oak on the outside. This provided a slot in the seat for the new back. I then cut a piece of ¾-inch plywood to fit into the slot in the seat and to provide the new seat back.

I reattached the upholstery using the original screws and brackets.

I had to cut the L-shape side piece and reupholstered it. The modifications cost less than $100 and took about a weekend to complete.

Now when we travel, I just pull the dinette seat back out of its slot and place it on the floor. I have full movement of the driver's seat. It allows various driving positions, eliminating my circulation problems.

Keeping Cool in Coach Seats

ROSEMARY THEURER, CORAM, NEW YORK

▶ Anyone who owns a motorhome knows how hot they can get during the summer — and how long it can take to cool down the entire interior. Since my husband and I sit up front while traveling, we realized we were wasting a lot of energy (and unnecessarily taxing expensive components) by air-conditioning the entire coach.

So, we created a way to get optimum results from just the dash air conditioner: homemade floor-to-ceiling privacy curtains.

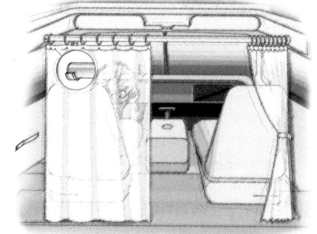

The "track" for the curtains is a ¾-inch-diameter metal electrical conduit pipe, mounted about 2 inches below the ceiling and extending wall-to-wall behind the driver and passenger seats. The painted pipe is held in place by two ¾-inch end caps similar to those used to hang shower curtains; one cap is cut in half so that the pipe can be easily removed.

For curtains, we used two twin-bed-size sheets. I sewed rings along the top edge and hemmed the bottom to within 1½ inches of the floor. I then sewed one part of hook-and-loop material to two tiebacks and affixed the other part to the wall.

When not in use, the curtains can be held back neatly and securely; when temperatures rise, they easily slide across the rod to close off the front part of the vehicle and keep the cool air where it's needed. The curtain also can be used for quick and easy privacy instead of drawing those heavy factory curtains around the front windshield.

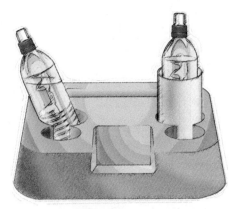

Customized Cup Holders

BOB JOHN, HOLLAND, MICHIGAN

▶ In our motorhome, my wife and I had a problem with our beverage holder. The can space was too small and the cup space was too large to hold 16- to 20-ounce plastic bottles without the possibility of the bottles tipping over.

To solve this problem, I cut two pieces of 3-inch interior-diameter PVC pipe to a length of 4 inches and inserted them into the cup space of the dash cup holder. This allows access to the drink without the possibility of the bottle tipping over while driving down the road.

All built-in beverage holders are different. I had to sand the pipe (to decrease the outside diameter), so it would fit into the cup holder.

Need a Shelf?

RICHARD SWANSON,
MORENO VALLEY, CALIFORNIA

▶ My wife wanted a shelf added near the couch to provide a place for her cup or glass when reading, knitting or watching television. My solution was to cut a piece of ¾-inch board in the shape of a teapot. (It can be any shape, but since she collects teapots, my choice was obvious.) I attached it to the wall (the back of the dinette) using a 2½-inch hinge; when not in use, it's held up and out of the way by a pair of flat magnets.

BUBBLE-WRAP BASICS

We have just recently become full-timers. In the past, we used only plastic dishes on our trips. Now that our RV is our full-time home, I find it necessary to take some glass items along.

I was concerned that we would get to our destination, only to find something broken. So, I purchased a roll of bubble-wrap and cut pieces to fit my various glass items.

The mugs are wrapped with the ends taped tightly, leaving the bottom of the mug clear so that it sits nicely in the cupboard, placed between the glass mixing bowls. I also wrapped the wine glasses.

I now travel worry free, knowing that I will be "saved by the bubbles."

SANDY TUPPER,
OLYMPIA, WASHINGTON

MUST BE A BIG BAG ...

Being less than happy with our RV manufacturer's idea of good décor, we set about to redecorate our RV's bedroom. We were able to easily and inexpensively change the look of the bedroom by buying a Bed In A Bag.

What's a Bed In A Bag? Sold at various linen supply stores (Bed Bath & Beyond, Linens-n-Things, etc.) The bag contains a comforter, top and fitted sheets, two pillow shams, two standard pillowcases and a bed skirt. Also available are matching valances and even drapes.

So out with the old, and with a few minutes' work with the Bed In A Bag items, you will have a decorating look that won't cause you to cringe (or worse) when you look at it.

JANET GLASER,
FREMONT, MICHIGAN

Editor's note: *Similar helpful products are also available from Travasak Sleep System (800-631-2000, travasak.com), and from Leisure Industries (208-345-9721, leisure-hacksack.com).*

FEET, DON'T FAIL ME NOW!

The narrow rungs on the ladder used to reach the bed in our Class C were killing our feet. At a local hardware store, we purchased a 4-foot section of foam pipe insulation. From it we cut smaller pieces to the same length as each rung of the ladder. These sections, when split lengthwise, fit perfectly over the rungs; cable ties were used at either end to secure the foam padding.

What a difference that makes when going up and down the ladder; no more pain in the feet!

FRAN WHITE, SHAWNEE, KANSAS

livability

Wine (Glass) Coolers

JAMES HART, HARRISONVILLE, MISSOURI

▶ Wine glasses may add a touch of luxury to an outing, but the fragile glassware can be hard to protect. One way to carry and store wine glasses in your motorhome is with large plastic soft-drink containers, or Styrofoam or plastic picnic cups of the proper size. Put

each wine glass in an adequately sized plastic cup for travel and/or storage. The glass won't turn over easily, which deters breakage.

Table Console

MAYNARD RICE, ENCINITAS, CALIFORNIA

▶ The floorplan of our gas-powered motorhome allows for the driver and copilot's seats to turn and face into the motorhome when we are parked. With the seats positioned rearward, however, the factory convenience console on the engine-compartment cover is not very useful.

To improve the situation, I made a small, simple table using pressed wood, then painted it. The table fits snugly over the engine console and provides added table space inside our coach. When we're on the road, the table stores beneath the dinette.

Booster Table

ED BURROWS, AGOURA HILLS, CALIFORNIA

▶ Our dinette table was not big enough to seat more than two people — or four very friendly folks. In my search for a means of extending the dining area, I found an unfinished table (at Ikea, $29) designed to be bolted to the wall as a drop-leaf table. The width was perfect and I could cut the length to exactly my needs. (A piece of plywood as thick as the original dinette table also would work.)

At Home Depot, I located a hollow, square-shape steel tube with a ¼-inch inside diameter. I also purchased a square rod that fit into the tube.

I cut the 4-foot-long tube in half, then mounted the twin tubes to the underside of the dinette table, spaced about 3 inches from its outer edge.

With the dinette table turned upside-down, line up the table extension and, by inserting the square rods (also cut in half) into the hollow tubes, ascertain the location of the tubes; the rods should extend into the tubes about 5 inches. Carefully drill holes through the rods, and screw them to the underside of the extension, using flat-head wood screws.

Then, center a simple catch to the edge of the extension and the dinette table to keep the two sections joined when in use.

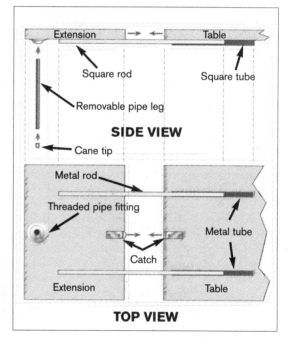

Finish the job by fabricating a leg support for the extension using a ½-inch removable length of pipe. Attach the leg with a ½-inch plastic pipe fitting (with threads on one end and no threads on the other, so the leg can be slipped into and out of it). Add a rubber cane-tip to the end touching the floor to prevent slipping.

To store the extension and leg, I use a bungee cord and secure it against the back wall of the clothes closet.

Letter-Perfect

HERMAN SCHLERF, REEDSPORT, OREGON

▶ We have found that buttons and switches in some motorhomes are not marked adequately, understandably — or, sometimes, not at all.

On the battery-disconnect switches in our coach, I could never remember which switch was for the engine battery and which one was for the coach battery. Plus, the ON/OFF switches for the water pump and the water heater were right next to each other, but the ON/OFF positions were opposite!

I wanted to mark these switches in a way that was small, readable and neat. One day while placing labels on videotapes, I came across some labels included with the new tapes that had small, self-adhesive alphabet-letter stickers. By using a small pair of tweezers to handle the individual letters, you can place them neatly on most any surface.

More Hang-Ups

ANDREW MANCINI, SYRACUSE, NEW YORK

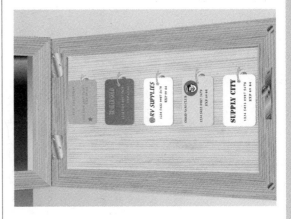

▶ I came up with this idea to keep track of all my discount cards, such as Good Sam Club, Flying J, etc., in the motorhome. I installed a row of cup hooks on the inside of a cabinet door near the entrance door. Then I punched a small hole in the end of each card. Now when I need a card, I just open the cabinet door and take the card I want as I exit the vehicle.

Entry-Step Carpet

WILLIAM WEBER,
HATBORO, PENNSYLVANIA

▶ To dress up and help keep dirt out of our motorhome, I bought a fancy outdoor mat and cut it to fit the entrance steps. These dressy outdoor mats come in a variety of designs and colors.

No Lost Ends

JEAN SVEUM, MOKELUMNE, CALIFORNIA

▶ A paper clip sticks to and saves the end of any roll of tape (think ubiquitous duct tape). No more lost ends. It also gives easy access to the next piece of tape when needed.

livability

Burner Cover

ANNETTE O'DONNELL, MESA, ARIZONA

▶ Do you have an old or new TV tray? You can have a work surface to place over the stovetop that is attractive, lightweight and easy to clean. Using finishing screws, screw short pieces of wooden dowels to the bottom corners of the tray, and cover the dowel ends with rubber feet. While I'm baking, this area is where I set my cookbook and baking paraphernalia.

Speed the Process

FRANK WOYTHAL, ANDOVER, NEW YORK

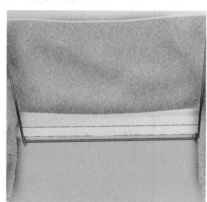

▶ After trying to quickly dry towels and other things in our RV bathroom, I came up with an idea to help speed the process.

I bought a clothesline reel at Camping World and secured it to the wall near the ceiling of the shower compartment. Then I ran the cord to a screw hook directly across the reel on the opposite wall. Next, I ran the cord to a screw about a foot from the first one. The cord then doubles back to a point a foot from the reel. This gives me two clotheslines on which to hang things, or I can hang them across two parallel lines for better airflow. If need be, the whole line can come down within seconds.

Bungees to the Rescue

ELLYN GRAEBERT, YUMA, ARIZONA

▶ As full-timers, we have found a way to keep from putting away countertop objects while traveling. Bungee cords solved our problem. We attached eye hooks along the walls among the objects we wish to store in place. Just hook on the bungees, and take off.

Keep It Cool

HARVEY HETRICK, TORRANCE, CALIFORNIA

▶ After purchasing enough reflective foil to cover every window in our RV (it does block out the heat), I had some left over. My wife suggested lining one section of our overhead  storage bins. Using hook-and-loop tabs, this foil is removable and the hook-and-loop allows the foil to be placed on all side walls, as well as on the bottom and top and on the cupboard doors.

Why bother doing this? If we open the compartments when we use the air conditioning, the cool air is trapped inside when we close them. Stored breads, rolls, etc., stay 15-20 degrees cooler inside the closed compartments when the air conditioning is turned off.

livability

10 minute tech
maintenance

Another Shocking Situation

THOMAS LEIK, PORTLAND, MICHIGAN

▶ Like other RVers, we have had "shocking situations" trying to service our batteries in a very cramped area.

The metal top of our battery storage area is only 2 inches above the posts of our batteries. When sliding in the batteries, which requires tipping them to fit under the exterior door opening, the posts occasionally would brush the metal top and a shower of sparks would occur.

Tightening the cables on top of the batteries produced the same dangerous situation; I never thought of wrapping the wrench with tape, as I have heard other RVers suggest.

We solved these problems by making two changes:

1. We glued a sheet of Plexiglas to the metal top of our

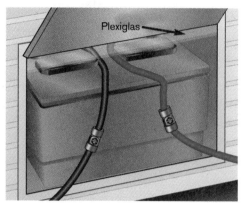

Plexiglas

battery compartment, using 3M weatherstrip adhesive. The top of the compartment is now a nonconductive surface, and no flash will occur if the posts should touch.

2. We cut the battery cables about halfway down the side of the battery and attached lugs to all four cut ends. Now we can slide the batteries into the compartment with the short cable ends already installed on the posts! After the batteries are in place, we simply bolt the matching lug ends together. Be sure to mark the cables before you cut them so there is no chance of error. Also, tape the positive ends to insulate them.

These connections are now made in front of the batteries (not the top), which is easily accessible and much safer.

Drain Completely

FRANK WOYTHAL, ANDOVER, NEW YORK

▶ When changing engine oil in my motorhome, I found that my oil filler-pipe location, like that on most motorhomes, is on quite a slope. That necessitated my holding each quart for quite awhile to completely drain the oil container. My tip is using a mini-bungee cord to hold the oil container at a nearly upright angle. Not only does that ease the task, but now while each quart is totally draining, I can be doing other chores.

Meet Your Marker

CHARLES MONTGOMERY, ENID, OKLAHOMA

▶ It is important to keep the tires on an RV properly inflated. However, it's quite difficult to read the very small print on the sidewall of the tire to obtain the tire manufacturers recommended tire pressure.

So, for a handy, quick reference, we painted the recommended tire pressure on each wheel hub. A permanent marker would also do the trick.

Now, when getting ready to hit the road, this quick reference helps us check the tires for proper inflation.

Squeeze Play

EDWARD HAGGETT III,
NEW BERN, NORTH CAROLINA

▶ I was faced with the same problem (filling all the cells in my RV batteries) as previous *10-Minute Tech* contributors, but had no room for using a funnel for the two rearmost cells.

My solution was to take a well-rinsed dish detergent bottle and attach a short piece of tubing. I actually inserted the tubing into the cap of the detergent bottle, where the push-to-seal top had been, and then filled the clean bottle with distilled water.

When I need to add water to the battery, I place the hose into the correct battery cell (but not into the battery acid) and turn the bottle upside down momentarily and give a slight squeeze.

Fill Me In

JOE BARRY, SAN DIEGO, CALIFORNIA

Cut

▶ Many RVers cut up plastic bottles to create funnels for various reasons. I recently cut a 1.75-liter liquor bottle in half and found that the bottle neck and cap threads will thread into the oil filler pipe on Ford Power Stroke diesel engines. One need not worry about the funnel slipping or falling over, and these easily made funnels may also fit the threads of oil filler pipes on other engines.

COSTLY NEGLECT

Having neglected proper care of my motorhome AC generator by not starting it periodically, and ending up with an unnecessary repair bill (my own fault), I decided to take better care of it. To remind me to perform the service, I placed a small calendar on the inside of one of the cabinet doors. This way, I mark the date each time, and can tell at a glance when I need to run the AC generator again.

JOE CAMPBELL, GOODWATER, ALABAMA

DIRTY PICTURES

I recently had difficulty identifying the source of a water leak under the shower of my trailer. The compartment under the shower had a small access hole in it, but the toilet was placed so close to the opening that I couldn't see into it. The old mirror and flashlight trick didn't work.

I solved the problem by using my video camera. I was able to place the camera into the access hole and slowly pan it around. I then took the tape to my television set and was able to clearly see the source of the leak!

RON ANDRESS, PRESCOTT VALLEY, ARIZONA

GOT BEES?

In the past, we have had problems with bees and hornets making nests in the refrigerator and water heater compartments. I hit upon the idea of putting mothballs in an old prescription bottle (with holes punched in the top and bottom), and placing these bottles in the outside effected compartments after arriving home from a trip. We have not had any free boarders since!

Just remember to remove the mothball bottles before you start the appliances.

JUDITH SIMON, SAGINAW, MICHIGAN

SLIDEOUT FENDER SKIRT

On my trailer, the slideout fender skirt was always coming loose. The dealership replaced the fastening screws with longer screws, which went through the rubber seal and into the wall. They then tried fatter screws, which didn't help either.

I called the factory about the problem and the service representative approved of my solution. I found some thick neoprene and rubber washers, which I put inside the fender skirt, and used ¼-inch bolts. This allowed me to snug up the bolts without cracking the fender, and also cut down on the vibration. I put silicone caulking on the bolt end and nut so the rubber seal on the wall doesn't puncture.

DALE NABBEN, BISMARCK, NORTH DAKOTA

SMOKE GETS IN YOUR EYES

A running joke in the amateur radio community concerns the smoke that manufacturers "place" in their components at the factory. When the smoke gets released, the device is broken. To keep the smoke properly inside your components, it's important to make sure that your 12-volt battery connections have the proper polarity.

Before disconnecting the RV batteries for servicing or replacement, note the color and position of each wire attached to each battery post, and then draw a diagram of the system. Be sure to clearly show which battery post each wire is attached to.

After you service or replace the batteries, you can keep this diagram with your RV papers, or laminate the diagram inside plastic sheets and attach it to the inside of the battery compartment door.

DAN DOLAN, LAYTON, UTAH

USE A TURKEY BASTER

On small jobs, I often need to transfer finishes or other liquids to smaller containers for mixing or use. To avoid messy spills when pouring from a larger container, I use a plastic turkey baster (less than $2 at most grocery stores). These are usually marked with ¼-ounce graduations and can be rinsed clean if using water-based products.

GEOFFRY CARLSON,
MANCOS, COLORADO

Editor's note: *Under no circumstances should you use the baster for food preparation after using it for other tasks involving toxic substances.*

RADIATING CLEANLINESS

On our diesel-pusher motorhome, engine temperature frequently elevated due to a dirty radiator. I found that by spraying the fan side of the radiator with a water-soluble cleaner (such as Simple Green or Gunk Engine Cleaner), letting it soak in and then flushing with a fine spray of water from a garden-hose nozzle, I could clean the radiator — and save the cost of having a shop perform the chore.

Care must be taken not to close the fins on the radiator by using too much water pressure.

The first time I did this, the engine temperature dropped 27 degrees!

JOHN MAGRATH,
GLENDALE, ARIZONA

Slip-Slidin' Along

EDDIE ADAMS, TORRANCE, CALIFORNIA

▶ Some spin-on oil filters are installed in locations that could stump Houdini, and the removal process becomes even more aggravating if a circus strongman put the last filter on so tight that the standard oil-filter wrench won't even budge it.

To avoid this, I fold a 3 × 8-inch piece of sandpaper (any grit number will do) lengthwise over the filter-wrench hoop.

Once the sandpaper is in place, its roughness imparts a non-slip surface to the wrench, ensuring a tight grip on the filter housing.

Funnel Function

TONY DANTZMAN, CRESCENT CITY, CALIFORNIA

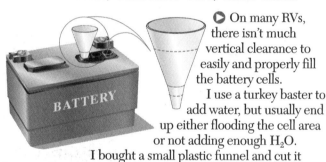

▶ On many RVs, there isn't much vertical clearance to easily and properly fill the battery cells.

I use a turkey baster to add water, but usually end up either flooding the cell area or not adding enough H_2O.

I bought a small plastic funnel and cut it down to the size needed for my batteries. Now I get the water into each cell without spilling.

Basic Instinct

ERNIE KLEVEN, STEVENSVILLE, MONTANA

▶ When I would change my vehicle's oil, it was always difficult to keep from spilling hot oil while unscrewing the old filter. Now I use an ice pick to punch a hole in the thin metal bottom of the filter to let the oil drain out before removing it.

ÁC Generator Oil Change

PAT KEOUGHAN, FORT WORTH, TEXAS

▶ To change the AC generator's oil on an extended trip, use a differential sump pump to suck the dirty oil out through the filler tube. We store the used oil in a covered (and marked) container until a proper oil-disposal location is found. Be sure to refill the AC generator.

Dipstick Door

CHARLES HYATT, MESA, ARIZONA

▶ As an owner of an older motorhome with a 454-CID engine, I quickly grew tired of having to remove the entire unwieldy cowling to check the transmission fluid level. So, I added a simple little door in the cowling.

To determine the location of the door, remove the cowling and measure the position of the transmission dipstick (use the indentations made by the cowling in the carpet as a guide). Transfer this measurement to the cowling, then scribe the cowling cover to mark out the door size you want — remember, it needs to be large enough to get your hand through (I made mine 5 inches square).

Cut out the door with a saw. The carpet should stay attached to the door; you are cutting through the carpet, cowling fiberglass and insulation all at once.

File the edges smooth, and then attach a hinge to the bottom of the cowling and the door using sheet metal screws (you may need to pry back the carpet to fit the hinge). Add a doorstop on the underside of the cowling, along with a small pull tab to the outside of the door.

I find now I'm checking the transmission fluid level each time I check the oil.

1,000 WORDS, 1,000 USES

I have found a number of practical uses for a digital camera around our RV. One, naturally, is to take photos of things that need to be repaired. This allows me to show (or fax) the images to a repair person, to better describe what needs to be fixed.

It's also great when I'm looking for a part. All I have to do is to show the photo (either printed or still in the camera) to the sales person to help me locate the exact component. When possible, I also take a photo of any identifying labels showing model and serial numbers. This has proven to be invaluable in getting the correct part the first time.

RAY CORBETT, PROSPER, TEXAS

GOOD EXTENSION

How many times have you needed to add air to the tires when the trailer is already hooked to the tow vehicle? In order to use a 12-volt DC compressor, you usually have to unhitch and drive around so you can pump up the tires.

I eliminated that problem by buying two 12-volt DC 10-foot extension cords. They are available at RadioShack. Now when my tires need air, I just use the extension cords and pump away!

ROBERT WYBLE,
CALEDONIA, NEW YORK

Editor's note: *Be sure the extension cord is rated for the current your pump draws, and that it doesn't overheat.*

WATER YOU WAITING FOR?

We all know that after a long winter break, the fresh water tanks in our motorhomes are in dire need of sanitizing. A bleach solution is the preferred treatment – but it can be messy.

Next time, try pouring a cup or two of bleach in your hose (using a funnel), rather than into the water inlet of your motorhome. Then, secure the male end of the hose in the water inlet, kink the other end of the hose near the end (to keep the bleach from running out as you lower the hose to faucet level), twist the female end onto your faucet and fill your tank. From there, it's easy to follow procedures for completing the sanitizing routine – and you've sanitized your hose in the process!

TOM ARCHULETA,
ALBUQUERQUE, NEW MEXICO

maintenance

Manageable Molding

ROBERT VALENTE, NOVI, MICHIGAN

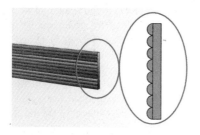

▶ I got tired of sanding and repainting the bottom of my trailer frame due to stone chips, and also of re-painting the rear bumper each season due to sun fading.

I purchased a 30-foot roll of 8⅛-inch ultra wide vinyl self-adhesive molding. I ordered it from J.C. Whitney; it can be found in either its catalog or on the Internet.

Go to the jcwhitney.com Web site, and in the upper-left-hand corner, a box asks for the SKU number, which is ZX124828W. This will show the sizes and colors available. You will know you are looking at the right ones when you see the red tape that covers the adhesive side.

For my vehicle, I ordered the 8-inch black, which was enough to do the lower front ends of my trailer, and enough to cover the top and rear surfaces of the rear bumper.

To install, sand and clean the affected areas, cut the molding to fit and apply.

Recycled Water Bottle

JAY KOOL, JENISON, MICHIGAN

▶ As we all should be doing, I routinely check the water level in the house and chassis batteries. I use a 22-ounce water bottle, with a sport cap attached, that was originally used for drinking water. This bottle, filled with distilled water, is usually sufficient to top off the individual cells. The squirt from the sport cap makes it very easy to fill the batteries without leaving a mess. The bottles take less room for storage, too.

We also use this type of bottle for soap for cleaning and for antifreeze (diluted to 50 percent) if needed in the reservoir. These bottles can be used for many things that come in gallon jugs and are not used all at once. We just refill any we used upon returning home.

Dual-Purpose Sun Shield

TERESA MARCHAND, FRONT ROYAL, VIRGINIA

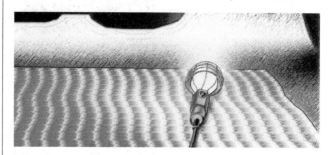

▶ Recently while traveling, we had a mechanical problem requiring my husband to crawl under the RV to repair it. Since we had no choice on where to stop, we ended up parked near a colony of ants and assorted road debris.

I was extremely concerned about him being bit or cut, so I quickly grabbed the sun reflector and laid it over the problem area. He was able to safely finish the repair — and a bonus was that when using the drop light, the pad reflected the light and made it easier to see and work.

Afterward, we just wiped the reflector off and rolled it up; once again, it sits on the windshield, serving its original purpose.

Milkin' It

O. GENE SMITH, CHESTERFIELD, INDIANA

▶ I devised my own battery-refill device by using an empty, well-rinsed half-gallon milk bottle, a 3-foot length of clear plastic hose and two straws.

In the cap of the bottle, drill two holes to hold the two straws snugly; pass the plastic tube through one of the straws and thread it down through the inside of the bottle handle (passing the tube through the bottle handle will help hold the tube on the bottom of the bottle).

Put the other straw through the second cap hole to provide air for the siphon. To start the siphoning action, rather than sucking on the hose, simply blow on the open straw. The air pressure will start the siphon. Place the bottle higher than the batteries to maintain the flow. You can use your finger to stop the flow, or simply move the end of the tube from one battery cell to another to fill all the cells.

maintenance

10

minute tech

mobile computing

Computer Slideout

DAVE VOGELER, VANCOUVER, WASHINGTON

▶ We usually take along our laptop computer and our printer, and we used to set it all up on the dinette table. At mealtime it proved a hassle to move the printer in order to clear the tabletop. My solution was to install an extension on the underside of the table that can slide out when needed. This extension spans the seat adjacent to the outside wall, extending out approximately 18 inches, sufficient to accommodate the 17-inch printer width. The laptop then fits on the seat, under the extension, freeing the tabletop and still providing seating space for three people.

The drawing shows roughly how it goes together. I used 24-inch drawer slides, available at any hardware store. For the extension, I used oak-faced ½-inch plywood with ¼ × ½-inch screen molding, glued and nailed to cover the rough edges of the plywood.

The 1⅛-inch cleats holding the slides were cut out of ¾-inch plywood and should be smoothed on the ends and on the outside edges to protect your knees. I finished the extension with varnish, but you could use Formica if preferred.

This same type of extension could be utilized at other locations on the tabletop to provide extra space for a variety of uses.

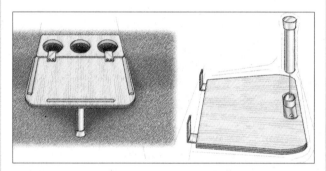

Hello, I Must Be Going

CURTIS HISSONG, ENTERPRISE, ALABAMA

▶ I have a Class A gas coach, so I took advantage of the engine's doghouse to create a shelf for my laptop (with a Garmin USB 235 antenna) so that both driver and copilot can read the GPS data easily. I used a piece of ⅜-inch cabinet-grade plywood, one inch wider and longer than my laptop. (This gave me room to glue small half-round trim on all sides to prevent the laptop from sliding off.)

Next, I attached two plastic L-brackets (using two small screws on each) that fit down in the back of the cup-holders — plastic will not mar the finish on the wood cup-holders.

I also added a removable post leg on the back of the shelf. This provides necessary support to level the shelf — and also provides ventilated space under the shelf for the inverter necessary to power the laptop.

Cleaning Up the Clutter

ALAN NOBLE, LIVINGSTON, TEXAS

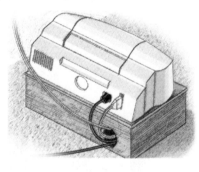

▶ We equipped our motorhome with a computer and a printer for e-mail and Internet access while traveling. However, I couldn't stand having all the wires scattered haphazardly on the floor and table.

To satisfy my need for neatness, I purchased a wooden box about the same size as the base of the printer and drilled a 2-inch hole in the back for the wires. (Smaller vent holes could be drilled in the sides, but with my equipment there was no need.)

The box holds the power strip/surge suppressor, plus the power cords for the printer and computer — and there's still room to store the extra wiring.

When placed in position, all that is seen is a short wire supplying power to the setup, and two wires going to my laptop on the table. A small piece of nonskid material keeps the printer in place, so it never needs to be disassembled. My wires are neat and my equipment is out of the way, permanently in place.

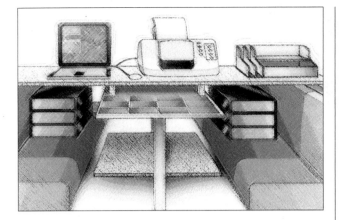

Computer Station

J IM S CHMIDT , S IOUX F ALLS , S OUTH D AKOTA

▶ Many older-model motorhomes aren't built with a workstation for a computer and printer. I needed such a workstation, so I did a little improvising with our dinette area and came up with a very workable office area.

I used a piece of 1 × 12-inch lumber and cut it to extend across the width of our dinette booth. The dinette table is approximately 2 inches lower than the backs of the seats, so I made a pair of 2 × 12-inch legs and attached them to the bottom of the shelf. I found some matching carpet that I glued to the top surface and, to protect the tabletop and dinette backs, I glued some rubber nonskid material to go under all points of contact.

We purchased an organizer to hold our mail, clock, stapler, stamps, etc. The shelf now holds our computer, a fax/printer and the organizer. We then obtained two three-drawer storage units to hold all our office supplies. They fit nicely under the shelf and rest on the dinette seats.

The back part of the area under the dinette table is used for more shelving. I put strips of hook-and-loop fasteners under the items on the shelf to keep them in place while the motorhome is moving.

IT'S IN THE BAG

I store the different cables needed for our laptop computer in individual resealable sandwich bags. I do the same with the power supplies and chargers for different cordless devices. The bags can be labeled. This keeps the cables from getting tangled up – and keeps me from forgetting which cable goes with what device.

B OB T OZER , B ROOKLYN P ARK , M INNESOTA

A DIAPER BAG?

One of a traveler's most-often-stolen possessions is the laptop computer. An effective way to reduce the chances of losing this expensive item is to disguise it.

Rather than carrying it in a standard laptop case, modify a diaper bag with Fome-Cor board and foam padding. The compartments for baby items in a diaper bag work equally well for the plugs and wires that laptop users need.

L ARRY F RANCIS , R ALEIGH , N ORTH C AROLINA

DESIGN YOUR LABEL

When registering at RV parks, instead of handwriting all of our information on the registration card, we've saved this information onto our laptop. We print out a sheet of 1 × 2⅝-inch sticky labels. We include the following information on each label:

Name
Address
Phone Number

Make, model, year and license numbers (for the truck, trailer, motorhome, dinghy, etc.)

Good Sam, SKP and/or other camping discount membership numbers

Depending on the font size used, there can be several lines on each label.

This speeds up the registration process, and the office staff really appreciates the printed version, rather than trying to decipher someone's handwriting.

B ARBARA R AECK , S EATTLE , W ASHINGTON

CLUTTER-CLEANER

We live full-time in our motorhome. There is never enough storage space, and I am always looking for ways to reduce clutter.

Since we use a notebook computer and a combination printer-copier-scanner-fax machine in our mobile office, once a month – after I have paid bills – I scan each of the credit card statements, bank statement and other bills through the scanner. I then save the file on a CD.

The CD can then be stored in a small disc container – and the paper shredded and tossed. If I need a copy of the statement, I can look at it on the computer or print out a copy. Periodically I make a copy of the CDs and send them to my son for backup and safekeeping.

B ARBARA N ELSON , M T . M ORRIS , I LLINOIS

mobile computing

Double-Duty Desk

WANDA SMITH,
CHESTERFIELD, INDIANA

▶ We bought a device called a Joto Desk (available though Assembled Products Corporation, 800-548-3373, jottodesk.com) for holding our laptop during travel.

It's almost infinitely adjustable, making it adaptable to all kinds of situations. It is very easy to adjust, holds the computer easily, is very stable and comes with straps to fasten the computer down — so that when traveling down bumpy roads, it won't bounce around.

Other accessories are also available, such as a phone holder, small light, etc.

I decided to make it do double-duty by fitting it with a round table top (attached with hook-and-loop fasteners) when we are parked.

mobile computing

10 minute tech
safety & security

AUTOMATIC PORCH LIGHT

For added security and convenience, I installed a motion detector on the curbside of our RV, just aft of the front awning arm and about 6 inches below the awning. I pointed the sensor toward the door of the RV.

Sixty-watt interior bulbs seem to provide enough light for my small yard area, and they don't protrude beyond the rolled-up awning.

I drilled a small hole through to the inside of the RV where the light assembly was fastened, passed the power cord through the hole and hooked into the 120-volt AC outlet with an in-line switch. Be sure to seal the wire where it enters the vehicle.

This automatic porch light works very well for me when I am out for the evening, or am expecting company after dark.

SCOTT STEWART,
HAMILTON, MONTANA

I CAN SEE CLEARLY NOW

In bad weather, if your windshield keeps fogging up, turn the defroster on high and pull your sun-visors down. This will keep the air directed toward the windshield and aid in keeping it clear.

LORENA O'CONNOR,
SILVER SPRINGS, MARYLAND

CHECK FOR LEAKS

In the past, to check for leaks when changing my LP-gas cylinders, I would mix the usual solution of dish soap and water and spread it on all the connections, making quite a mess.

While cleaning my eyeglasses with lens cleaner from a small spray pump bottle I purchased at Wal-Mart, it occurred to me that it would also work to check for leaks on the gas connections. A few pumps at each connection does the trick, and leaves virtually no mess.

CONRAD LIND,
SPENCERPORT, NEW YORK

NO-SLIP GRIP

I wanted a small, non-slip rubber mat for the shower floor in my motorhome, but most of them were too large. Instead, I purchased a Rubbermaid kitchen-sink mat. They come in different sizes — and work great.

CHERYL EVERETT, SWANTON, OHIO

A Close Shave

JOAN COTTERELL, LEAGUE, TEXAS

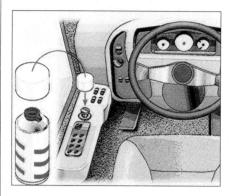

Our motorhome is a diesel-pusher with an Allison transmission. The controls for the transmission, parking brake and other items are on a ledge to the left of the driver. We sometimes park the motorhome in our driveway, which has a slight incline.

Having a dog that gets excited — and small children who are sometimes in our coach — I worried about the parking-brake knob being accidentally pushed down, which would then release the brake and allow the coach to roll into the street!

I solved this possible problem by covering the knob with the plastic cover from an aerosol shaving-cream can. Be sure to use one that is deep enough, and doesn't have that extra cup inside.

Editor's note: *Under such parking circumstances, the use of adequate wheel chocks is the safe and prudent thing to do as well as using the coach parking brake.*

Áqua Alarm

VIC McCAULEY, SPOTSYLVANIA, VIRGINIA

Some of us have had the very bad experience of a water leak. With an inexpensive ($5 to $10) alarm device, the damage and cleanup can be minimized.

It is 3×4 inches in size and has its own battery. The sensor, which is about the size of a quarter, is placed within 5 feet of the 85-decibel alarm. It takes only $\frac{1}{32}$-inch of water to activate the alarm by completing the current path between the two contacts on the sensor.

The alarm can probably be purchased from several sources; I found mine at harborfreight.com (part no. 42702).

Heads Up

WILL LANIER, AURORA, COLORADO

▶ Unlike our previous motorhome, our new coach is equipped with slideouts. To remind our children (and ourselves!) to watch our heads when walking around the new motorhome, we placed red reflective tape on the slideout edges.

When we have to park close to another motorhome, it also helps alert people who are walking through the campsite to be aware of the slideout.

See Them Rungs

DARRELL FEVERGEON,
COSTA MESA, CALIFORNIA

▶ Motorhome roof ladders with the extruded metal steps tend to extend beyond the coach body in the back, creating potential danger to inattentive pedestrians.

My motorhome's ladder is close to the sidewalk when parked on my driveway. In the interest of safety and visibility, I added red reflective tape to the ends of the rungs.

Inexpensive self-stick red reflective tape is available at auto-parts stores. After making a template, I simply cut and attached as many tape pieces as needed, affixing them to both sides of the ladder rungs. These smart-looking reflectors also increase nighttime visibility.

PLATFORM FOR SAFETY

Some of my friends have fallen off the roof of their motorhomes while washing or working on the front end. I have eliminated that possibility by building a hanging scaffold against the front wall of my garage. That makes it easy to wax, clean the windshield, etc.

I used 2 × 4s for the framing (be sure there are no large knots or weak spots) and 2 × 10s for the platform surface. The assembly hangs from the garage roof rafters. If your garage ceiling is covered and you cannot get to the rafters, you could construct the platform so that it sits on the floor. Be sure to cross-brace the supports and fasten the assembly to the wall, so it will not tip over.

Because it is about head-high, I padded the ends and covered them with red cloth for visibility. I hope this prevents a few accidents.

HAROLD STERZBACH, LOUISVILLE, OHIO

PROTECTION

Valve-stem extenders, also called dual-tire inflaters, make checking air pressure and inflating inner-rear duals a lot easier. However, some users have serious problems with air leaks. It seems the extenders can chafe or wear through if they touch the edge of the wheel hole or the wheel-cover hole. The chafing is caused by vibration and slight movement of the wheel cover while traveling. Loss of air can occur, and serious situations might be encountered.

Having heard of these incidents, I decided to check my extenders. Even though mine were of the woven-steel type, they had started to rub through. Rather than discard them, I cut four 2-inch pieces from an old ⅝-inch-diameter garden hose. These pieces were slipped over the extenders to the point where they touched the edge of the hole in the wheel liner. Now, any chafing will occur on the pieces of hose, not the extenders. I check them periodically for wear.

HERB JERRELL,
HOMOSASSA, FLORIDA

WATCH YOUR HEAD

As a retired truck driver, I'm well aware of low underpasses, clearance at gas stations and low-hanging branches at campsites. I also see a lot of motorhomes with severe damage due to drivers trying to go under places without enough clearance.

Here is an idea that works: Mount an antenna on the front of your motorhome that is a little higher than anything mounted on the roof (a CB antenna works well). Ease forward into a questionable spot. If the antenna hits, stop and back up.

BOB COLLEY, CASPER, WYOMING

safety & security

Slow Leak Detection

ARTHUR WAGNER, KERRVILLE, TEXAS

▶ Sometimes a tire will develop a slow leak that's hard to find. Often the leak is in the tire valve core, which is a tiny spring-loaded device inside the tire valve stem.

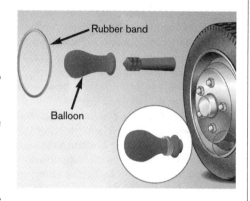

Frequently the leak is so gradual that it won't immediately show up. Here is what you can do with a suspect valve stem core. Slide a small balloon over the valve stem and secure it with a rubber band. If the balloon inflates after being in place for several days, you have found your leak.

Safer Hookup

FRANK WOYTHAL, ANDOVER, NEW YORK

▶ When hooking up an extension cord to your motorhome's shorepower cord, there is a risk of rain getting into the connection if this is simply plugged in and laid on the ground.

My tip is to make this connection within a plastic storage container with a tight-fitting lid. Simply cut two narrow slots in the sides of the container to accommodate the two cords. Slide the cords into the slots, as shown in the illustration, and snap the lid tight. When the container is not in use to keep the connection dry, it is a great place to store the various adapters we use to complete our electrical hookup.

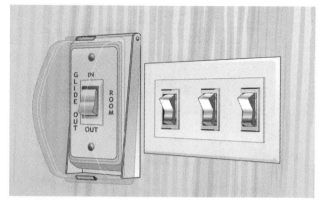

Slideout Savior

PHIL TURCOTTE, CLINTON, MASSACHUSETTS

▶ We have a fifth-wheel with slideouts. The switch for the slideouts is mounted inside near the door, along with three other switches. On some occasions when it's dark, we come into the trailer and accidentally flip the slideout switch instead of the light switch.

A simple solution to this problem is to go to a home-improvement center and purchase a wet-location electrical switch plate, which comes with a clear flip-up cover, and install it over the slideout switch. This has not only solved our problem, but it also keeps curious grandchildren and people not familiar with our trailer from accidentally flipping the slideout switch.

Lost My Brakes

MARK MAJERUS, MIDDLETOWN, DELAWARE

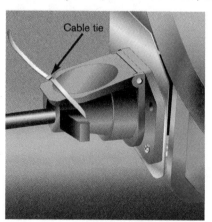

▶ While descending a 7-percent grade, my trailer's brakes failed (thank goodness for anti-lock braking systems). The culprit was the trailer wiring harness plug — it had popped out of the receptacle on my truck. Having a small spring clip is not the most secure means of holding such a critical part in place. Ever since then, I make sure to secure the flap and plug in place with a simple cable tie.

LP-Gas Reminder

PHIL TURCOTTE, CLINTON, MASSACHUSETTS

◉ On our fifth-wheel, the compartment for the LP-gas cylinders is covered by a door.

We try not to travel with the LP-gas on, and have sometimes found that we have forgotten to shut off the gas valves. Once the compartment door is closed, it seems to be a matter of out of sight, out of mind.

Our simple solution was to make a colorful sign on card stock, printed on both sides. We then laminated it and put it into a luggage-tag pouch.

Then we attached a screw eye on the inside of the top front edge of the LP-gas compartment and hung the tag.

When we turn the LP-gas valves on, we just pull the tag out over the door and close it. The door-jamb stops are partially cut out to allow for ventilation so that the hanging tag does not make the door hard to close.

When we're ready to leave, the tag serves as a bright reminder to shut off the LP-gas.

Short Step

ARDELL PETERSON, BELLINGHAM, WASHINGTON

◉ The extendible door step on many RVs is quite shallow and can present a safety hazard when you're entering or exiting the rig.

I overcame this problem and increased my step's dimension by bolting a piece of 2 × 2-inch wood to the step flange with ¼-inch bolts. Also, I wanted to improve visibility, so I painted the extension bright yellow and the rest of the step light gray.

Finally, I sprinkled some fine-grain sand in the wet paint to improve skid-resistance.

CAUTION

Caution must be used when adding a 12-volt DC receptacle, such as a cigar-lighter socket, to a lighting circuit. Normally, lighting circuits use smaller-gauge wire than does a circuit designed to support a lighter socket. The reason for the heavier wire is that some appliances and/or tools use a significantly higher current than is available in a lighting circuit.

If you are considering adding a 12-volt DC receptacle to any circuit, the following should be done. First, determine the highest current rating of the appliances to be used. Second, isolate the circuit where the socket is to be added and check the fuse capacity for that circuit. If the current needed is higher than 80 percent of the fuse rating, the socket should not be added to this circuit.

Under no circumstances should an existing fuse be replaced with one rated at a higher current capacity. If you need more current than the existing circuit can supply, add a new fused circuit, using the proper wire size to ensure safety.

LYLE NAISH, FRENCHTOWN, MONTANA

KEEP YOUR LEGS UP

I recently had a problem with the landing legs of my fifth-wheel malfunctioning and being forced down to the road while the vehicle was in motion.

After driving in a very heavy rainstorm, the road spray was so thick that it filled the control switch box with water. This caused the switch contacts to short in the down position, and drove the legs down to the highway. As on many fifth-wheels manufactured before 2000, the control switch is located on the vertical surface of the trailer, directly back of the tow truck rear wheels.

There are basically two solutions to this problem. You can either relocate the control switch to the side of the trailer, or you can go to RadioShack and purchase a rubber cap (part no. 225-1598), package of two, for $1.29. Each cap comes with a rubber-coated locking nut that replaces the existing switch locking nut. Remove the existing lock nut, install the new locking nut, slip the rubber boot over the switch bat handle and you are done.

The switch is totally functional without removing the rubber boot.

HOWARD ROSSER, WALWORTH, NEW YORK

PROTECT THE STEPS

There was a problem with the outside RV steps accumulating ice and snow when I was driving my motorhome in inclement weather. So I attached a mud flap just in front of the steps. It only has to be large enough to protect them from road spray. Mud flaps are available at auto- and truck-supply stores.

JOSEPH VOLK, GARDNERVILLE, NEVADA

Double Header

NANCY MONK, BELLEVUE, IDAHO

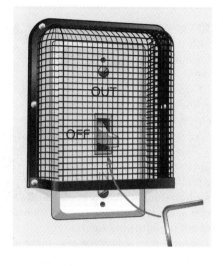

▶ Our new fifth-wheel is wonderful, except for the fact that the control switch for the living room/kitchen slideout is located just inside the front door, near the switches for the interior and porch lights.

On more than one occasion, we have entered our home and reached for the light switch and pushed the slideout switch by mistake, which causes our cat to evacuate the premises at high speed and disappear for days! Small children also have a ball with this switch and head right for it when they see the commotion it causes if they push it.

To prevent this, I purchased a 4-inch square metal mesh "office note holder" from an office-supply store. I drilled tiny holes in the corners and attached it to the wall, covering the slideout switch and preventing it from being accessed by mistake.

To activate the switch, I use a small Allen wrench (stuck in the note holder's mesh while traveling) to push through the mesh and press the button.

BOB BRANSON, BASTROP, TEXAS

▶ I've seen several suggestions for covering slideout switches, which many manufacturers insist on placing right next to light switches with the predictable result. I have stolen — uh, I mean — adapted these suggestions to use an attractive picture frame.

First I purchased a suitably sized frame. Second, to accommodate the length of the switches sticking out from the wall, I built up the thickness of the frame by making a simple box frame out of scrap wood strips, the same outside dimension of the picture frame.

After attaching this "spacer" frame to the wall over the switches, I mounted the picture frame to it with small brass hinges at the top. The picture frame hangs closed in the natural position, covering the switches, but can easily be raised when needed.

For the photo in the frame I wanted to use an actual picture of the switches, but my wife didn't see the humor in that!

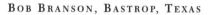

Surprise, Surprise!

FRED BRUDER, CLEARWATER, FLORIDA

▶ One night, my wife got out of bed and turned on the living-room light from the switch on the wall in the motorhome bedroom. On returning to bed, she went to turn off the living-room light and flipped off the wall switch she thought was the light switch. We were both surprised when the bedroom slideout started moving in.

The next incident occurred in my parents' motorhome when my father, going out the door, stepped out into thin air. He hit the ground hard, rolling, tumbling and uttering a few "gosh-darn-its." He still claims, "Your mom pushed the step switch the night before, when we went to bed," and he's sticking with that story.

The solution to both problems proved simple. I went to my local home center and purchased some wet-location electrical switch-plate covers. They come with a clear cover, which you have to lift up in order to get to the switch itself. They fit perfectly over the existing switches.

Now, no more unexpected rides on our beds and no more gymnastic practice for my father!

Don't Use Your Head

ROGER KIRKPATRICK, MOBILE, ALABAMA

▶ The hitch kingpin on every fifth-wheel can present a safety hazard to anyone who goes near it, especially children.

To reduce this hazard, my solution was to hang a plastic five-gallon bucket on the kingpin. I straightened and reformed the bucket handle so that it fit in the formed lip in front of the pin box. I also drilled a few holes in the bucket bottom so rainwater would not collect.

The bucket is easy to remove and store, and does not come off in high winds or when you push on it in any direction. A coat of bright-colored paint aids in seeing the bucket before accidentally running into the kingpin.

Ropin' the Wind

LEE RUPEL, KERNVILLE, CALIFORNIA

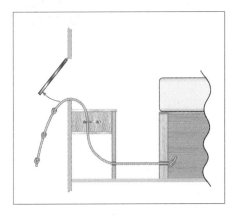

▶ How many of us have practiced exiting through our emergency escape window? Some RVers might have difficulty using the fire-escape window, which, in fifth-wheels, is a good 7 feet above the ground.

To help with this exiting problem, I bought a 12-foot length of ¾-inch soft flexible rope and fastened it, inside the bedroom, beneath the escape window, to the bed-mounting timbers. Either a good-size eyebolt mounted to a strong component of the RV's framework or drilling a hole through the mounting timber, and then passing the rope through the hole to tie a knot inside will securely fasten the rope.

The rope then can be curled up on the floor. I tied a knot every 18 inches along the length of the rope to make it easier to climb down. Each overhand knot will use 4 or 5 inches of rope.

FIRE-SAFETY UPGRADE

The smoke alarms in most RVs are logically positioned at the highest point on the ceiling. However, they are often set off by the slightest amount of smoke from cooking, which can be very annoying. Like too many other RVers, I disabled my detector by removing the battery because the detector that came with the vehicle did not have a "silencer" button, and to have to climb a stool to temporarily remove the battery every time I wanted to cook was inconvenient.

I corrected this problem and stayed safe by replacing the original smoke detector with a First Alert model ($20) that can be temporarily turned off simply by pointing the TV remote at the detector and pushing the volume or channel button. I was able to use the original holes in the ceiling to install the new mounting bracket.

This is a small price to pay for the safety of your family and equipment.

THOMAS ROSS, SHEBOYGAN, WISCONSIN

SAFE AT HOME

Security is a concern for all RVers. Here is a no-cost idea that will add to your peace of mind.

Many vehicles have a remote door opener/lock for their tow- or dinghy vehicle on their key chain. Most of those remote devices feature a panic button. When you shut down for the day, your keys should be with you inside the RV. If your security is threatened during the night, push the panic button on the remote. The honking and flashing lights of the vehicle will likely cause the intruder to flee.

RED STEVENSON, BIXBY, OKLAHOMA

SOUND THE ALARM

One morning my wife was getting out of bed and put her foot on the floor, only to jump right back into bed. The carpet was soaking wet. The water tank under the bed had sprung a leak and, because of its location, we had no warning.

To prevent a reoccurrence of this problem, I went to a hardware store and purchased a water alarm.

The unit, (model no. 00700), manufactured by Sonin Inc., cost $19 Canadian. I also installed another alarm by the hot-water tank and the plumbing.

Now, we will have no more unwanted wet surprises.

EDWARD MEUINER,
TECUMSEH, ONTARIO

Wrong Type of Open-Door Policy

CLINT LAND, SALEM, MISSOURI

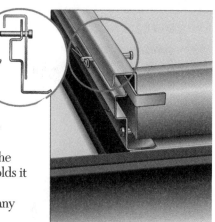

▶ There we were, traveling down the interstate, when I looked in the rearview mirror, and boy, did I get a surprise!

The slideout tray of the storage compartment in our fifth-wheel was sticking out about 2 feet. It had pushed hard enough against the compartment door to bend the latches, and the door was wide open.

Apparently, the spring that holds the latch for the tray was missing, letting the tray slide one way that, luckily, was on the passenger side.

I remedied this problem by drilling a ¼-inch hole through the top portion of the tray and its frame. I then inserted a pin, with a hole in one end, so a cotter pin holds it in place.

The moral of this story is don't trust those latch springs. If the tray had come any farther out, there could have been a lot of serious damage!

Save Your Noodle With a Noodle

BARBARA RAECK, SEATTLE, WASHINGTON

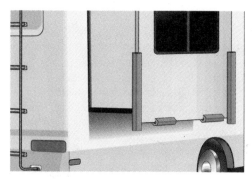

▶ We recently discovered a way to cushion the blow of accidentally head-butting the kingpin box and bedroom slide on our fifth-wheel when parked at a campground.

I purchased two regular swim noodles with a hole through the center. We cut the noodles lengthwise down to the center hole, and then cut each noodle into three pieces. We fit three pieces over the hitch kingpin box edges. The other three pieces are used on the sides and bottom of the bedroom slideout.

It may not keep you from hitting your head, but it won't hurt as much.

Safe Storage

FRANK WOYTHAL, ANDOVER, NEW YORK

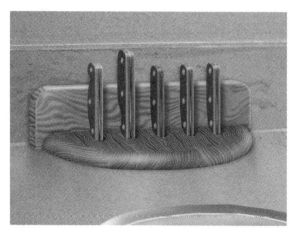

▶ Occasionally our grandchildren go camping with us. We needed a means to keep our sharp knives readily accessible, yet out of their reach.

My quick fix was to cut a series of ¼-inch slots in the back of our countertop, extending about 2 inches from the back wall, using a sabre saw with a flush cutting blade. Using adhesive, I then fastened a piece of oak paneling to the wall behind the slots. A piece of solid oak with matching slots butted against the plywood is cemented and/or held down with screws from below. Predrilling the screw holes will keep the oak from splitting. This keeps the knives out of reach and keeps them secure when traveling.

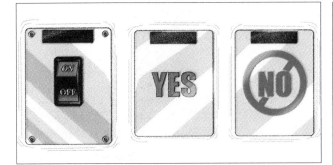

In or Out?

R I C H A R D   M A R R I N S O N ,   T U L S A ,   O K L A H O M A

▶ After seeing the damage done to slideout rooms because safety devices had not been removed prior to extending the rooms, I devised a simple reminder for myself.

I made a small laminated card with "YES" on one side and "NO" on the other. To mount it, a small strip of hook-and-loop fastener is applied on each side of the card as well as near the in/out switch for the room. Now, when the room is out, I turn the card to read "YES" — or, conversely, "NO" when the room is in and the safety bars are in place.

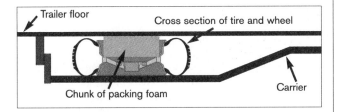

Spare-Tire Restrainer

J O H N   I R W I N ,   A U S T I N ,   T E X A S

▶ Many travel trailers now store the spare tire in a carrier slung just behind the A-frame. These carriers are generally "one size fits all." For some smaller wheel-tire combinations, you will find that the tire can slide around and bounce quite a bit in the carrier. This may ultimately cause the carrier welds to break and the spare tire may drop to the road and cause a driving hazard and it may be run over and/or lost.

I solved this problem by placing a large chunk of salvaged packing foam inside the spare-tire wheel, so that it presses tightly upward against the trailer floor when the carrier is locked in place.

This prevents any unwanted bouncing or sliding of the spare tire in the carrier.

Fire-Extinguisher Storage

F R A N K   W O Y T H A L ,   A N D O V E R ,   N E W   Y O R K

▶ I wanted to supplement the factory-installed fire extinguisher that is mounted at the entry of my motorhome with a larger, easily accessible one. My idea was to mount it behind the driver's seat, just inside that door. I simply fastened an empty metal juice can to the floor with three screws and washers through its bottom. There, it is easy to get at whether I should need it inside or outside the motorhome.

Key Safe & Secure

A R L E N E   C H I A R O L A N Z I O ,
F L O R H A M   P A R K ,   N E W   J E R S E Y

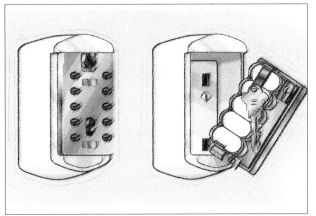

▶ Like many people, I'm afraid of losing or misplacing my keys. I found a simple device that is worth its weight in gold: a push-button key safe that can be mounted anywhere around your RV.

It will safely store two keys and allow for thousands of possible combinations to ensure privacy.

Aside from alleviating the fear of losing a key when participating in outdoor activities, this also provides my family access to our motorhome when coming to visit. I installed the box inside the LP-gas compartment, which, of course, is never locked.

Noodle Soup

WILLIAM HOLTZ SR., BERLIN, MARYLAND

▶ Use your noodle — your swim noodle, that is! After almost losing my TV antenna, I found I needed a reminder to let me know it was still up. I had a small piece of noodle left over from a different project. I cut a lengthwise slit in it and found that it fit on the front edge of the fifth-

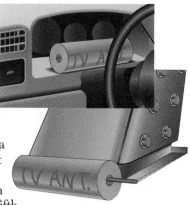

wheel hitch. If I do not unhook the trailer, I place it in the area of the speedometer. Either way, I cannot miss the noodle, and it reminds me that the antenna is up.

Keep 'Em Closed

ESTHER OVESEN, WILTON, IOWA

▶ Due to rough roads, there is always a chance of drawers in the RV coming open, which could seriously damage the sliding mechanism.

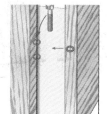

Three small eye screws solved the problem for me. I placed one into the side of the drawer, and put the other two above and below it into the cabinet face.

Now a small bolt dropped through the three eye screws keeps the drawer securely closed.

Pincher Bug

KEVIN DISBRO,
MILROY, INDIANA

▶ The emergency breakaway cable on our fifth-wheel somehow managed to get pinched in the hitch, bringing things to a sudden stop.

To prevent this problem from happening again, I took an old water hose and cut about an 8-inch piece and slid it over the cable to the center, where it touches the bed of the truck.

Since doing this there have been no more sudden stops.

BABY FLAT

During one of our trips, a trucker pulled along side and gave me the air horn and pointed down. I pulled over and, to my horror, found that the rear tire on my trailer had been reduced to a mass of shredded rubber and steel. In addition, the sewer-drain connections were cut off, and there was a large hole in the floor of the bathroom. I had been driving on that flat tire for miles without knowing anything was wrong.

To prevent future problems, I bought a tire monitor for the trailer. However, the manufacturer of the monitor said that the monitor's maximum range was 15 feet.

The distance from the trailer tires to the cab is 42 feet. I put the tire monitor in the trailer's mid-section next to a 900 MHz baby monitor receiver/transmitter. I take the portable receiver to the cab with me, turn the monitors on and am alerted to any loss in tire pressure by an audible beep.

JOHN PETERSEN, BEARSVILLE, NEW YORK

Security Bar

NORMAN BORDO, WARREN, MICHIGAN

▶ Our coach was manufactured with a deadbolt on the central exit door, but no security on the inside for the driver's door. I could not locate a deadbolt and I did not want to drill any holes in the lower part of the driver's door, so I fashioned one out of an oak spar that works just fine and made my wife very happy! Even if the door lock is pried open, the bar would prevent the door from opening. When it is not in use, I store it under my seat.

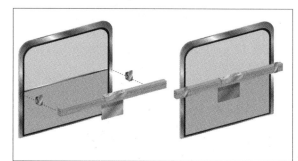

10 minute tech

sanitation

Two More Hose Holders

JOHN TERRELL, GREEN VALLEY, ARIZONA

▶ To keep our sewer hose firmly in place, I purchased a cement paver slab, a machine-threaded eye and hook (long enough to go through the slab) and a 2-foot-or-so length of light chain from our local home-supply store. With a masonry bit, I drilled two holes through the slab and installed the hook in one hole and the eye in the other. Then I attached the chain permanently to the eyebolt. At the campground, I place the slab by the sewer opening and lay the sewer hose on the slab. I put the chain over the hose and slip a link onto the hook. I now have an adjustable weight that will hold the sewer hose in place under any condition.

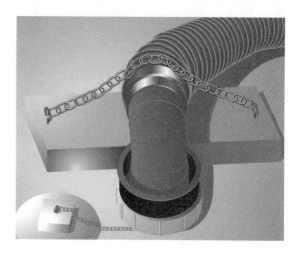

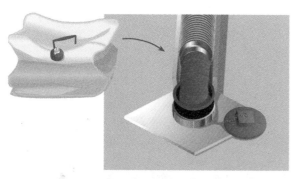

DON FREDRICKSON, BEAR LAKE, MICHIGAN

▶ On our first few RV trips, I found that all parks have different sewer-pipe heights. Putting our 3-inch elbow into a 4-inch sewer pipe never seemed secure; it always wanted to pop out or fall over.

My solution was to buy a 5-gallon collapsible water bag at a camping store. At the campground, I fill the bag about two-thirds full of water and place it over the end fitting of the hose. The bag forms over the elbow, thus distributing the weight evenly. With the cap off, I then press down on the top of the bag to remove the air, and when the water comes to the top, I put the cap on.

When I'm ready to break camp, I pour out the water on the nearest tree, and collapse and store the bag. The neat thing about the water bag is that, unlike a sand bag, I don't have to haul that extra weight down the road.

A Pungent Problem

FRED ROSI, VINELAND, NEW JERSEY

▶ There are few things more embarrassing than having spillage from an accidentally disconnected sewer hose. I know, because it happened to me. To avoid this problem, I made a simple weighted hold-down device. It consists of four 8-ounce fishing weights and a 12-inch piece of plastic-coated electrical wire to hold them together. To use, I just drape the weights over the sewer connection. When I take up the sewer hose, the weights are easy to wash and store. If needed, more weights can be added.

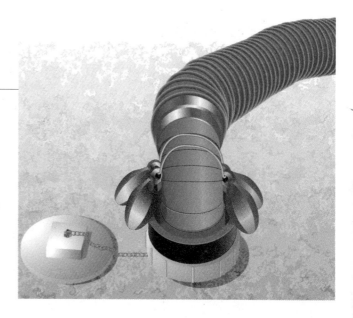

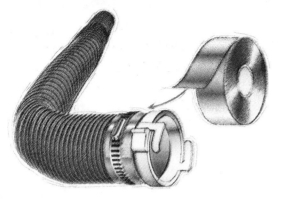

No Leaks Since

KEN RUHLAND, MIDDLETON, WISCONSIN

▶ The sewer hose always leaked near the connection. We unscrewed the metal clamp that secures the connector to the hose. There was a tear in the hose at this location. The metal clamp had worn through the hose material, creating a tear, and thus the leak.

Our solution was to cut off the bad section of the hose (or, depending on the condition of the rest of the hose, replace it). We installed the connector into the hose, wrapped duct tape on the beginning of the hose where the metal clamp would secure the connector, and then reinstalled the metal clamp over the duct-tape area. We've had no leaks since.

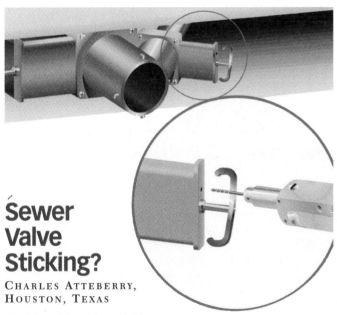

Sewer Valve Sticking?

CHARLES ATTEBERRY, HOUSTON, TEXAS

▶ I found that if you drill a ⅛-inch hole in the front of the sewer valve above the pull handle and use the long plastic tube to spray WD-40 into the hole, it will lubricate the inside of the valve. To close the hole, use a ½-inch-long sheet-metal screw.

BAG THE BOWL

On a recent trip in our motorhome, the toilet bowl seal would not hold water — worse yet, it was allowing odors to come inside. Even with a good cleaning and using petroleum jelly around the seal, the water continued to seep out. Immediate help was needed.

We filled a plastic one-gallon-size freezer bag about ¾ full of water and then placed this freezer bag inside a larger plastic bag. After letting all the water out of the toilet, we placed the plastic bag in the toilet, thereby sealing the drain. When the toilet was needed to be used, the plastic bag was set aside in a plastic bucket until the toilet was flushed, then once again placed in the toilet.

This proved so effective that we continued using the plastic bag until we got home and had time to get the toilet properly repaired!

EARL JENNINGS, BEND, OREGON

SEAL-A-LEAK

I had difficulty finding a durable, yet economical, way to seal a leak coming from a small crack in one of the polyethylene holding tanks in my motorhome. Polyethylene is a thermoplastic; not having a solvent base, the best repair is made by melting the plastic. Though there are kits available to make this repair, not every hardware store stocks them — but then it occurred to me that the plastic adhesive in our common household hot-melt glue gun is polyethylene. I use the clear or slightly opaque glue sticks.

When plastic welding, it is important to ensure that the repair plastic actually gets melted into the object to be repaired. Since our household glue gun does not get hot enough to do that, I helped it along with my electric soldering iron. After cleaning the area to be repaired, I first used the soldering iron to slightly melt the surface of the tank around the crack. Then I applied plastic adhesive, from the hot-melt glue gun, which I thoroughly melted and blended into the holding-tank plastic, using my soldering iron.

The repair sets immediately, once the heat is removed. Since the repair is now part of the tank, it should last indefinitely. If you need more strength from the repair, just place a piece of fiberglass drywall-joint tape or wire mesh into the melted area to be repaired prior to applying the hot-melt glue. If you wish, you can first test this method on a plastic milk container, which is also made of polyethylene.

JOHN BAXTER, SAN DIEGO, CALIFORNIA

sanitation

Reverse Your Thinking

GEORGE DE SHAZER, FRESNO, CALIFORNIA

▶ Carrying the drain hose, plus the right amount of spares, took up a lot of valuable storage space. I had a large plastic bin used for just this purpose. As many of my fellow campers have done, I experimented with using a large PVC pipe to contain the hoses, but the inside diameter wouldn't accommodate the end fittings.

It finally dawned on me that the hose didn't have to go into the pipe, the pipe could go into the hose! For a couple of bucks I bought a 10-foot-long, 2-inch-diameter PVC pipe. I drilled a ¼-inch hole through both sides and at both ends of the pipe. I slipped the hose over the pipe and inserted an eyebolt in each end, which keeps the hose from slipping off. I fastened a pair of hooks on the side wall (or ceiling) of my storage compartment and hang the eyebolts on them.

It worked so well that I bought longer eyebolts and put a second hose under the first, completely eliminating loose sewer hoses in bins and using space that was previously wasted.

Store It ... but Where?

PAUL SHIPLEY, CROSSVILLE, TENNESSEE

▶ Here's how to store a 20-foot sewer hose and a 3-inch funnel in an unusual place ... on the LP-gas cylinder platform!

At the front of the platform, between the LP-gas cylinders, drill a ¼-inch hole. Cut a ¼-inch threaded rod a few inches longer than the length of a fully compressed 20-foot sewer hose. Insert the rod into the hole and fasten with a nut and washer above and below the platform.

Place the hose over the rod and then slide the funnel, pointed end down, over the rod and down against the sewer hose. Secure with a large ¼-inch washer and wing nut.

You might also want to cut a piece of scrap PVC plastic water pipe to fit over the threaded rod. Make the pipe long enough to protect the inside of the sewer hose from abrasion damage when it contacts the pipe threads, but short enough to allow the funnel to compress and secure the hose.

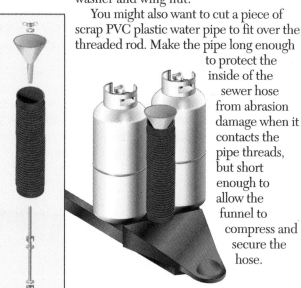

Replace the Wheels

JOHN SPEAR, VIA E-MAIL

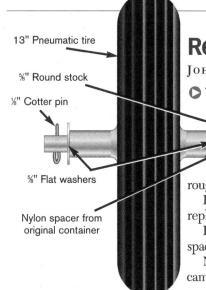

13" Pneumatic tire

⅝" Round stock

⅛" Cotter pin

⅝" Flat washers

Nylon spacer from original container

▶ When camping where there are no sewer connections, one of the few options available is to use a portable dump tank and haul it to the nearest dump station. As almost everyone knows, the blue container comes with small, loud plastic wheels that seem to allow for limited ground clearance. You have to be very careful when moving the container over rough or dirt terrain, or you could have quite a mess on your hands.

I have solved this problem somewhat by removing the existing wheels and replacing them with 13-inch pneumatic wheelbarrow tires.

First, I used ⅝-inch solid round stock to replace the existing axle. I used the wheel spacers from the original axle to keep the new wheels off the tank.

Now when the holding tanks need dumping, I can haul the dump tank through the campground much more easily.

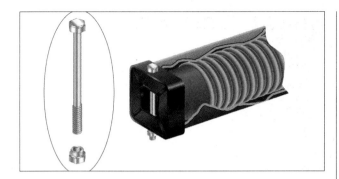

They Stole My Hose!

STANLEY FREDERICK, TUCSON, ARIZONA

▶ Imagine after a period of camping, pulling up to the dump station and finding that someone has stolen your sewer hose.

After replacing the hose, my thoughts turned to preventive measures. My solution was to pass two ⁵⁄₁₆ × 4⅜-inch bolts through the existing holes in the bumper, down through holes that I drilled in the rubber end plugs. I secured them using acorn nuts with nylon lock-washer inserts.

The nylon inserts hold the nuts tight enough so wrenches must be used to get the bolts out, yet the nuts don't have to be snugged up against the bumper.

This system is not foolproof; however it does make it harder for would-be thieves to get to the sewer hose. Of course, I do have to get out the wrenches every time I want to use the sewer hose, but at least it is there every time I need it.

Pleasing Portable

TIM STAATS, MILWAUKEE, WISCONSIN

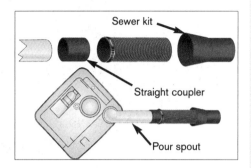

Sewer kit

Straight coupler

Pour spout

▶ Like many campers who pull a pop-up trailer, I carry a portable toilet. I'm very pleased with this method, but dumping can be a problem, especially if I'm not near an outhouse.

Most campgrounds forbid dumping portable toilets in a flush toilet. Regular RV dump stations are also unsuitable because the liquid starts pouring from the unit before the short built-in pour spout can be inserted into the sewer drain.

The simple solution was to construct an 18-inch sewer hose. My RV dealer gave me a section of sewer hose, and I bought a straight sewer coupler for one end of the hose from Camping World. Its diameter is a perfect fit to slide over the portable toilet's pour spout. On the other end, I installed a funnel-shaped connector to fit into the drain hole of the RV dump stations.

I can now use the regular RV dump stations found everywhere. Additionally, I have found that using the short hose allows for faster, cleaner and more-convenient dumping than using campground outhouses.

DOPE HEAD

After 10 years of faithful service, my RV's toilet began to leak water. A short time after using the toilet, the water would pass around the flush trap and through the rubber groove.

I bought a small tube of pliable, plumbing pipe-thread dope. It's non-hardening and it remains flexible.

While holding the flush trap open, I dried the area thoroughly to ensure a better bond. I then pressed the pipe-thread dope into the rubber groove. This makes a tight seal for the flush trap.

One application should last the entire camping season. The best permanent fix is replacing the seal, of course, but the pipe dope works in a pinch, too.

BILL DYE, MIDWEST CITY, OKLAHOMA

FINAL DRAIN VALVE

Our fifth-wheel has three separate waste tanks with valves plumbed to one drain-line outlet. After we had towed the trailer, a couple of pints of liquid would leak in the lines to the drain-cap area. When opening the cap, I tried to catch this liquid in a bucket. What a mess!

My cure was to install a final drain valve. With a hacksaw, I removed the end of the dump pipe (with the notches that accept the bayonet hose adapter) about 1 inch from the end. I then installed a 3-inch slide valve (available from any RV-parts supplier), and then reattached the hose adapter and cap. It was a 20-minute job for about $10. No more mess or drips.

Be sure to use the correct ABS plastic cement for black drain pipe when assembling, and make sure you have the additional room necessary to make such a modification.

RICHARD WIEBE, MESQUITE, NEVADA

sanitation

Stop, Thief!

BUDDY HATCHER,
SHREVEPORT, LOUISIANA

◯ After losing my sewer hose twice, once to theft and once due to the rubber bumper cap falling off, I came up with this idea.

I cut a small slot out of each opposing side of my rubber bumper cap. I then replaced the cap with the slots aligned with the existing holes in the bumper. I then inserted a long shank lock (sometimes called a bicycle lock) through the bumper. These locks are available at hardware stores.

The process was repeated at the other end of the bumper. This completely prevents the removal of the hose by accident or theft.

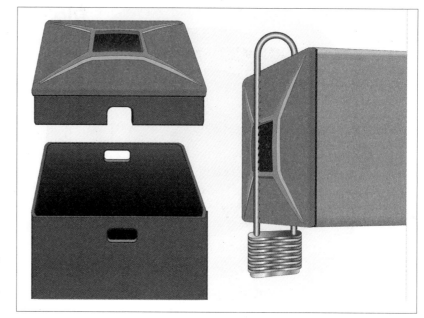

Abracadabra

EDDIE KNIGHT,
GREEN COVE SPRINGS,
FLORIDA

◯ Over time, all kinds of "stuff" collects on the inside walls of the black-water tank. This creates sanitation problems and gives false readings on the monitor.

An easy-to-make, affordable pressure-wash "magic wand" can cure this.

Using ¾-inch PVC pipe, cut a piece long enough to go from at least 6 inches above the toilet to the bottom of the black tank. On the top end, glue a 90-degree elbow, a short nipple, a shut-off valve and a female garden-hose adapter.

At the bottom end of the wand, glue a PVC cap. Since the tank has four sides, drill four ³⁄₁₆-inch holes at the 12-, 3-, 6- and 9 o'clock positions, about one or two inches from the bottom of the pipe.

Next, drill a hole in the middle of the cap. You might have to come up with your own size of the holes, depending on your water pressure.

I recommend cutting the pipe longer than you might consider necessary, so you can cut, recap and redrill if necessary to achieve a more desirable water pressure.

Make sure the tank is empty and hook a garden hose to the wand. With the RV water pump off, open the toilet-flush flap and carefully inset the wand until it reaches the bottom of the tank. Open the PVC valve and move the wand up and down in a rotating motion for several minutes and then empty the tank.

Do this several times and you will be surprised at how much unwanted material will be removed, leaving a fresh tank and more accurate monitor readings.

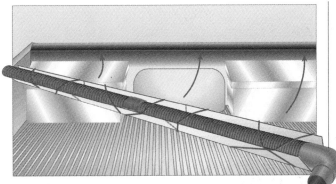

Always in the Way

G.L. BLANCETT, LIVINGSTON, TEXAS

▶ We are full-timers and move quite often, so I carry several sewer hoses to accommodate all the different campground layouts. I carried them in the back of the pickup and they were always in the way and getting holes punched in them.

My solution was to buy a 10-foot rain gutter and cut it to fit in the bed of the truck over the wheel well. Now I just lay the hose in the gutter, and crisscrossed bungee cords keep it in place. This keeps them out of the way and looks far better than before.

Got Leaks?

BO BOHMAN, LANCASTER, CALIFORNIA

▶ Tired of that leaky sewer dump valve causing a nasty surprise and a messed-up compartment every time you remove the sewer valve cap?

Until you can have the valve replaced, try this: From any store selling garden hose, buy a hose shut-off valve and screw it on to the hose connection of the motorhome's sewer-dump-valve cap. Caps thus equipped can be purchased at your local RV parts supplier.

Now, when ready to connect the sewer hose, just open this new shut-off valve and drain any accumulated liquid into a can. No more mess!

Mold Prevention

JOHN DONAHUE, CHULA VISTA, CALIFORNIA

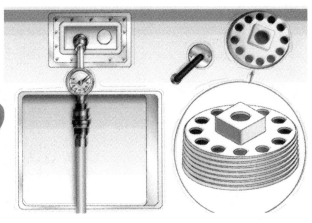

▶ The storage area provided for our RV's sewer hose is located inside a 5-inch-diameter PVC pipe, with a PVC pipe cap to retain the hose inside the pipe. It works fine — except returning the wet hose to its enclosed storage can create a breeding environment for all sorts of germs, to say nothing of mold. To minimize this, I drilled 12 holes, each ⅝-inch diameter, along the outside front of the cap, then added a one-inch-diameter hole in the cap center. This simple fix keeps our sewer hose secure in its storage area, while allowing it to dry out.

Vermin Veil

MARVIN BRYANT, LITTLETON, COLORADO

▶ When my RV is not being used, I have found it advantageous to leave the sewer open and the cover off to allow the tanks to be vented. I was concerned about insects or whatever getting in the tank.

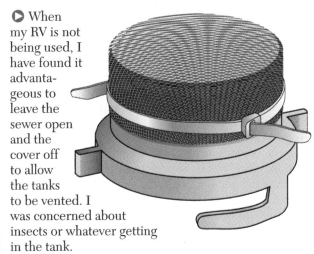

Using a couple of cable tie wraps, or a hose clamp, I fastened a small piece of screen to an extra sewer hose connector and this has worked out great.

Crimp It

GERALD VOGEL, ONTARIO, CALIFORNIA

▶ I kept losing the sewer-hose restraint caps on the end of my rear bumper until I came up with this idea.

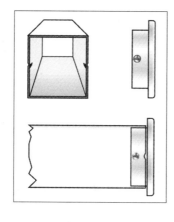

I put sheet-metal screws on opposite sides of the cap, as near the outside edge as possible. With a pair of pliers, I crimped (or bent) the sides of the bumper inward between ⅛ and ³⁄₁₆ inch on opposite sides of the bumper.

Push the cap with the screw heads past the crimps, and the cap stays firmly in place.

Smooth Sliding

FRANK MARELLI, LIVINGSTON, TEXAS

▶ My sewer hose was being destroyed by the rust and rough bottom surface of my bumper storage. I simply cut a piece of 3-inch plastic "lawn and shrub edging" the length of the bumper and slid it into the bumper. Now the sewer hose slides on the smooth plastic liner. Problem solved.

Rinse That Tank

FRANK WOYTHAL, ANDOVER, NEW YORK

▶ This is a method I've been using to access my motorhome's bathroom when I want to rinse the black-water tank. It's simply a straight section of a gasoline-tank filler neck and a locking gas cap.

First, determine a location in the bathroom, and confirm the location on the exterior wall. Check to be sure that there are no pipes, wires or other obstructions in this wall section. It may be tricky, but you also need to avoid any structural framing members in the wall; a local RV-repair facility might be able to help determine where these are before you cut. Then, cover the locations with masking tape to protect the surfaces before going to work with a hole saw, a drill bit and/or a sabre saw. The flange of the filler neck already has holes or small screws to secure the tube to the wall. Run a bead of silicone around the flange to seal it to the wall.

This method allows me to insert the cleaning wand, shutoff valve and hose without going through the door and dragging the hose assembly through the living space.

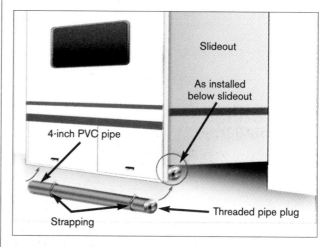

Black Hose Down

BILL WRIGHT, SAN JOSE, CALIFORNIA

▶ Need another location for storing longer lengths of sewer hose? PVC pipe works, but there are only so many places you can stash a sizable length of pipe. Fortunately, many motorhomes include storage bays below their slideouts — which offer ample space to mount a 4-inch-diameter PVC pipe (with end-fittings). Check for clearance and, using metal strapping, fasten the pipe of the desired length to the floor of the bay. Make sure that the screws will not hit anything critical, and remember to seal all holes with silicone sealer. I used black PVC, and it is hardly noticeable.

A Hose by Any Other Name ...

EARL ROGERS,
FORT WAYNE, INDIANA

▶ My fifth-wheel came with enclosed storage for a single 10-foot sewer hose. At many parks, this is not long enough. I needed a way to store the additional hose so that it was not in the way, but that allowed it to dry properly.

I found the solution in 4-inch plastic drain tubing. This tubing is normally buried in the ground and used to drain water away from buildings. It can be purchased with slots cut into the tubing at intervals, and a cap is available to close the end of the tubing. The slots allow air to circulate, keeping the hose dry.

I used long plastic ties to fasten the tubing to the front legs of my fifth-wheel, inside the storage area. The tubing is made with ridges, which makes it flexible, so it readily bends to fit the available area.

I cut an 8-foot piece in two sections and fastened them to the legs, and I now carry two additional 10-foot sewer hoses.

Sewer Hose Support

HARVEY HETRICK, TORRANCE, CALIFORNIA

▶ On a recent trip to the hardware store, I purchased two 10-foot lengths of vinyl rain gutter and eight nylon

bolts and butterfly nuts. I cut the 10-foot sections in half, leaving four 5-foot sections. They nicely telescope inside each other. I drilled holes every 3 inches along the top edges of all sections. I can use any length of gutter from 5 feet to about 20 feet by adjusting the sections inside each other and fastening with the nylon nuts and bolts.

The end of the gutter assembly, under the motorhome, is held up by a bent metal strap through the bolt holes on the end and passed up through the sewer-hose opening in the floor of the hose compartment. The standard sewer hose fits snugly inside the rain gutter and stays in place with no hassle.

Meanwhile, Back at the Toilet

CHARLES GILBERT, JOHNSTOWN, PENNSYLVANIA

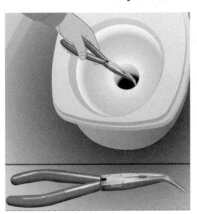

▶ It seems the most common cause for the water to leak out of the RV toilet is paper caught in the sliding valve. The toilet paper collects near the pivot pin, around the outer rim.

A pair of 90-degree needle-nose pliers is the perfect tool to remove the paper without taking the toilet apart. Turn the water off, depress the pedal to hold the valve open, and remove the paper. You don't even have to touch the inside of the toilet.

Another Sewer Idea

MARCEL DeWULF, LAKE BLUFF, ILLINOIS

▶ To hold the sewer-hose discharge elbow securely in place when dumping and to eliminate scrambling from the dump valve to the hose elbow, I filled an old stretched-out sweat sock with pebbles and tied the end with wire. I then pulled the other sock over the first one, but in the opposite direction, and again secured the end. (A sturdy canvas bean bag or shot bag would be an upgrade.) Rocks, boards and hole covers do not conform to the hose, but this bag works like a charm.

He Used to Lash

HARRIET LUCE, JOLIET, ILLINOIS

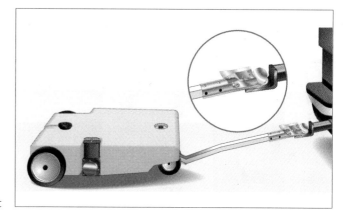

▶ When it was time to empty our four-wheeled black-water tote tank, my husband used to lash it to the truck's trailer hitch with straps. Last summer, on our way to the dump station with a full tank, it came off the hitch and very nearly went through someone's campsite.

He went to the parts store and bought a 1⅞-inch coupler, and then cut off the loop on the end of the tote handle. The coupler was then bolted on the end of the handle.

Now we can make the trip to the dump station without a side trip through someone's campsite.

10 minute tech

storage

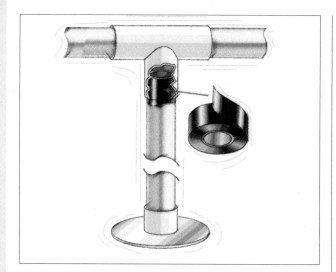

A Weighty Situation

MALCOLM GRAY, CINCINNATI, OHIO

▶ Like many folks, we are full-timers living in a coach not really designed for full-time living. Our closet pole was marginal at best, barely able to handle the load we placed on it. We solved the problem by purchasing a more substantial one-inch-diameter steel pole to replace the original, reinstalling the support cups with additional screws.

We then fabricated a floor-to-pole center support using materials from the hardware store. We cut this second pole to the appropriate length and slipped the upper end into a one-inch inside-diameter plastic T, which was slipped onto the closet rod before installation in the closet. (A little electrical tape will shim up a loose fit.) Some filing inside the T was needed to allow it to slip over the closet pole.

The lower end of the vertical pole was capped with a plastic foot designed for this purpose, while the closet floor was protected by resting the capped rod on a round steel electrical box cover to distribute the weight over a larger area.

Handy Hang-Ups

ROBERT SORENSEN, MAPLEWOOD, MINNESOTA

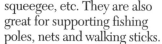

▶ To organize our motorhome storage space, I attached broom clips to the ceiling of the basement compartments to hold our broom, wash brush, squeegee, etc. They are also great for supporting fishing poles, nets and walking sticks.

The entryway steps inside our motorhome have grooved rubber treads and need to be swept often. I attached a broom clip on the wall just inside the door (near the floor) to secure a small whisk broom.

I also put hook-and-loop fastening on the lower wall to hold a flashlight. That keeps everything off the floor, but handy.

NELDA SEIVER, PORT ARTHUR, TEXAS

▶ When it's raining and the RV awning is extended, use a removable suction-cup hook on the outside of the coach to hang up a wet umbrella. This keeps it handy when needed, and the dripping umbrella doesn't have to be taken into the coach. If the awning is not extended, place the suction-cup hook in the shower enclosure, so the wet umbrella will drip into the tub.

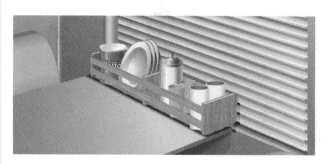

An Ex CD Holder

BARBARA DOUGHERTY, POWELL, TENNESSEE

▶ When I saw this inexpensive CD holder at a flea market, I knew it was just the thing to use for storage on my dinette table. I store paper plates and napkins, eating utensils, a sugar bowl, salt and pepper shakers and many other little things that get mislaid during moves. I put strips of nonskid material underneath to keep it in place while on the road.

A Galley Shelf

BOB BINGHAM, SANGER, CALIFORNIA

▶ Like most motorhomers, we needed additional counter space around our galley sink. To provide this space, I built a three-tier removable shelf that fits over the back part of the sink. It has three shelves and two cubbyholes to store brushes and so forth. The outside shelves are about 5 inches above the sink, and the center shelf is about 5 inches

higher to provide space to use the faucet. The exact dimensions will vary, depending on the available space in each motorhome. I used ¾-inch oak-veneered plywood, but other woods may be used and stained or painted to match the existing cupboards. When traveling, the shelf can be stored under the table or in another handy area.

A Simple Solution

RICK ZELLER, COVINGTON, LOUISIANA

▶ We never seemed to have enough closet space for the shoes we carry in our motorhome. To provide additional space, I purchased a hanging cloth storage bag with pouches to accommodate 12 pairs of shoes, and cut it in half to fit into our closet space. Hanging one of the two sections on each side of the closet not only organized the shoes, but it also freed the shelf space we had used for shoe storage. The pouches also could be used to store a curling iron, a hair dryer and/or other small objects.

Bend Me, Shape Me, Fold Me Over

DELLA WAYNICK, WARREN, MICHIGAN

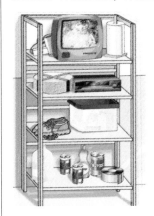

▶ As you know, we ladies never have enough counter space — which can be a problem in a motorhome. Since our coach has a slideout, we added folding shelving to the wall. When the slide is extended, we have extra shelves; when we're traveling, the folded shelves fit between the wall and the retracted slide. I found the shelving at Target, for just $29.99!

Blank-Wall Storage

BETTY CHAPMAN, VIDOR, TEXAS

▶ Here's an attractive solution to the need for additional storage in motorhomes that have a blank wall when the slideout is open.

Use a three-drawer plastic cabinet that can be purchased at most discount stores. Top it with a circular board (available at many hardware and home-center stores), and then drape it with a round tablecloth.

When traveling, the top is taken off and stored and the cabinet is placed out of the way, wherever there is room.

EVERY PICTURE TELLS A STORY

My "better half" was looking for a certain item she knew was in an outside compartment, but by the time she found it she had searched through every compartment.

So, she asked me to make a list of what is in each compartment. She only asked for a written list, but I think a picture is worth a thousand words — so I photographed every compartment and, utilizing my computer and a drawing program, created a diagram of the compartments and then listed all the items in each.

The diagram is displayed on the inside of a cupboard, easily viewed when needed.

HARVEY HETRICK, TORRANCE, CALIFORNIA

FLAT AND STACK

As a full-timer, I know how important it is to get as much space out of your freezer as possible. One way I do this is by stacking. When I buy a five-pound package of ground beef, I slice it into five equal slices and then put each into a freezer bag. Then I flatten each bag before sealing, and I am able to stack them on the freezer shelf with no problem.

PAT PULLUM, ROGERS, ARKANSAS

HANG IN THERE

We found that our diesel motorhome has a lot of space in the front of the coach, above the AC generator. Even better, the area has two support brackets above the AC generator. We've found that the brackets are perfect for storing all sorts of needed equipment — including a 6-foot folding ladder, three sewer-hose supports, our telescoping window squeegee and (being an amateur artist) a folding easel.

Each item is secured by bungee cords to both the braces and the item lying beneath or beside it.

Your coach probably has similar space by the AC generator; if you don't have the metal support brackets, it's a small matter to attach a pair of them to either end of the firewall. Items stored there must be able to handle the heat.

CHRISTINE DAVIS, MADISON, WISCONSIN

RECYCLE JARS

To make the most of the limited space in my RV refrigerator, I recycle jars that fit in the refrigerator door shelves. I transfer various food items into them, rather than filling the main refrigerator shelves. Between uses, I wash the jars and store them and their lids in a designated spot in the refrigerator door.

COLEEN SYKORA,
RAPID CITY, SOUTH DAKOTA

Better Storage

LEONE TEEL, LIVINGSTON, TEXAS

⬤ Our new motorhome has lots of basement storage space, but one compartment is only 26 inches deep. As an alternative to using stackable storage tubs, I inserted in our basement bin two off-the-shelf 21 × 21 × 21-inch wire-basket frames, available in the shelving section of home-improvement stores.

Each frame can hold from one to four sliding baskets. For one frame, I chose 7-inch and 11-inch-deep wire baskets. The other frame holds two 7-inch-deep baskets and one 3-inch-deep basket. All baskets are 20 inches square. The basement bin measured 46 × 23 × 26 inches, and this storage-frame setup leaves me with room on the side, top and rear for more seasonal items. Now I can find and access my stored items quickly and with much greater ease.

Utilizing Storage Space

NEIL JOHNSON, PENSACOLA, FLORIDA

⬤ Being full-timers, my wife and I try to utilize every bit of available storage space in our motorhome. For bedroom bureaus, we each have a cabinet 22 inches wide, 27 inches high and 9 inches deep. Each is divided horizontally by one shelf.

To make the area more useful, we built cubbyhole partitions using ¼-inch-thick Fome-Cor (which can be found at RV supply stores and arts-and-crafts stores). Once we determined the sizes of the various cubbyholes and cut the Fome-Cor board to size, the partitions were glued together (and to a vertical backboard for strength) using a hot-glue gun. After 18 months of use, the partitions show little wear.

storage

Handy Storage Shelf

LADDIE LeBLOND, BELMONT, MICHIGAN

◐ There is a lack of storage space in my motorhome for all the videotapes, campground directories, tour books and related publications I want close at hand, but not in the way.

I made a handy storage shelf that fits against the wall under the dinette. I cut a piece of plywood 8 inches wide and exactly as long as the width of the dinette table, so it fits on the tabletop supports that are used to make it into a bed. To keep the books from sliding off, I fastened to the front edge a strip of molding a couple of inches shorter, so it doesn't rub against the seat cushions.

A road test revealed that the shelf assembly tended to slide away from the wall. That was resolved by drilling a small vertical hole in the support on each side and using a cut-off nail as a retaining pin. On the rare occasions when we need to convert the dinette into a bed, the shelf assembly can be quickly removed.

Card Table Storage

EDWARD LYCHWALA, WARE, MASSACHUSETTS

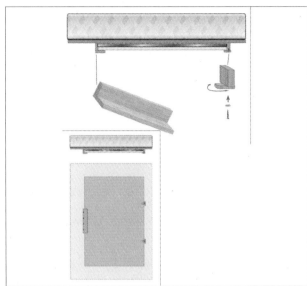

◐ We take a folding card table with us on trips. We used to store the table under our bed with everything else packed on top of it — meaning we had to unpack half of the rig every time we needed the table. Then we tried packing everything else first and putting the table on top — which meant we had to remove the table every time we needed to get to the other items.

To solve these problems, we now hang the table from the underside of the bed platform using a few scraps of hardwood, glue and screws.

Small Motorhomes & Square Bumpers

BERNARD OSTERBERGER, NILES, ILLINOIS

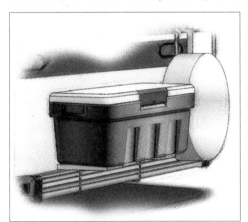

◐ For those of us with small motorhomes and square bumpers, I found a great solution for extra storage of lightweight items. It's the Rubbermaid Action Packer, available in 25-, 35- and 50-gallon sizes. All packers are lightweight and lockable.

U-bolts attach two 2 × 6 × 19-inch pieces of treated lumber to the bumper. The Action Packer is screwed to the lumber, using several 2-inch deck screws with wide fender washers, through two 1 × 4 × 16-inch boards on the inside bottom of the container.

When mounting the container on the bumper, be sure to leave enough room for the lid to open, and do not cover the license plate. If necessary, just move the license plate and bracket to another location.

Because of the leverage and twisting action of this kind of mount, the container should be used for storing lightweight items only; no bowling-ball or river-rock collections.

MORE STORAGE SPACE

My husband, Reid, and I, along with our two cats, travel in a 27-foot trailer. After our last trip, I came up with an idea to give us more storage space.

Since we do not use the hide-a-bed, I asked Reid to remove it and build in a storage chest. He found the assembly quite easy to take out. He built a box 47 inches long, 27 inches high and 10 inches deep, with a hinged top to open up under the seat cushions. It makes a wonderful storage chest.

We kept the hide-a-bed assembly in the event we ever sell the trailer and the buyers prefer the bed. This alteration does not change the sofa's appearance, and it's much more comfortable to sit on.

PATRICIA JACOB, BELLVUE, COLORADO

PERFECT PANTRY

We have bench-type dinette seats in our motorhome. The space under the benches was just a deep, narrow area that made reaching/finding anything a real problem. On the other hand, this seemed like the ideal space to store canned goods.

I found a large plastic container, about 8 inches high (shorter than the height of the access door), and a couple of feet long. It slides out just like a drawer – and makes a perfect pantry!

PATSY JOHNSON,
RED LAKE FALLS, MINNESOTA

SKEWER STORAGE

In the process of transferring supplies from our old RV to the new beauty, storage of the well used – but indispensable – marshmallow-roasting skewers arose.

Seeking to keep things clean and tidy, I hit upon storing the skewers in a mailing tube (available at any office-supply store). The tubes are available in a variety of sizes and have removable caps, which can be taped at either end if needed.

RALPH MARTINEZ, ARCADIA, CALIFORNIA

Editor's note: *Do you think the marshmallow skewers would mind if we stored the shish-kabob skewers in the tube with them?*

SURF'S UP!

I have a ¾-ton truck that pulls a fifth-wheel. I also own a folding boat, and wanted to carry it on the top of the truck. Metal supports for rooftops cost more than $200, so I devised a cheaper solution.

I found a soft-top carrier made by Sun Rise that is used by surfers to carry their boards. These cost about $35 and work great. They can be purchased at surf shops or on the Internet.

GEORGE FIPP, JACKSONVILLE, FLORIDA

A Place for Everything & Everything in Its Place

HORACE SEARCIE, CINCINNATI, OHIO

▶ When living in tight quarters, storage is anywhere you can find it. The most underused areas tend to be the backs of cabinet doors, which can be easily converted into storage for a hair dryer, a curling iron, etc.

Using small screw-in hardware hooks, make a hook rack (like the type for hanging keys), and attach it to the chosen door. For items that have no loop for hanging, a plastic cable tie can be fastened to the object (or its cord). Of course, a small wire tray can be attached to the door bottom for bottles, brushes, etc.

Extra Storage

ROBERT LADD, NIPOMO, CALIFORNIA

▶ For trips where extra enclosed storage may be needed, purchase appropriate-sized plastic storage containers, the kind with lids and latches, available at all of the mass merchandisers. Position them in the bed of your pickup and mount them on long strips of wood such as pressure-treated 1 × 4s or 2 × 4s. Short screws with washers attach the storage containers to the wood. The containers are held in place and there is a means for air circulation. When not needed, the whole assembly lifts out easily.

More "Found" Storage

MARY WAGNER, LIVINGSTON, TEXAS

▶ Storage space is always at a premium in a motorhome, and some items are particularly hard to stow and retrieve. I found that the space above the edge of the slide-out storage tray in one of the basement-storage bays was just the right size for one of the PVC tubes I use to store a sewer hose.

I fastened it to the wall just high enough to clear the sliding tray. In it we store fishing rods, the long handles for washing tools and parts for a weaving loom.

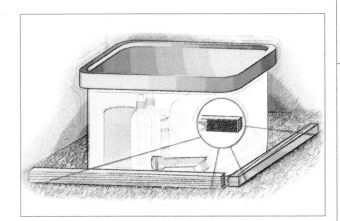

Slip-Sliding Away

MARY CORSARO, WALDORF, MARYLAND

▶ Items moving around in our storage compartments quickly became an irritation when traveling, but permanent partitioning isn't practical since the items stored change with every trip. Our solution was to cut a few pieces of 1 × 2-inch lumber into bars about 2 feet long. Along one side of the wooden strips we added several lengths of the "hook" portion of hook-and-loop fasteners; for longevity's sake, we secured the fasteners with a few staples to keep the material in place. When these bars are pressed hook-side-down against the carpet in the storage compartment, they provide enough grip to keep even heavy items from sliding.

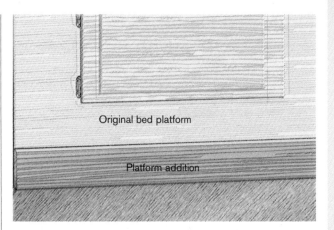

Original bed platform

Platform addition

Pedestal Bed Storage

FRANK WOYTHAL, ANDOVER, NEW YORK

▶ To create more storage space under the bed in our motorhome, I simply unscrewed the bed platform from the carpeted floor and slid an additional frame of stained and varnished 2 × 6-inch boards (on edge) under it. I then screwed the existing structure to the top of the new frame and secured the new support to the floor using angle brackets.

Out of Sight

ARLENE CHIAROLANZIO,
FLORHAM PARK, NEW JERSEY

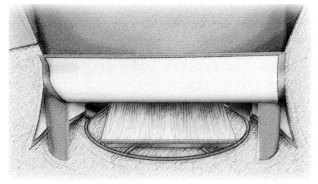

▶ Our recliner chair has a chair skirt that conceals anything beneath it, and it's next to the door.

This combination means that we tend to stuff everything from outdoor shoes to the dog's brush beneath it. The problem is, the chair can move, so we cut a piece of plywood to fit onto the circular steel base of the chair, turning the area beneath it into a "shelf." Now, anything placed beneath it is secure even when the chair is moved.

storage

No More Digging

HERBERT SUTTON, SUN CITY WEST, ARIZONA

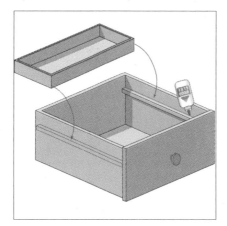

▶ My RV has several large drawers that are in convenient locations. The problem is that small items always settle to the bottom, making it a nuisance to retrieve them.

This nuisance was cured by installing strips inside the drawers on either side. I constructed trays from scraps of wood to fit on top of the strips. The trays slide back and forth for access, and can be lifted out if needed. All the parts were assembled using carpenter's glue. When the glue was cured, I finished the pieces to match the original drawers.

Rubber-Glove Storage

RICHARD DUCCI, LITCHFIELD, CONNECTICUT

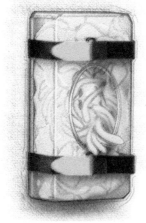

▶ While attempting to find a convenient storage method for disposable rubber or vinyl gloves used for refueling or emptying holding tanks, I noticed that the box of gloves was almost identical in size to a standard tissue box.

A tissue dispenser with a snap-off bottom was purchased, and the snap-off base was attached to a vertical surface inside a storage compartment, along with two hook-and-loop straps.

The box of gloves was carefully cut open and the contents placed in the dispenser box. It was snapped together and the straps secured. Some glove boxes are exactly the same size as the tissue dispenser, and glove removal is not necessary; simply place box and all into the dispenser. Gloves are now always handy.

Round Cans in Square Holes

CURTIS NODOLF, JANESVILLE, WISCONSIN

▶ I tend to stock cans of soda, water bottles, etc., in excess of what could be accommodated in the refrigerator, in a cardboard box in my basement storage. Once I started removing items from the carton, however, the remaining cans and bottles rolled around the box.

To prevent this, I purchased an old wooden soda case (with 24 compartments) from an antique dealer. I fill each compartment with individual cans and bottles — and they are held in place during travel.

Be careful what you buy; some of the old wooden cases will not accept a soda can without modification (the individual compartments were originally sized for glass bottles, which were smaller than present-day cans). If that proves to be a problem, just round out the square compartments.

Oak-y Dokey

JUANITA DOBBS, CLARKSVILLE, ARKANSAS

▶ Our fifth-wheel trailer features a storage ledge that's useless while we're on the road. To make it functional, we attached a length of decorative oak rail — available at any home remodeling and supply center — to the edges and then added simple baskets from a crafts store to hold small items. Now the ledge looks great and the baskets are useful for easy-access storage.

storage

Laundry Storage

PHILLIP CRONK, NAMPA, INDIANA

▶ Here is our alternative to storing dirty laundry in the shower. The bedroom in our RV has an island bed with walking space at the foot and sides. At one of the corners, I was able to install a clothes hamper without restricting passage around the corner of the bed.

Using 1 × 4-inch boards, I built a 48 × 18-inch frame. I made the frame as high as I could, allowing a 12-inch space below the overhead cabinets. Enough space was left at the bottom to allow the trap door to fully swing down. The two side boards were beveled where they meet the walls.

To allow air circulation, I covered the inside of the frame with a piece of decorative perforated aluminum sheeting available at hardware stores and home centers. I also matched the cabinet hardware in our RV.

Since these sheets are available only in 36 × 36-inch size, I put a brace across at about the 34-inch mark where the upper and lower pieces would meet, attaching them to the frame with a staple gun.

For the bottom trap door, I used a piece of ½-inch plywood cut to shape. A brass chest-type-catch holds the trap door closed. The wood was stained to match the rest of the woodwork and given two coats of varnish.

The finished frame was installed with six brass wood screws and plastic wall anchors.

Level That Crate

BILL JONES, SALOME, ARIZONA

▶ Plastic office crates, designed for hanging files, make a good way to organize the "stuff" that tends to accumulate in the back of an extended-cab pick-up. However, the rear floor of the vehicle often is not level and cannot firmly support a file crate.

The solution is to use storage boxes that can be leveled. I found a brand of box called a Space Crate at Staples, the nationwide office-supply chain. The crate is designed for stacking and uses hollow legs at each corner. By using wooden dowels, plastic tips, furniture coasters and some small screws, the box can be fitted to be level on the floor of your vehicle.

After cutting the dowels to the required lengths (long enough to reach from the bottom of the crate to the truck floor), install the plastic tips. Then insert the dowels into the holes in the bottom of the crate. A little masking tape wrapped around the dowel rod will provide a snug fit if the diameter is slightly small.

Next, install the coaster after having first drilled a pilot hole in the dowel and a clearance hole in the coaster. Screw the coaster loosely onto the dowel to allow for any minor adjustment on your truck floor. The teeth on the coaster will settle into the carpet on your vehicle, keeping the box firmly in place when loaded.

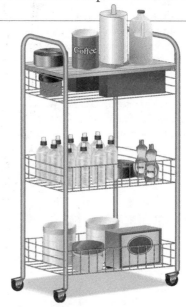

Cart Sharp

JUDY BRENHOLT, CUSHING, WISCONSIN

▶ I needed additional space in my RV, so I bought a small utility cart at Wal-Mart. The spare cutting board from my sink fits perfectly between the top handles, providing additional space. The baskets below it provide additional storage.

It is lightweight and easily moved, and the baskets keep things contained while I'm on the road.

HARDWARE ON THE MOVE

Because there is always a need for a nut, bolt, nail, screw or washer while on the road, we carry a hardware case when we travel. It is a collection of peanut-butter jars filled with an assortment of "stuff." The contents are written on each lid. We use a retired suitcase to hold this collection of "stuff."

FRED HIGGINS,
STERLING HEIGHTS, MICHIGAN

IT'S IN THE BAG

To end some of the clutter in our motorhome's basement compartment (that houses our electrical and water connections), I purchased some plain cotton tote bags. These bags are very inexpensive and are found readily in the crafts section of large department stores and fabric stores.

The bags come in varying sizes. I use two of the largest bags to contain my 30-amp and 50-amp extension cords. A medium-size bag contains the water hose, while smaller, separate bags contain the TV cable and phone lines.

We mark each of the bags with permanent marker so we can tell at a glance which bag contains what item. With the items stored this way, I don't have to separate and re-coil items that I don't need to set up camp.

NEIL JOHNSON,
PENSACOLA, FLORIDA

LURES FOR LADIES

Lightweight clear-plastic fishing-lure boxes were the answer to my earring-storage and organizational problems.

Some boxes are no bigger than a paperback book. They are all compartmentalized to isolate pairs of earrings, (or any small items) and I can see at a glance what's in them. The lids snap securely so that they can be stored at any angle without spillage. Even when full, they weigh only a fraction of a traditional wooden box.

You can find these multi-use fishing-lure boxes in any store's camping/fishing section.

RITA DANIELS, SUNDANCE, WYOMING

Editor's note: *Similar boxes are found at hardware stores, where they are used to store small items.*

Behind Bars

MAGGIE CHAMBERLAIN,
WOODLAND PARK, COLORADO

▶ I was having problems with items falling off the shelf above the closet bar while we were driving. I bought 18-inch spring-loaded curtain rods and mounted them vertically in front of each pile of towels, clothing, etc., to prevent them from coming down.

This size can also be used in the medicine cabinet, refrigerator and side shelving in the closet.

Handy Storage

LOIS LAFERRIERE, ELK POINT, SOUTH DAKOTA

▶ While looking for places to store things, it occurred to me that I could utilize the space below the shelf provided for our television.

Since our TV shelf is supported by two diagonal shelf supports, I took a dowel rod, wider than the shelf supports, and sewed two rows of clear plastic pockets to the rod. I was then able to hang this assembly below the TV shelf, from the shelf supports.

In these pockets I store pencils, paper, a small tool kit, scissors, a sewing kit, etc. Now, these small things are out of the way, yet are still handy to get to.

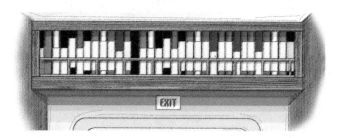

Video Storage

ARLENE CHIAROLANZIO, FLORHAM PARK, NEW JERSEY

▶ Our motorhome came with a wooden key-holder over the door. Knowing that we would not be hanging keys in this alcove, we removed the hooks to make a safe and easy place to store our videos.

Drinking From a Glass Slipper (Holder)

DANNY LINDSTROM, CASTROVILLE, CALIFORNIA

▶ My wife and I, from time to time, enjoy a bottle of wine. We have found that a vinyl shoe holder we purchased from a camping store works perfectly as a storage aid. It keeps the opened bottles upright and prevents all the bottles from banging together.

We used short wood screws to attach the shoe holder to the inside of a closet door, near the kitchen dining area. When empty, the vinyl holder takes up no room.

Traveling Dish Holder

MARION MILLENDER, IOWA PARK, TEXAS

▶ For years, we had been trying to come up with something that would hold dishes for traveling, but allow easy usage when camped. One day, while cleaning out the closet and disposing of the old plastic

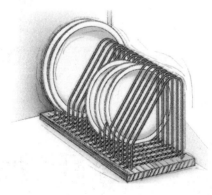

hangers that had begun to sag, I happened to turn one on end, and it dawned on me how the hangers can be cut and used for dish holders.

We used a ¾-inch-thick piece of plywood, 9 × 17 inches, drilled holes on ⅞-inch centers for the hangers to fit in, and cut grooves for the dishes. The hanger sections are about 8 inches tall, and the plywood base can be cut to fit any motorhome's available space.

The plates do not bang together, but can be easily removed or replaced for use. The plastic hanger section flexes, so you do not damage your plates.

Increased Capacity

PAUL MALLY, CLINTON TOWNSHIP, MICHIGAN

▶ We discovered that we could increase the storage capacity of our pantry by installing wood strips across the open side of the pantry shelves. These wooden strips retain the items on the shelves.

I cut the wood strips to length using shade bottoms (available anywhere shades are sold), and used hook-and-loop fastener to anchor them to the pantry framework. The hook part of the fastener was added to the inside of the framework, and the loop part was wrapped around the ends of the wood strips.

We are able to adjust these wood strips (up or down) as required, depending on the items stored.

Thin Is In

JO ANN SODEN, PAHRUMP, NEVADA

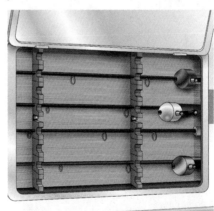

▶ What do you store in that skinny storage compartment, on your slide-out, which is located behind your couch? Try fishing gear.

We purchased two fishing-rod holders and then mounted them on the back wall of the storage compartment, one above the other. Rods go into the holders, while reels are stored on the bottom of the compartment at either end.

All of our fishing gear now rides safely and securely, and it remains easily accessible.

Bag It

DOUGLASS KEOWEN, WOODLAND, CALIFORNIA

▶ Got a lot of plastic grocery bags lying about? Take an empty gallon water or milk container and cut an "X" across the bottom. Then, insert the plastic bags through the X until you have enough to fill the container.

You can pull the bags out, through the uncapped top, one at a time, as needed. If you can't get the next one out, just dampen your finger and pull the bag out.

Rack 'Em Up

ALVORD HUTCHINSON, AGAWAM, MASSACHUSETTS

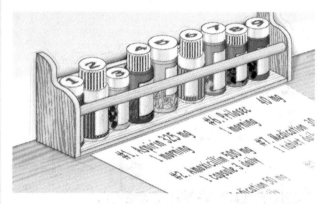

▶ My wife takes a number of different prescriptions daily. When we traveled in our motorhome, we had a problem finding a convenient place to keep them in an orderly fashion.

So, I purchased a rack made to hold spice containers. It is 12 inches long, 1¼ inches wide and 2½ inches deep. I secured it to the inside of one of the wardrobe drawers.

Using a marking pen, I numbered the caps from empty prescription bottles. I then made a list showing each prescription by number, name, strength, amount taken each day and when to take them.

Now she loads each bottle with the required number of pills for the days we will be away from home.

Hang It Up

PAUL BECKER, SAN ANGELO, TEXAS

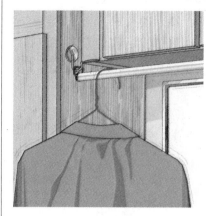

▶ My wife enjoys the washer-dryer in our coach and uses it often. However, she likes to remove some items from the dryer early and hang-dry them to prevent wrinkles. Of course, this isn't as easy as it sounds while traveling in a motorhome. Finding a place to hang them outside (if allowed) was always a problem. The clothes usually ended up draped in all manner of places inside the coach.

It was a real mess, until I came up with the following idea. As in most RVs, our motorhome's floorplan included storage cabinets above the head of the bed, with longer compartments on either side. I mounted two brass coat hooks on the side of the vertical cabinets, and hung a removable clothes rod between them. Now, the clothes hang next to a window, out of the way, until dry.

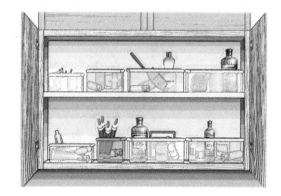

Medicine Man

JANET LYNCH, SURPRISE, ARIZONA

▶ While traveling in our motorhome, I have found that the medicine cabinet becomes very unorganized because of the stored items sliding around.

To prevent this from happening, we store the items in plastic containers recycled from such products as facecloths and reusable wipes. These containers are a perfect fit for the medicine cabinet shelves.

Are You Packin' a Rod?

JOHN CRACCHIOLO, DELRAY BEACH, FLORIDA

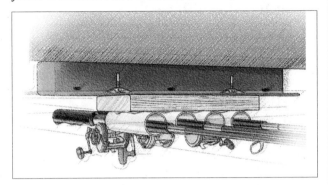

▶ Fishing is one of many RVers' favorite hobbies. The problem is where to store the rods securely and out of the way while protecting them from shifting loads in the storage bays.

After trying various store-bought gadgets with little success, this simple idea came to me. It has proven so useful, I want to share it.

All you need is:
- 4 1½-inch PVC T-fittings
- 2 toggle bolts
- 1 2 × 4 about 15 feet long
- 1 bungee cord
- epoxy adhesive

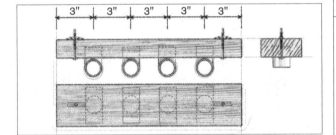

First, cut holes in the 2 × 4, sized to be just slightly larger than the outside diameter of the PVC T-fitting. Cut the holes only deep enough to receive the length of one of the T-fitting ends, not all the way through, as this will add strength and make gluing much easier. (I used an adjustable circle cutter, which made a nice snug fit.) The holes should be about 3 inches apart, center-to-center.

Mix up a batch of epoxy and fill the holes in the 2 × 4 with enough to provide good coverage on the T-fitting end. Press the T-fittings firmly into the holes, making sure they all point perpendicular to the 2 × 4 and parallel to each other.

Install this assembly with the toggle bolts to the ceiling of the storage compartment, in existing holes if there are any.

Finally, a bungee cord toward the front of the rods will help hold them up and out of the way. Secure the bungee cord to the existing holes in the next rib of the chassis.

Pipe Dreams

MARK BOARDMAN, TAYLORSVILLE, KENTUCKY

▶ We like to use a large (7 × 15-foot) patio rug when we camp. The problem is storing and transporting a sometimes wet and muddy rug inside the RV.

We installed a piece of 8-inch PVC pipe under our trailer. The pipe has a female adapter glued to each end with a screw-in plug for easy removal. The rug can be removed or inserted from either side of the RV.

We mounted the pipe using ⅜-inch threaded rod bent into a "U" shape to fit around the pipe.

Holes were drilled in the RV's frame to match the "U" bolt ends. I used lock nuts to eliminate the possibility of the tube coming loose.

A piece of treated 4 × 4-inch lumber, cut to match the shape of the pipe, makes a very good mounting bracket.

To prevent the screw-in plugs from getting lost, I used a short piece of stainless-steel jack chain to attach them to the frame.

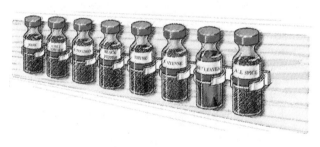

Spice Up Your Coach

MICHELE WATTERWORTH, PROSPECT, CONNECTICUT

▶ I have discovered a new storage helper that I have found very useful in our RV. The items are called "Spice Clips" (available through Harriet Carter Gifts, (800) 377-7878) and are self-adhesive, plastic tension clips that will hold and tightly grip various sizes of spice bottles and/or jars — in any serviceable size place you find.

You can cut them to fit and customize their use for any size or shape of space. My husband has used them for securing small jars of screws, nails, tacks and fuses; they're also useful for fishing hooks and tackle!

storage

A Clothes-Rod Idea

JOE CAMPBELL, GOODWATER, ALABAMA

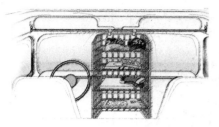

▶ Regarding my clothes-rod idea that you published in a previous issue, I thought of a way to expand its function. I purchased a plastic shoe rack, the kind that has adjustable shelves, and use the appropriate number of shelves that will fit hanging from the rod in the space between the seats of my Class B motorhome when camped. It is great for holding caps, maps and brochures and, of course, the latest issue of *MotorHome!*

When I'm ready to hit the road, I remove the rod and hang the rack on the rod in the shower/tub area.

FILLING THE GAP

We have a large pass-through exterior-storage compartment in the rear of our motorhome. It is cumbersome, however, to access the middle of the compartment. We found the most convenient way to utilize this space is with a large plastic storage bin on wheels. We can easily load the bin – then wheel it into the middle of the compartment; almost anything small can be used as wheel chocks to prevent it from moving while the coach is in motion. When we need anything packed into the bin, it's an easy matter to wheel it back out.

BRENDA GUETTHOFF, ELBURN, ILLINOIS

TWO QUICKIES

We live full-time in our motorhome and have relatively little space for storing important documents we need to keep with us. So, we began using resealable plastic freezer bags to store the papers. The bags are durable, water- and spill-proof, thus allowing storage almost anywhere in the coach, including spaces not ordinarily associated with this usage, such as under drawers.

Also, we use our laptop computer for our Global Positioning System (GPS) applications. However, the computer and the GPS receiver tended to slide readily when placed on the dash. We solved the problem by placing easily found rubber jar-lid grips under them.

FRANK GRISWOLD, TAMPA, FLORIDA

Upside-Down Storage

ELLE & PETER LACQUES,
GLENEDEN BEACH, OREGON

▶ We traveled across the country for three months and found that we needed extra storage for our CDs, VCR tapes, books, etc., so we came up with this inexpensive, very convenient and good-looking addition.

From a local home-improvement store we purchased two bathroom vanity cabinets in finished wood that color-matched our existing cabinets. They were about $45 each. We turned them upside down and bolted one to each side of the wall-mounted table-support shelf. The top (formerly the bottom) was also finished and matched our cabinets.

We added ¼ × ¾-inch wooden strips across the open tops (originally storage cubbies below the cabinets' two doors) to hold loose items, and then added door snaps at the bottom to ensure that the doors stay closed while we are driving down the road.

Not only does this arrangement add to our storage, it gives additional surfaces for convenient use. And best of all, it looks great — like twin dining-room buffets.

It's Part of Life

MARY WAGNER, LIVINGSTON, TEXAS

▶ Laundry is a necessary part of life, and quarters are a necessity at the self-serve laundry. We store our quarters in a box meant for sewing-machine bobbins. The quarters are stored neatly, so it is easy to see how many there are. The box is small and easy to slip into a pocket to carry. Bobbin boxes are available in the sewing department of your favorite fabric store.

storage

Know When To Hold 'Em

PAMELA THOMPSON, LIVINGSTON, TEXAS

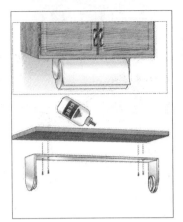

▶ Our cupboard floor was not thick enough to support a paper-towel holder without having the screws pop through. My husband cut a piece of ½-inch-thick board (sized to accommodate the holder) and used wood glue to secure it to the underside of the overhead cabinet floor.

We now have a place to securely mount the paper-towel holder!

Wood It Work?

STEVE SHELDAHL, ESTES PARK, COLORADO

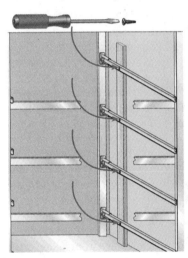

▶ Many of the RV manufacturers are using a drawer-glide system that utilizes a metal runner slid into a plastic support piece in the rear of the cabinet. My experience has been that this plastic support piece breaks very easily, allowing the guide and the drawer to fall.

My answer to this problem was to buy some 1 × 2-inch lumber and cut it long enough to reach from the floor of the cabinet to about 4 inches above the highest drawer guide. I placed one length on the outside of each set of the metal drawer guides in each cabinet, as close to the plastic piece as possible. The wood strip must rest on the cabinet floor.

I then screwed each drawer guide to the new vertical wood support using an existing hole in the drawer guide and a ¾-inch No. 6 flat-head wood screw. If the plastic support piece is already broken, the metal guide has to be repositioned to its correct location before screwing it to the new wood support. Broken or not, I left the plastic support pieces in place to maintain the side-to-side alignment.

With this arrangement, the weight of the drawer is now supported by the wood strip, and not by the easily broken plastic.

Store Those Lids

BERT JASTER, RALEIGH, NORTH CAROLINA

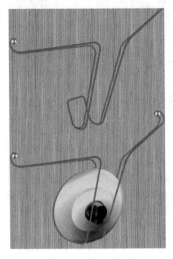

▶ Does storing the lids to your pots and pans drive you crazy? Here's a quick and inexpensive solution. Purchase plastic-coated wire coat hangers at your favorite discount store. Use wire cutters and pliers to bend the wire to the shape and size of each individual lid handle, forming a U-shape stirrup at the bottom. Then form a small loop at each end, and use a small wood screw to fasten the wire shapes to the inside of the cabinet-door rails. Be sure to place them so that the lids won't hit any shelves inside the cabinet when the door is closed.

Off the Floor

BILL READING,
LENHARTSVILLE, PENNSYLVANIA

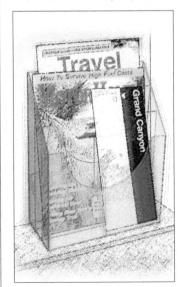

▶ Maps, guidebooks and other literature always seem to end up on the floor and underfoot when we're traveling. To help keep things tidy and organized, I went to an office-supply store and purchased a six-pocket brochure-holder with removable dividers that can accommodate magazines. I then mounted it in a convenient location near the copilot's seat. Now maps are easy to find and within easy reach.

Sun-Visor Shelf

RON NORBIE, SIOUX FALLS, SOUTH DAKOTA

▶ My wife wanted a place to put family pictures while we were parked. She came up with the idea of using the sun visors, set flat and lowered. We don't put heavy picture frames on them, but this uses a previously empty spot and gives the motorhome a more homey feel.

Sun-Visor Shelf Plus

JAN MILLER, SUNSET HILLS, MISSOURI

▶ For years I have been using the sun visors for shelves. Using a piece of ⅛-inch plywood, my husband added a third shelf. He used decorative chain from our local hardware store to hang it from the visors, and I made a patriotic cover for it.

What's a Drawer Cake?

MRS. J. HUDSON, LIVINGSTON, TEXAS

▶ Yesterday I baked a cake in a drawer! Today the drawer is back in place, under our dinette table, where it holds napkins, a calculator, pens, paper clips and other stuff.

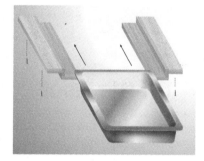

We purchased an 11 × 14-inch cake pan. Wooden L-shape glides were glued and screwed to the underside of the table close to the wall. A loaf-size pan, on the other side, holds medication bottles, and neither pan interferes with seating four people. Be sure to use pans with wide rims.

Simple Storage Shelf

MARVIN LAXTON, PORTLAND, OREGON

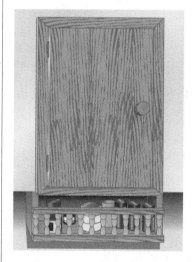

▶ The medicine cabinet in our trailer never had much storage, but one day we hit on a way to increase it. We screwed a new shelf under the cabinet to hold larger makeup bottles and other "stuff," and stained it to match the original cabinet. On the front edge of the new shelf, we attached a 4-inch rail to keep things from falling off.

Eliminate the Struggle

CLARENCE EY, BEL AIR, MARYLAND

▶ To eliminate the struggle in reaching the groceries stored in the back of a deep pantry cabinet, I installed heavy-duty slider baskets. These coated steel-wire baskets glide out on smooth-rolling ball-bearing rails, providing easy access to everything in the cabinets. This type of basket can be purchased at most hardware or home centers. Installation instructions come with each basket.

storage

Depth Perception

FRANK WOYTHAL, ANDOVER, NEW YORK

▶ Stretching wall-to-wall in the bath area, the medicine cabinet in our motorhome was quite wide — but its shallow depth and lack of a second shelf limited its usefulness.

To double its depth, I first removed the entire unit from the wall. I then cut a 1 × 4-inch wood plank to the same length as the stock floor of the cabinet, refinished it and mounted it alongside the original (using wooden dowels and glue). In our motorhome, the sides of the cabinet are actually the bathroom walls, simplifying removal/ replacement. Because many of the cabinet's contents are in short containers, I also added a second shelf.

Hidden Hamper

HENRY NUNEZ, GRIFFITH, INDIANA

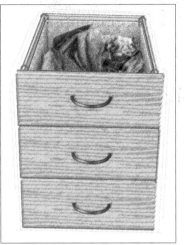

▶ Of the two nightstands in the bedroom of our motorhome, one had three drawers that were rarely used. Rather than let the space go to waste, I decided to make a clothes hamper out of it.

After taking out the drawers, I removed the bottoms from the top two drawers, leaving the lowest drawer intact.

To fasten all three drawers together (and form a single unit), I attached a piece of plywood to the back of the drawers and another to the inside faces. I also put hooks along the inside top edges to hold the laundry bag, which helps for easy lifting in and out.

Shoe Storage

RICHARD HINES, WALWORTH, NEW YORK

▶ One of the things we've done to improve storage capacity in our coach is to construct inexpensive units for shoes, installed in the lift-up storage area under the bed.

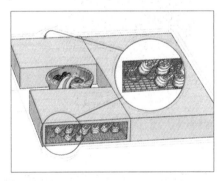

All that's needed is to remove an equal length of the existing bed box and replace it with one or two of the newly constructed shoe-storage units. I made ours of laminated pinewood, with hard-wire shelving on the inside.

The height of your shoebox will be determined by the height of the existing bed box. The length can be as long as you like, but may also be determined by the lift-and-support system already under your bed. We added two new boxes and left a center storage area that we now use for our laundry basket.

Out of Sight, Out of Smell

ROBERT SWADELL, HENDERSON, NEVADA

▶ Have you ever noticed how the laundry bag gets bigger and bigger — and invariably spends most of its time in the shower? Our solution was to install a trap door in the floor of our coach, leading to a hamper in an outside storage compartment. Not only does this remove dirty clothes from the living quarters, but it also eliminates any accompanying odors.

Obviously, this will not work in every motorhome, but we have had no trouble finding a location that works in our latest Class C coach.

Wineglass Rack

CLAIRE ROGERS, TUCSON, ARIZONA

▶ After moving from house to motorhome, we found we missed our wineglasses. Bringing them along and using them was more fuss than we liked. We had to wrap and box them for storage each time we used them.

We found a simple solution at a home store in the form of laminated molded-fiber threshold, such as used for Pergo or Shaw flooring. That allows us to hang the glasses from tracks in a convenient location underneath the overhead cabinet.

Before installing, we lined what would be the tracks with thick felt on both the threshold and the underside of the cabinets. (Be sure the felt is thick enough to hold the bases snug.) We measured the base of the glasses to determine the spacing of the threshold pieces, and then attached them to the cabinet bottom with brass screws. We covered the exposed ends with woodgrain tape. For extra security, wedge a wood shim into the tracks before getting underway.

Handy Keys

ANNETTE O'DONNEL, MESA, ARIZONA

▶ We like having our various keys handy, but not in plain sight. We have a mid-entry coach and have hung a wooden key bar on the wall, behind the free-standing dinette chair. To prevent the hanging keys from marking up the wall, we placed a piece of matching leather under the key bar and stapled the  bottom edge to the wall. It's hardly noticeable and is very convenient. We also have hung our dog's leash and collar here, which is handy when stopping at rest areas.

Space Organized

JOYCE STONER, GRAND ISLAND, NEBRASKA

▶ I organized the space under the bathroom sink using baskets — personal needs in one, cleaning supplies in another. They are easy to pull out when something is needed. For more light in this area, we installed one of those handy tap lights.

What a Mess

KAREN LOCKWOOD, OKLAHOMA CITY, OKLAHOMA

▶ We always had maps and travel books all over our RV. Because our entry door is behind the front passenger seat, there is a gap between the seat and the wall of the coach.

It was in this space where we constructed a map box; it holds a lot of maps and directories right where it is convenient for the passenger to access. The box measures about 5 inches wide and 28 inches long, but it could be built to any size that the space in the RV allows.

Does Your Load Shift?

Ron Gross, Wilsonville, Oregon

▶ When opening storage compartments after traveling, I found that frequently the load had shifted and some items would fall out. To prevent this from happening, I fabricated a "T" out of wood strips. The crossbeam goes on the bottom just inside the door, with the plain end up. That allows the compartment doors to be opened without stuff falling out.

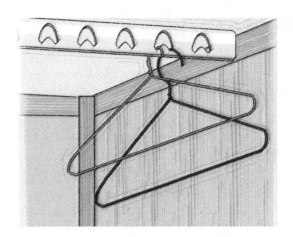

Short & to the Point

Harold Sterzbach, Louisville, Ohio

▶ We have a clothes closet located on the wall above our bed, and as can be expected, it's really not tall enough to be completely useful.

To help make it more functional, I cut the top of the hangers off, then bent the remaining wire to create an abbreviated hanger hook.

This shortens the hook by about two inches, and increases the length of the hanging space.

Four on the Floor

Peggy Kerbaugh, Keene, New Hampshire

▶ We put four plastic storage containers under the sofa in our motorhome to keep shoes and other items neat and separated. To access these containers, I

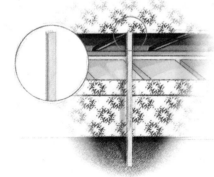

have to lift the sofa seat and then struggle to try and keep the seat from sliding back down on my head.

My husband thought of making a brace of wood to keep me from bashing my head. He used a 1 × 2 × 24-inch piece of wood with a V-groove cut in the top edge (to more securely grip the front edge of the sofa seat). It is stored under the sofa, near the front edge, for easy access when needed.

Slide Show

Charles Juran, Prescott, Arizona

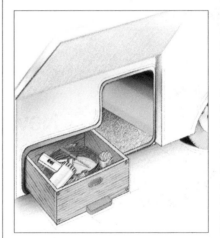

▶ Slideouts dramatically increase a motorhome's living space when open, but the space under the slideout mechanism itself is awkward to use effectively. I solved this by installing a drawer. The tray rides on center-slide-drawer hardware, available at any home-center or hardware store. The components are screwed to a piece of plywood that rests below the drawer. I also added what looks like a handle at the end — but it's actually a foam block to prevent drawer movement while on the road.

storage

Sag Be Gone

BRUCE BAKER, MARTINEZ, CALIFORNIA

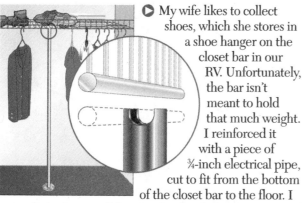

▶ My wife likes to collect shoes, which she stores in a shoe hanger on the closet bar in our RV. Unfortunately, the bar isn't meant to hold that much weight. I reinforced it with a piece of ¾-inch electrical pipe, cut to fit from the bottom of the closet bar to the floor. I cut a slit in the top of the pipe for the clothes bar to rest in and the bottom end rests on a 3-inch metal plate on the floor.

This is a very inexpensive way to reinforce a closet bar, and now my wife can hang shoes, coats and whatever else she likes without worrying about the bar sagging.

Amazing Storage

ROBERT RIMBEY, MOUNT AIRY, MARYLAND

▶ We recently purchased a new motorhome. Every feature on it is great except the lack of a large pantry for canned goods.

My remedy is shown in the drawing. It rolls in and out with ease and holds an amazing amount of goods. The dimensions of the slide-out drawer will vary with each motorhome, but the basic concept remains the same.

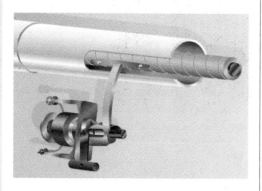

Store Those Rods

BOB SUTTON,
SANTA CLARITA, CALIFORNIA

▶ I fastened lengths of PVC drainpipe (with plastic pipe straps) under the coach floor, at the top of one of our pass-through basement-storage compartments. That allows me to carry a variety of fully assembled fishing rods for quick use when we arrive at our favorite fishin' holes.

In order to accommodate the mounted reels, I cut a slot in the lowest part of each pipe at the end where the reel hangs. The rods are always ready, protected and out of the way.

Vertical Files

BOB GAIDO, IRVINE, CALIFORNIA

▶ In our RV, as in most others, overhead storage in the cupboard above the sink is limited. We found that small, medium and large-size plates and paper-plate holders can stack vertically very nicely in a plastic vertical-file divider, allowing easy access to the size of plate desired.

Never Stay Put

JAMES HAMILTON,
LAKE CITY, FLORIDA

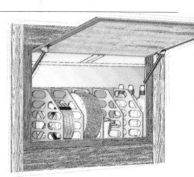

▶ Storing paper plates, plastic cutlery, wax paper, aluminum foil, reclosable plastic bags, etc., has always been a problem in our motorhome. They never stay where they're put. My wife, Lena, came up with this idea to keep everything in its place.

She got some plastic magazine files, which can be purchased from Wal-Mart or any office-supply store, and I fastened them together with quick ties. Voila! Now everything is where it should be.

10 minute tech
systems

FAST AND HOT

We have a 40-foot motorhome, and it takes awhile for hot water to get to the kitchen from the rear, where the water heater is located.

To remedy this, I chose a very good 2½-gallon auxiliary water heater, In-Sink-Erator model no.152. I mounted it under the kitchen sink, and it solved the problem. It has a 1,500-watt heating element to quickly bring the water to the desired temperature, so we need to be plugged into shorepower or running the AC generator to use it. No more wasted time and water, waiting for hot water at the sink!

JOHN SPIRO, SALIDA, COLORADO

HOW'S YOUR FREQUENCY?

Many RVs have auxiliary generators, providing alternating current (AC). Here in North America, appliances that use AC are designed to use 60-cycle power, which is the intended output frequency of the AC generator.

If the frequency is too low, there is the danger of electric-motor burnout. There is less danger if the frequency is too high, but then the voltage may also be too high. Here is a simple way to check the frequency.

With the AC generator running, plug in an electric clock. The clock speed is established by the frequency of the electricity. Compare the second hand of the clock (or the rate the colon blinks on digital clocks) to the second hand of an accurate wristwatch. If both hands agree during one complete revolution, the frequency is correct.

For a more accurate measurement, do this for several consecutive revolutions. There should be an adjustment on the engine governor to correct a frequency error. Consult your generator service manual.

ALVIN WYLAND, WILLIAMSBURG, IOWA

TANK DRAIN

My RV has the freshwater tank mounted under the bed in the rear of the motorhome. To drain this tank, the factory has installed a drain valve – also under the bed! I found this, to say the least, very inconvenient.

At the end of the factory discharge hose, I attached an extension that ended just inside the outside compartment, where I added a new drain valve and routed the discharge under the compartment floor. I now leave the factory (under the bed) valve, open all the time. I no longer have to go into the bedroom and raise the bed to drain the water.

DONALD ROGERS,
WHITTIER, CALIFORNIA

Good-Bye Pump Noise

HOWARD MEYER, PLYMOUTH, MICHIGAN

▶ We love remote, quiet campgrounds. However, primitive campgrounds require that we use our freshwater holding tank — and its noisy pump. I always felt the pump could be heard all over the campground.

I went to the hardware store and bought the cheapest foam kneeling pad they had. A small section (slightly larger than the pump mounting holes) was cut from the pad and glued to a scrap piece of wood paneling.

I removed the pump from its original mounting location in the motorhome, glued my new pad/paneling piece to the original mounting location (foam side toward the wall). Finally, the pump was reattached to the scrap paneling using wood screws.

Since there is no solid connection between the pump and the motorhome, almost all of the noise and vibration is absorbed by the foam kneeling pad. The size of the pad (mine measured 4 × 5 inches) distributes the stress on the glue bond and keeps it from peeling away.

Now, when I turn on the water in the kitchen, I find myself constantly checking the panel light to make sure the pump is turned on!

So Where Is It?

STEVEN SHAPIRO SR.,
ROSEBURG, OREGON

▶ I have had a problem keeping track of my 30-amp power cord's 20-amp plug adapter when not using it. I solved the problem using three 10-inch cable ties.

By linking the ties together and attaching them to the cord and the adapter, the adapter is always where I can find it when I need it.

A Sticky Situation

Joe Stapleton, Colbert, Washington

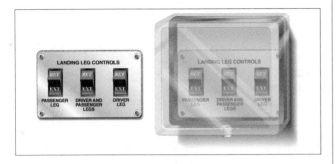

▶ I had to replace the landing-gear-switch set on my year-old fifth-wheel because the switches kept getting stuck in the ON position due to dust and moisture build-up.

To avoid this problem, I purchased a Home Universal Thermostat Guard and installed it over my switch set with four screws.

The thermostat guard is clear plastic and has a lock and two keys included. When you unlock the cover from the frame, the whole cover comes off so you don't have to hold it up to operate the switches. When on the road or parked, the cover is locked in place, so debris or unwanted tampering can't affect the switch.

There are vent holes around the bottom mounting plate of the cover, so I used a standard foam weather strip to seal them.

Make It Simple

Bob Burrill, Austin, Texas

▶ I've noticed all kinds of ways for hanging water filters in RV campsites. Some are in trees, others in stands or on the ground. I hooked mine up permanently in the basement of my motorhome. All I have to do is pull out the water hose and hook it up to the hose bib. I used PVC pipe and various fittings to semipermanently plumb the filter to the coach. The filter does not have to hang straight down; it could be at an angle or even horizontal, but you must leave enough room to unscrew the container to change the filter cartridge.

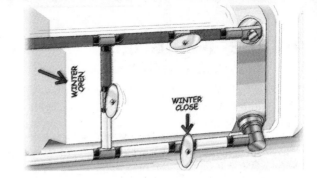

Twisting Spigots

Arlene Chiarolanzio, Florham Park, New Jersey

▶ Every year when winterizing our motorhome, my husband would ask me, "Which valves do I close?" Finally, I had him take an indelible marker and, on the side of the hot-water-tank insulation (and near the valves in question), add notations and draw arrows showing which valves to open/close. Now, the information is always available — and makes the job so much easier.

Waste Not, Want Not

George de Shazer, Fresno, California

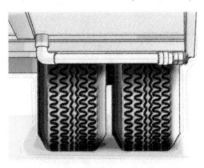

▶ The low-point drain on my motorhome's freshwater tank was an unthreaded length of PVC pipe descending about 4 inches below the floor of the service compartment. With the water shortage in our area, I was unhappy with wasting so much water when emptying the tank. By adding a few fittings, I am now able to use this water for other things.

I began by buying a ½-inch PVC elbow, but found the existing drainpipe was slightly too big in diameter to accommodate the ½-inch elbow. By slightly sanding the end of the pipe with coarse sandpaper, the elbow slipped on easily; a dab of PVC cement made the attachment permanent.

I then cemented an 18-inch section of ½-inch PVC pipe to the other end of the elbow, which extended to the side of the motorhome. A garden hose-threaded nipple, cemented to the end of the pipe, completed the installation. It's now easy to drain the tank into my flower beds — with no water wasted.

Another Night-Light

RENE LORD, RICHMOND, BRITISH COLUMBIA

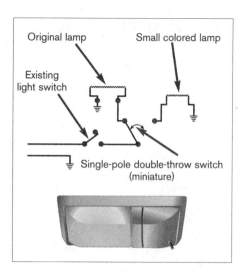

Original lamp   Small colored lamp

Existing light switch

Single-pole double-throw switch (miniature)

▶ We recently bought a new trailer and never had a problem with interior lighting until now. As it turns out, the bathroom lighting is too good. When getting up in the middle of the night, we found the overhead light was so bright it was blinding.

To create a night-light, I installed a simple two-way switch and an additional 12-volt DC colored bulb in the existing fixture. The additional bulb socket was purchased at an auto-parts store and I bought the two-way switch at an electronics store.

After disconnecting the power, I removed the light fixture and fastened the extra socket near the existing bulb. I then drilled a small hole on the side of the fixture for the switch. The hot wire goes to the center pole on the switch. One terminal of the switch goes to one light, and the other wire goes to the other bulb. The last wire is the ground wire for the new bulb, which was connected to the negative wire in the fixture. Reinstall the fixture and you are in business.

At night, I leave it set so that the colored light goes on when using the bathroom light switch. During the day or early evening, I leave the new switch set to let the regular white light go on. When we are hooked up to shorepower, I leave the colored light on all night.

Change the Order

RONALD AAVANG, UNION, ILLINOIS

▶ On my trailer, I rearranged the order of the brackets for the LP-gas regulator and installed a spring under the assembly. This keeps the hardware from sliding down the hold-down rod, which makes it harder to put a refilled cylinder back in place.

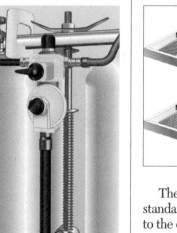

Now I do not have to hold up the hardware and install the cylinder at the same time. When I loosen the hold-down wing nut, everything raises up and out of the way. Then I can tip the cylinder away, lift it out and lower it, then tip the refilled cylinder back in and re-tighten with ease.

I bought the spring at the hardware store and used a cable clamp on the rod under the spring to support and adjust it. I also added some flat washers where I thought they should be, and added a nut at the bottom of the rod as a jam-nut to keep the rod from turning.

Go First-Class

ROBERT SWADELL, HENDERSON, NEVADA

▶ With the advent of ducted air conditioners in RVs, a simple opportunity has arisen to install a really first-class filter system — one capable of killing smoke and pollen, etc.

I have shown two versions, one that does not share an outlet and uses a 20 × 20-inch filter, and one that has an outlet associated with it, in which we used a 16 × 20-inch filter.

The frame is made from painted ¾-inch wood, in which a standard return-air grille has been installed. It can be fastened to the ceiling with inside-mounted L brackets, and foam weatherstripping is used to seal it up.

Several manufacturers sell these "Ultra Filters," but I have found the 3M Filtrete units to be the best. They are made in two grades — 1000 and 1250, with the latter capable of filtering out the smallest particles. They come close to matching the efficiency of electronic air filters.

Because these filters are designed to handle much larger volumes than found in RVs, they will last for several months.

The improvement in air quality is dramatic — which is especially helpful for pet lovers with allergies and for non-smokers who live with smokers.

systems

A Status Light

BOB GLAZER, HUNTINGTON WOODS, MICHIGAN

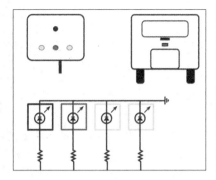

▶ Going down the road with the trailer's water pump left on can lead to an unintentional floor wash if a plumbing fitting should come loose. Too many times, after a roadside pit stop, my wife and I scratch our heads and ask each other, "Did you turn off the pump?" You know the drill: Hop out, go back, open the door and check the switch.

A status light mounted where it can be seen in the rearview mirror helps eliminate most of these fire drills. And as long as I was going to put a signal box back there, lights to show brake and turn-signal activity seemed like a logical addition as well. A 1,000-ohm resistor in series before high-output LEDs does the trick for 12-volt DC input. (Ask about this type of setup at an electronics store, such as RadioShack.)

The box was a plastic throat-lozenge container. The total cost was about $10.

Turn Around

ROBERT WILLIAMS, LIVINGSTON, TEXAS

▶ One of the most dreaded tasks in our fifth-wheel is taking out an LP-gas cylinder to have it filled.

The door opening is 25½ inches wide, but the width of the two cylinders is 27 inches. This means I have to lift the cylinder and move it toward the regulator and center post to remove it. The gas hose is stiff and is yet another obstacle.

To make the removal easier and quicker, I turned the regulator around and placed the hoses in the rear of the compartment. I placed a mirror, attached with hook-and-loop fastener, on the back wall of the compartment so I can still read the RED/GREEN indicator and know when I have an empty cylinder.

Sleep Aid

HARVEY HETRICK, TORRANCE, CALIFORNIA

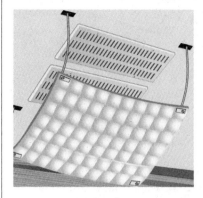

▶ We seldom need to use both our air conditioners, but when necessary we do. However, we have found that even on low fan, with the temperature set to higher settings, the air blows much too strongly on us as we sleep. A simple cure that we worked out is to make an air deflector from a sheet of any lightweight material.

Cut the sheet to be slightly larger than the size of the air outlets. Cut four lengths of monofilament (lawn-edger, fishing line, etc.). Make a hole in each corner of the deflector and insert one piece of line into each. Using a heat source (iron, soldering iron, etc.), melt the filament ends enough to keep the filament from coming out of the holes.

Do the same to four small male hook-and-loop tabs: make holes, insert line and melt the ends. We have carpet material on our ceiling, so the hook-and-loop sticks firmly. If you have a solid-surface ceiling, a small tab of female hook-and-loop will be needed. The device is completely adjustable by varying where the tabs are placed.

Venting His Frustration

MARIETTA KREBSBACH, ELKHART LAKE, WISCONSIN

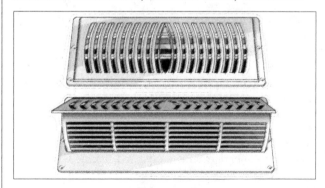

▶ I have found another solution to the problem of air conditioning blowing directly down on you. I bought adjustable heating vents in a department store for less than $5. They fit precisely into the vent openings; even the screw holes match!

systems

Coffee Talk

James Jipping, Holland, Michigan

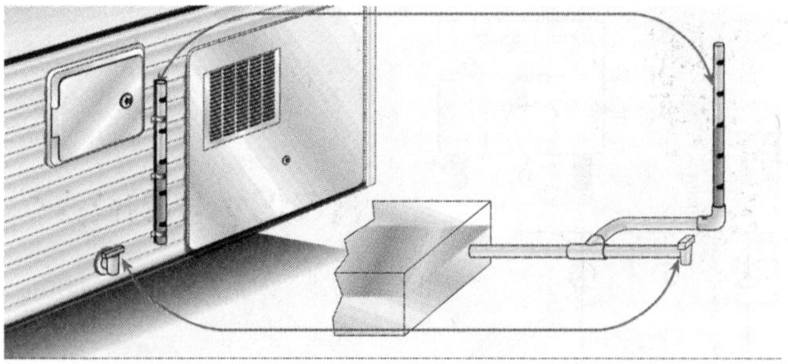

Despite my best efforts, I could never tell how full the freshwater tank was. Not only were the electric-sensor readouts not visible from where the tank was being filled, but sometimes they didn't work that well. In addition, how much precise information can you really get from ⅓-⅓-⅓ readouts?

The answer appeared one night while having coffee at a social function — the sight glass on a coffee urn.

All I had to do was add a sight glass to the side of my RV by connecting it to the drain line on the freshwater tank.

My drain line is ⅜ inch ID (½ inch OD), so I purchased a ⅜ × ⅜ × ⅜-inch plastic tee, a ⅜-inch elbow and a length of ⅜-inch clear plastic hose. This length needs to be enough to go from the tee, which I inserted in the drain line, to the elbow plus 1 or 2 inches above the water tank.

I opted to mount the sight glass on the outside of my RV, a few inches from the existing exterior drain valve. I cut the drain line, inserted the tee and ran the hose from the tee through the hole in the wall. Then, in order to make a sharp right-angled turn, I used the ⅜-inch elbow and attached the rest of the plastic hose. I caulked around the hole in the RV wall and used small hose clamps to seal the hose at the fittings.

The sight glass hose is mounted vertically, and is fastened to the wall of the RV with a couple of plastic clamps. The top of the plastic hose is about 2 inches above the top of the water tank. A permanent marker was used to put a scale on the gauge.

Editor's note: *Perhaps inside the compartment where your water fill lines are located, or the compartment housing the water tank, might be better locations for the sight gauge. Remember, you cannot seal the top of the sight glass hose because as the water level rises it has to push the air out of the hose. A pin hole should work.*

LP-Gas-Cylinder Turn-On

Ernest Rainey, Pensacola, Florida

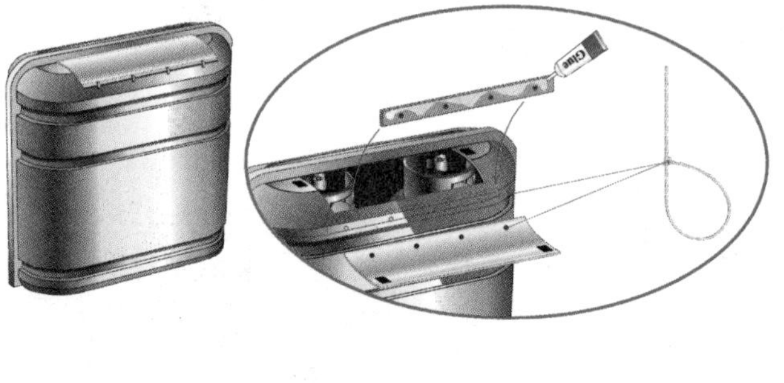

I do not like to tow my RV with the LP-gas turned on. Therefore, in order to turn the cylinder off, I would have to lift the cover to access the valve each time I hit the road or set up camp.

I made an access door on the LP-gas-cylinder cover. In order to reach both valves, the opening on the top of the cover had to be 16 inches long by about 5 inches wide. I centered it on the front half, and forward of the center seam by at least ½ inch. I marked this and cut the opening with a sharp tool.

Then I cut a lid from an old white storage container box. I outlined the cutout section on the container top and added another inch on all sides for overlap.

Next, I cut a piece of wood (you could also use plastic) ¼ × 1 × 17½ inches. I used a good adhesive to glue this piece under the front edge of the cutout and clamped it until it was dry. That reinforced the edge to hinge the new door.

To form the hinges, I placed the door over the opening and made four marks equally spaced. These should be over the area supported by the reinforcing piece of wood or plastic. I drilled these out with a 7/32-inch drill bit on the door first, then marked the position on the tank cover. Then I drilled two holes through the reinforced area, one over the other, at each of the four locations.

Using 7½-inch cable ties, I looped the ties through one of the holes in the reinforced area, up through the new door and back down through the second hole, leaving slack in the tie so the door will hinge without binding. I trimmed the tie ends neatly. To hold the door down, I use several pieces of heavy-duty hook-and-loop fastener.

Knuckle Sandwich

NORM WELCH, PORTLAND, OREGON

▶ After barking my knuckles countless times when trying to drain the RV's water heater, I finally hit on the solution.

I removed the petcock, and at the hardware store I bought a 2-inch length of galvanized pipe and a sleeve the same diameter as the petcock. Using Teflon tape as a thread sealant, I screwed the sleeve onto the pipe and the petcock into the other end of the sleeve, and then screwed this assembly into the RV's water heater.

Now the original petcock projects past the air-mixture tube and can be easily used without banging my knuckles. Makes you wonder why the manufacturer didn't do this in the first place.

Water Filter System

GORDON BROOME, LOUISVILLE, OHIO

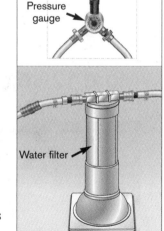

Pressure gauge

Water filter

▶ My inexpensive water-purification system consists of a single filter. The base is a plastic floor drain, which, when attached to the water-filter container with a plastic coupler, can be set on the ground and connected to the water hose. A pressure gauge, a Y-connector and a short hose to use for a variety of things complete the system.

The water hose connects to the water filter using metal connectors because the plastic connectors tend to break more easily. Stainless-steel worm clamps were also used where necessary.

Editor's note: *Remember the pressure reducer and the gauge should be attached directly to the hose bib, not at the end of a hose before it enters your RV. Hoses are not designed to carry the static pressure of unregulated water.*

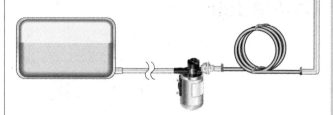

Noisy Pump?

JOHN STROTHER,
NEW MARTINSVILLE, WEST VIRGINIA

▶ The water pumps in RVs can get noisy. Most of this noise is caused by the vibrations the pump makes being transferred to the RV walls by the existing hard-plastic piping.

I have used the arrangement pictured on two different RVs to help quiet down the pump. I could hardly hear it working after I was through.

On the first one, I used a 5-foot supply hose of reinforced white vinyl with ½-inch connections. On the second one, I used a 5-foot piece of high-pressure reinforced vinyl tubing, which was also ½ inch. They were installed with double crimp rings on each end.

Both times I looped the hoses in approximately 4- or 5-inch-high diameter loops and secured them with tie wraps. The looped section absorbs the vibrations from the water pump, and nothing is passed on to the solid piping.

No More Drips

MARVIN BRYANT, LITTLETON, COLORADO

▶ The freshwater tank drain on my fifth-wheel has never worked satisfactorily. It has always been very difficult to open or close, and when closed, it still dripped.

I finally found a solution that works perfectly. I cut off most of the valve from the mounting plate and replaced it with a male garden-hose connector and then added a garden-hose shut-off valve.

Besides providing an easy on-and-off point, it also yields a garden-hose connection that can be used to drain the fresh water on to flowers or garden.

Be sure the fitting you buy is the proper size to fit the tubing that remains on the mounting plate. Mine was a tight fit, but with a little effort, it worked fine.

Go With the Flow

LARRY BLACK, SNELLVILLE, GEORGIA

▶ Water pressure is a common problem with RVs. I noticed that, with my RV, I seemed to have less pressure when connected to city water than when using my

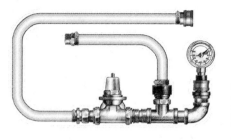

on-board water pump. Further investigation revealed that it was not a pressure problem, but a flow problem.

The standard RV pressure regulator, while holding the pressure at or lower than 50 PSI, has only an opening between ¼- and ⅜-inch in diameter. This greatly restricts water flow.

I found that the standard household pressure regulator (available at all hardware and home-center stores) has a larger ¾-inch opening and has adjustable pressure. By using standard brass plumbing components, a household pressure regulator and pressure gauge, I now have control of my water pressure — and good flow!

Editor's note: *Any type of water-pressure regulator must always be connected at the source, not where the water hose enters the motorhome. The incoming pressure, going through an unprotected hose, may eventually cause it to burst.*

Also, the use of a ½-inch ID hose will restrict flow no matter what regulator you use; ⅝- or ¾-inch ID hoses will allow your RV's water system to perform as designed.

Set a Screen

EDWARD HESS, YUMA, ARIZONA

▶ Sometimes my trailer's water hoses get dirty, collecting sediment and particles of who knows what. I eliminated this problem by buying and installing cone-shaped screen washers in the end of each hose. They trap a lot of unwanted "stuff" before it gets to your RV.

They are available anywhere garden hoses are sold.

Increase the Water Flow

JAMES BROWNING, LIVINGSTON, TEXAS

▶ The water flow in most motorhomes, with the usual RV water-pressure regulator, is very low, making normal things like washing dishes or taking a shower a slow process.

We cured our water-flow problems at the hardware store. We purchased a residential water-pressure reducer and the simple fittings required to adapt it to the water hose we all use. This setup will increase the water flow without increasing the pressure. If not so equipped, you'll also need a pressure gauge (as pictured) so you can adjust the regulator to 45 PSI at maximum. The reason for this increase in flow rate is that the RV pressure reducer as a ¼-inch opening and the residential version has a ¾-inch opening. Therefore more water can come through the pipes with no increase in pressure.

Some motorhomes have a pressure regulator installed within the water system. If so, it will likely have to be removed to gain the benefits of the new regulator.

More 12-Volts

RICHARD SCHRADER, AURORA, INDIANA

▶ I was having trouble getting my car in position to use its dash-mounted 12-volt DC outlet so I could plug in my portable air compressor to keep the proper pressure in my motorhome's tires. The solution was to install a 12-volt DC outlet (I hooked mine up to the light circuit) in the center storage compartments on each side of my motorhome. Now I don't need to depend on my RV's 12-volt DC dash outlets or the car's.

10

minute tech

towing

SHOW ME THE WAY

For many years, I have used a cost-free method to show me when my fifth-wheel hitch is in the correct position to be latched.

I use four 4 × 1-inch pieces of yellow electrician's tape. Two are placed on the hitch table perpendicular to the pin hole. I then placed the other two pieces of tape in a vertical position on each side of the hitch pin.

This allows me to see at a glance if I am in proper position to latch. When the pieces of tape line up, I am ready to latch up.

CARL MCPHERSON,
MOUNT VERNON, ILLINOIS

MONITOR THE TRAILER

When I first bought my trailer, it seemed to have wear problems with tires, springs and so on. The worst part was that I didn't always recognize that there was a problem.

To improve my ability to keep track of what was going on, I got some small colored self-adhesive dots sold in stationery stores. I parked the trailer on a flat area with a typical load of food and water.

I put one black dot each in the upper right and left corners of my tow vehicle's back window. Then I sat behind the steering wheel with the inside rearview mirror adjusted so that I could see the whole rear window. I had my wife affix two orange dots to the trailer, in such a position that they would be hidden from view by the black dots. To protect them, I waxed over the dots.

I now have the means to quickly notice if the trailer is leaning to either side. If the orange trailer dots become visible, I have a clue that something is wrong.

ED STOREY, EL PASO, TEXAS

SNOWBIRD TIP

Last year, with the wind blowing at 30 MPH, producing a wind-chill factor of minus 20 degrees, it was past time to hook up the Sunline for our snowbird journey from upstate New York to Florida.

My wife, Donna, directed me rearward to line up the coupler with the ball. We lined up perfectly on the first try! Next, all I had to do was lower the trailer on the ball and we would be on the road, heading for the warmth.

Forty five minutes later, using Donna's hair dryer and a plastic mallet, I finally managed to dislodge the last piece of ice from the trailer coupling. Next time, I'll be putting a freezer bag over the trailer coupling in order to keep the assembly bone-dry and ice-free.

JOHN PETERSEN, BEARSVILLE, NEW YORK

A Much-Needed Safety Reminder

FRED HIGGINS,
ROYAL OAK, MICHIGAN

▶ Having arrived on more than one occasion at our destination without the fifth-wheel hitch handle locking latch padlocked, I now store the padlock below the control for the landing legs. Now, when hitching up, I can't miss seeing it. The cost is less than 25 cents for a screw eye.

Fuse Panel

RICHARD HUGO, LIVINGSTON, TEXAS

▶ Before pressing our car into service as a dinghy, we have to pull four fuses to make it towable. After doing this the hard way (one at a time, with a fuse-puller),

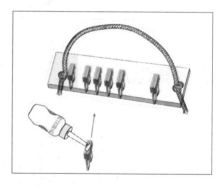

I fabricated a device that will remove all four fuses at once — and, later, reinstall them as a group.

First, I identified the fuses that needed to be pulled, then cut a piece of ⅛-inch-thick clear Plexiglas large enough to cover them (I chose Plexiglas in order to see through it). I put a dab of super glue on the back of each fuse, placed the Plexiglas panel against the fuses and held it in place for a few seconds. After it sets (about an hour), I pulled the appropriate fuses by pulling the Plexiglas straight out.

To make it easier to pull, I drilled ⅛-inch holes at each end and knotted a piece of twine to form a handle.

The fuses remain attached, in place, to the Plexiglas. When ready to drive the dinghy, I simply line up the fuses in the proper position and gently push against the panel.

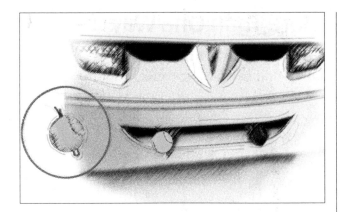

Another Use

CURTIS NODOLF, JANESVILLE, WISCONSIN

▶ Use of tennis balls as a cover for ball hitches and to hold wiper blades off of the windshield is commonly seen. Here is another use.

My towed car is equipped with a Blue Ox towing package. I cut tennis balls to fit over the towing baseplate "horns," which extend in front of my dinghy bumper. A pin through the tennis balls keeps them in place. This reduces the chance of damage to another vehicle that might back into my dinghy's bumper, and it helps protect the legs of anyone who walks too close to the car.

Pin Savior

RICHARD PREVALLET, LIVINGSTON, TEXAS

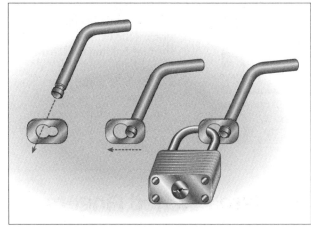

▶ I have heard stories by fifth-wheel owners of someone pulling the "hairpins" of the pull pins that hold the hitch to the truck bed, which allows the trailer to separate from the truck. Reese Hitch sells a product that keeps this from happening. A Reese Pin Lock Plate takes the place of the hairpin. A lock is then put into the hole to keep the plate from being removed. Each package comes with four lock plates, and can be ordered from your local RV dealer.

Rock Guard

TOM MCNAMARA, PENSACOLA, FLORIDA

▶ On the back of our motorhome, we have a brush-style splash guard. While this guard is great with mud and dust, it was not much help in deflecting pebbles, stone chips and other small road debris.

I went to the hardware store and purchased a sheet of punched-metal galvanized screening (used by plasterers), and some plastic cable ties. I cut the screening to the same size as the splash guard. Then, with the cable ties, I attached it to the inside surface of the brush guard.

Now, my towed car is ding free.

Rock Guard II

DICK ADAMS, WILLISTON, FLORIDA

▶ A while back, we had a hard rubber mud flap installed beneath the rear bumper, running the full width of the coach. At my insistence (and against the manufacturer's recommendation), it was installed so it barely cleared the ground.

Well, I paid for that mistake with dings on the front of my new towed car, due to the "tiddly-winking" of pebbles when the mud flap dragged across gravel.

I reinstalled it to clear the ground by the recommended 4 inches. This eliminated the dings — but lots of road spray passed under the mud flap and onto the towed car.

I finally solved the dilemma by mounting one of the "grass skirt"-type mud guards inside the hard rubber flap, and extending it all the way to the ground. Now we have no dings and minimal road spray on the towed car.

towing

Lock-Pin System

WILLIAM WRIGHT, SANTA ROSA, CALIFORNIA

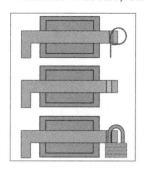

▶ To help protect your equipment from being stolen, discard the clips that "secure" the pins holding the hardware in place. Then enlarge the existing hole in the pin ends to accommodate a padlock shaft. Now there will be no pin removal, accidental or otherwise, without the key!

No More Pinched Fingers

JIM UBOLDI, SANTA ROSA, CALIFORNIA

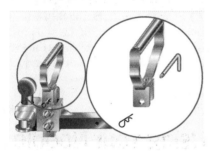

▶ For those who have adjustable hitches, the top hole makes a great place for a handle. I had a removable handle made that will slide over the top of the unused hole. I slip the locking pin through the holes in the handle assembly and the hole at the top of the hitch.

Now it's easy to pick up and install the hitch with no more greasy hands, pinched fingers or strained back.

Protect Yourself

JAMES SCHAFLA, LANCASTER, NEW YORK

▶ An easy way to protect yourself from bumping into the fifth-wheel kingpin and also help avoid kingpin grease is to simply take a foam can cooler and slip it over the kingpin. Pick a brightly colored can cooler, so it will be seen more easily.

More Than One Way One Man's Trash ...

LOREN ROBERTS, GLADSTONE, MICHIGAN

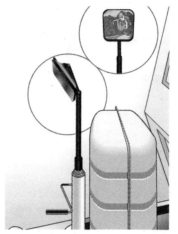

▶ The illustration shows a handy device I made from "junk" to make it easy to hook up my trailer.

The mirror is attached to a steel rod, which is then inserted into PVC pipes, and a fitting which will slide over the trailer-jack housing.

I placed a strip of white tape on the top-center of the tailgate. Using the inside rearview mirror, I line up the tape with the pipe as I back in. When the ball comes in view, it's simply a matter of stopping when the ball passes under the coupler.

Stop Getting In and Out

GERRY HALE, ROATAN, BAY ISLANDS, HONDURAS

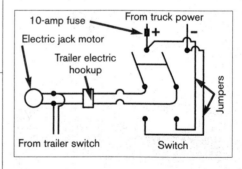

▶ I enjoy the electric jacks on my fifth-wheel trailer, but I don't like having to get in and out of the truck in order to adjust them.

To solve this problem, I installed a 20-amp switch inside the cab of the truck and wired it as shown in the diagram.

When I unhook, I get in the truck and prepare to pull ahead. If I need to raise the fifth-wheel to clear the tailgate, I simply do it from the truck.

When I prepare to hook up, I plug in the electrical connection. From the truck, I can then raise or lower the fifth-wheel until the hitch is engaged. Then I get out and finish raising the jacks, using the switch located at the fifth-wheel.

Caution: make certain no one is operating both switches at the same time or you will have a short circuit.

Adjust the Level Sensor

MARVIN BRYANT, LITTLETON, COLORADO

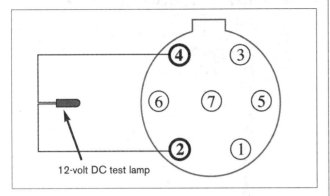

12-volt DC test lamp

▶ To properly adjust the level sensor on my truck's brake controller for use while towing a fifth-wheel, the truck must be level and the trailer has to be connected.

Sometimes it is difficult to find an area large enough to have the trailer connected on a level surface, so I connect a 12-volt DC test lamp to simulate the trailer. This allows me to make the level-sensor adjustment in my garage or on any other convenient, level area.

Hard-To-See Hitch

WES TALLMAN, LIVINGSTON, TEXAS

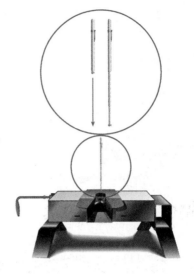

▶ After installing a 30-inch-wide tool-box in my pickup, I found that I could no longer see the fifth-wheel hitch in the truck bed. I came up with this simple, inexpensive, no-drilling-required idea.

I place a telescoping pocket magnet, magnet-end down, on the center edge of the fifth-wheel hitch. The extended length of the magnet is visible from the driver's seat. When the hitch-pin plate comes in contact with the magnet, it just pushes it out of the way.

Never Lose It Again

JAMES JIPPING, HOLLAND, MICHIGAN

▶ It seems that I am always misplacing the tool that I use to lift the spring-bar into place. When I'm done hitching (or unhitching)

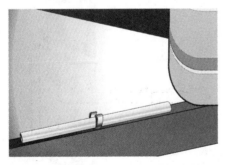

the trailer, the tool usually gets placed on the rear bumper, while I do other chores, and — you guessed it — I drive off without it.

For about a buck and a mere 15 minutes, I solved the problem. All I needed is a broom clamp (from the hardware store) that was large enough to snugly fit the tool. One metal screw attached the clamp to the trailer's frame near the spring-bar bracket.

In the two years prior to adding this clamp, I had lost four tools. In the two years since I've had it, I've lost none. And this says nothing about how convenient it is to have the tool at arm's length when it's needed.

Using Your Noodle

TERRY NANCE, NIXON, TEXAS

▶ I got tired of hearing my fifth-wheel hitch clunk when I was driving without the trailer. I also found it difficult to hitch up the fifth-wheel when the trailer was tilted.

To solve both problems, I went to a Wal-Mart and bought a noodle, which is a styrofoam tube generally used to float on in water.

I cut two pieces, each about 6 inches long. I placed a noodle section on each side under the fifth-wheel hitch to help keep it level. I trimmed the excess from the noodle pieces with a knife.

Now it is easy to hitch up the fifth-wheel, and there is no more noise when I'm driving without the trailer. When, after a period of time, the tubes get a crease, I rotate them.

towing

One Problem, Two Solutions

WILLIAM BYL, JENISON, MICHIGAN

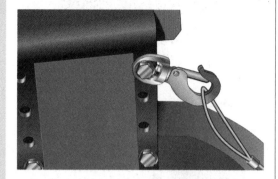

◉ Securing the loop of the breakaway cable was a problem on our fifth-wheel. I solved it by mounting a snap swivel in one of the unused adjustment holes on the hitch.

Now it is a "snap" to hook or unhook the cable when hitching or unhitching the trailer.

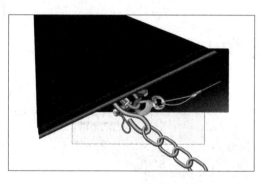

MARVIN VOLZ, HOUSTON, TEXAS

◉ We all know how important it is to properly attach your trailer's emergency breakaway-switch cable to your tow vehicle, but it doesn't have to be a chore.

I attached a "screw tight" chain link to the loop on the hitch receiver where the safety chain hooks. I also ran the loop at the end of the breakaway-switch cable through a stainless spring-loaded clip, which I now just clip onto the link on the hitch receiver. I also readjusted the switch wire by cutting it to just the right length, so as not to trip on sharp turns, and secured it with a small cable clamp.

Now it's just a "click" to adjust or remove the cable.

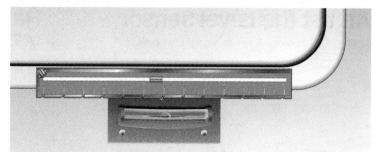

Determine the Height

JACK FOX, CARTHAGE, TEXAS

◉ I have a suggestion about how to determine the correct height of the fifth-wheel's kingpin when backing to hook up to the trailer. In a craft, fabric or sewing store, buy an inexpensive sewing gauge and attach it beneath a level on the side of the trailer. After lifting the trailer to the correct height to remove the tow vehicle, slide the sewing-gauge's indicator to the center of the level's bubble. When rehitching, place the bubble at the center point of the indicator. You will now be at the correct height and do not need to readjust the hitch height again.

Reference Library

DOROTHY SEMTANA, SALEM, OREGON

◉ I am a 76-year-old single RVer, and I was not impressed with commercial solutions to help hitch my 24-foot trailer, so I developed some reference points.

The rock guard with the diamond designs on the front of the trailer centers the truck to the hitch. On the rear window of the truck canopy, I have a sticker that I match to the large level that is on the trailer window-guard cover.

The remaining problem was to know when the ball was under the A-frame coupler. I solved this using PVC pipe. I bought a length of ¾-inch PVC pipe, a 90-degree elbow, and a pipe flange.

I centered and glued the flange to the A-frame. Then I cut two sections of the PVC pipes. The dimensions will vary for each vehicle set up. I then joined the two sections with the elbow and press the assembly into the flange on the A-frame.

Now after cutting the pipes to the correct lengths, all I have to do is back toward the A-frame and when the pipe bumps the canopy window, the ball is under the coupler.

Mirror Adjustment

E. Lloyd Medlin, Livingston, Texas

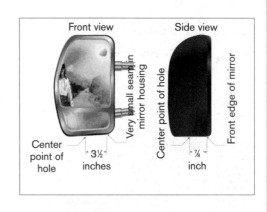

▶ As the owner of a Ford F-550 pickup, I have nonadjustable outside convex mirrors. The left-side mirror enabled me to see the left outside dual tire and little else. A fellow RVer gave me this solution.

From the electrical department at a hardware store, purchase a 1-inch knockout cover (just ask, they'll know what you want). A little black spray paint made it ready to use on my black mirror housing.

Using a 1-inch-hole-drill bit (spade bits are cheap; once again, just ask), cut a hole at a point 3⅛ inches from the small seam on the underside of the mirror and ⅞ inch from the front edge of the mirror. (Old saying: Measure twice, cut once!)

The hole will reveal the prongs that are the mounting point of the convex mirror. Using needle-nose pliers, squeeze the prongs together and move (tilt) the mirror to a more acceptable position.

Sit in the driver's seat to confirm proper positioning. When it's positioned just right, drill a small pilot hole for a screw to hold the new position permanently. Snap the previously purchased knockout cover into the hole in the mirror body, and the job is done.

Use O-Rings

Robert Bittel, Largo, Florida

▶ I found a way to stop the electric cord from being disconnected from my trailer during towing. I slipped several 1½-inch O-rings (available at any hardware store) over the connector, on to the power cord. When hooking up to the trailer, I slide the O-rings over the connector lid.

When unhooked, the O-rings are left on the electric cord, where they are always handy.

Slick Disc Fix

Charles "Ken" Rudolph Jr., Las Cruces, New Mexico

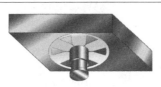

▶ Many fifth-wheel owners use a nylon disc between the hitch saddle and the pin box as a lubricant in lieu of messy grease. After a while, the friction fit that holds the disc on the kingpin becomes worn and the disc will not stay in place.

My remedy is to remove the disc and place it on a hard surface (such as concrete) and hammer the disc, on the edges where it contacts the kingpin, enough to spread the nylon a little.

My disc is 12 years old and still going strong.

Bed-Cover Burrito

Leeun Werner, Little Falls, Minnesota

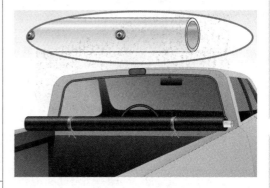

▶ I have a truck-bed cover for my tow vehicle that fastens with snaps. When rolling it forward prior to hooking up our fifth-wheel, it would take two people to make a decent roll. Then after tying it in place, it would sag and look bad.

To solve this I purchased a 6-foot piece of 1½-inch black (to color-match) PVC pipe and a package of snaps the same size as the snaps on the cover's back edge at the tailgate. I screwed six of the snaps to the PVC pipe to match the snap spacing on the cover.

Now when I want to roll the cover back, I snap the cover to the PVC pipe and roll it forward. I can roll it myself and when tied, it makes a neat roll and stays put.

towing

BAD VISION

After installing a toolbox in the back of my pickup, I could no longer see the hitch in the truck bed. This made it difficult to connect to the fifth-wheel kingpin when backing up.

So I taped a piece of reflective tape across the center of the toolbox lid (from front to back) and ran another up the center of the fifth-wheel's pin box.

Now when backing up, I have only to line them up in the rearview mirror.

The reflective tape also helps in dim light. In the dark, the outside cab light on the truck lights the tape up.

GEORGE FIPP, JACKSONVILLE, FLORIDA

COVER YOUR ENDS

To keep water and snow out of your hitch receiver and to prevent rust build-up, install a hitch cover over both ends of the receiver.

FRED ALTRIETH,
ROCHESTER, NEW YORK

HEAVY METTLE

I was confronted with the problem of removing the 86-pound fifth-wheel hitch from my truck. Tapping into my experience as a sailor, I set up a block and tackle to lift the hitch out, and lowered it on a wheeled platform to be easily stored in our garage.

I used ⅝-inch double-braid line and a set of four pulleys (in dual blocks) to make the lift. This gives us a lifting weight of only 25 pounds, since the block multiplies our effort by the number of pulleys in the system.

I attached this block and tackle set to the garage-ceiling-support beam. (Be sure to pick a main support beam, not just a stud.) I put a locking hook on the end of the line.

Now, when ready to remove the fifth-wheel hitch, I simply close the hitch and put a line around its head, which comes out the closed hole. I attach the hook on a loop of the line and lift away. Then I tie off the line, before I pull the truck out of the garage. Now, with the truck out of the way, I slide the platform under the hitch and lower it on to the platform.

The blocks and hook can be bought at any marine store and at many hardware and home-center stores.

The more pulleys you use, the less effort required, although you lose a bit of "gain" because of the line drag on the additional pulleys.

BILL BATES,
HIGHLANDS RANCH, COLORADO

Laser Tag

WILLIAM ROBERTS, HANOVER, MARYLAND

▶ I once saw a tip about using a laser pen to help hook up a trailer. That made me think about applying a laser pen to the task of hooking up a fifth-wheel.

I came up with the hardware shown in the illustration. The orange wire tie is slid along the laser-pointer barrel to turn it on. The blue wire ties fasten the pen to a scrap-aluminum framework that fits on the bed rail behind the cab.

The target is a piece of 2-inch PVC pipe that is mounted above the kingpin box. It is held in place by a length of electrical conduit, fitted inside the pipe. To mount the pipe in a vertical position, cut the bottom of the PVC pipe at an angle to match the angle of the kingpin box.

The nice part of this set-up is that you can back the truck to the fifth-wheel from almost any angle. Just watch the truck tailgate!

Tow-Bar Protector

JOHN KIRKNER, FOREST CITY, IOWA

▶ When traveling with a towed vehicle, the crosspiece of the tow bar accumulates road dirt and grime, requiring cleaning before the tow bar can be slid into the closed position.

From the hardware store, I purchased a piece of 1½-inch foam-pipe insulation, cut it to the proper length, and slipped it over the crosspiece (as shown in the illustration). When the foam insulation is removed, the bar is clean and easily folded.

If You Build It ...

DON DUNSTAN, BEASLEY, TEXAS

▶ Perplexed with the problem of how to remove the fifth-wheel hitch from the bed of my truck by myself, and where to store it, I came up with this solution.

Leaving the hitch attached to the kingpin box, I removed the pins that hold the hitch to the bed rails and raised the front of the fifth-wheel until the hitch was free of the truck bed.

After driving the truck out from under the fifth-wheel, I lower the landing jacks so that the hitch is resting on the stand.

I built the stand using two treated 2 × 6-inch boards, each 8 feet long. I cut the pieces for the upper and lower brace into eight pieces, each 24 inches long. In addition, I cut a treated 12-foot long 2 × 4-inch board into four pieces, each 34 inches long. Measurements can be adjusted to fit each individual installation.

The wood stand takes the place of my tripod stand and gives me a very convenient place to store my hitch.

Throwin' In The Towel

OLENE BRAME, LIVINGSTON, TEXAS

▶ Most motorhomers — those who tow a dinghy, anyway — worry about towing with the dinghy's steering column locked. We had a routine of checking through the back window of the motorhome to make sure that the steering wheel of our towed car was turning after we started down the road.

When we purchased a diesel-pusher, we could see the towed car in our back-up camera — but we couldn't determine whether the steering wheel was turning or not. Our solution was to tie a small white dish towel around the top of the steering wheel. Now we can watch the back-up camera and see the towel move as the steering wheel moves. This little bit of extra assurance makes us more comfortable as we hit the road!

More Laser Tag

THOMAS MITSOCK, WHARTON, NEW JERSEY

▶ I devised a simple device to take the guesswork out of hitching a tow vehicle to a trailer.

I bought a cylindrical laser pointer with a push-button ON/OFF switch (available at RadioShack, Brookstone and many other stores) for less than $30.

Into a piece of wood, I bored a hole that was ⅛-inch larger than the diameter of the pointer. I also bored two ¼-inch holes perpendicular to the pointer for ¼-20 screws and two concentric ½-inch diameter recesses (do these before the ¼-inch holes) to hot glue in two ¼-20 nuts.

The screw to the rear is used to hold the pointer in the oversize hole, while the front one is used to depress the ON/OFF button on the pointer.

To mount the assembly to the trailer hitch, I used two inexpensive magnets, also glued in place. Hook-and-loop fastener could also be used. The size of the wood used will vary as to your hitch arrangement.

To use, simply turn it on, attach it to the hitch and have your partner tell you which way you have to turn to make the red dot come to the center of the trailer hitch, and then keep backing straight until the ball is under it.

When you're done, be sure to turn the laser off so the batteries don't run out.

Scratch No More

PAT KEOUGHAN, FORT WORTH, TEXAS

▶ To keep the magnetic light wires from scratching your dinghy vehicle's paint job, wrap the wires with sheepskin and secure them with electrical ties.

towing

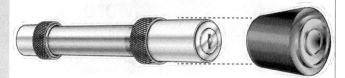

A Tip About a Tip

LARRY CORDER, BEDFORD, TEXAS

▶ For those of us who cannot keep from losing the small lock covers that come on the receiver-lock assembly, there is a cheap solution: rubber walking-cane tips.

I found that a ⅞-inch rubber walking-cane tip fits snugly over my ⅝-inch-diameter receiver lock — and unlike the lock cover that came with the part, it will not come off until a considerable amount of pressure is applied to remove it. Most hardware stores stock various sized rubber walking-cane tips that should fit any size receiver-lock assembly.

Hitch Hidden?

RAYMOND NEESLEY, FLORENCE, OREGON

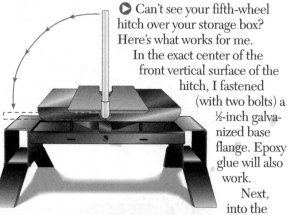

▶ Can't see your fifth-wheel hitch over your storage box? Here's what works for me.

In the exact center of the front vertical surface of the hitch, I fastened (with two bolts) a ½-inch galvanized base flange. Epoxy glue will also work.

Next, into the base flange, I screwed a ½ × 2½-inch PVC pipe nipple, and to it, I screwed on a 90-degree PVC elbow that's been hand tightened. Slip a length of ½-inch PVC into the slip side of the elbow, or it can be glued.

The length of the pipe will be determined by the height of the hitch, your viewing position and other factors.

Next, I painted a 1-inch white stripe down the center of the gooseneck. I turned the pipe to the vertical position and, using the rearview mirror, lined up the pipe and stripe and then backed onto the hitch. I then turned the pipe counterclockwise, to cause it to lie down out of the way. If it's not glued, you could even remove it to store until needed again.

Kind of a Drag

ROBERT WHITE, FRANKLIN, KENTUCKY

▶ It is important to manage safety-chain drag while still maintaining sufficient turning length when towing a trailer. Winding up the chain greatly reduces its available length, so I wove a heavy-duty screen-door spring through the links of each chain. The spring's end loops were fastened to the last link on each end of the chain with heavy-duty nylon wire ties.

This mechanically gathers the chain on the spring to hold it off the pavement, yet it still allows the chain to stretch to its full length whenever necessary.

You Would Even Say It Glows ...

JACK PHILLIPS, MEMPHIS, TENNESSEE

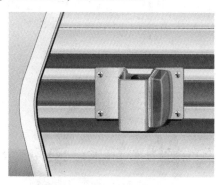

▶ I own a trailer and pull it with a pickup. For years I have experienced problems on multi-lane highways. Cars and trucks will pull up close to the rear of my trailer and refuse to pass or fall back. If I wish to change lanes, other drivers can't see my turn-signal lights, and I often have to cut them off. Boy, do I get cussed out a lot!

To calm everyone's nerves, I added turn lights to the front of my trailer that also act as stoplights. I had a metal shop bend two pieces of ⅛-inch metal. The lights came from an auto parts store.

I wired the lights to the power cord that connects to the tow vehicle.

Now, even when following closely, drivers can see my signaled intentions and avoid accidents.

towing